Beyond Epistemology

Beyond Epistemology

A Pragmatist Approach to Feminist Science Studies

Sharyn Clough

ROWMAN & LITTLEFIELD PUBLISHERS, INC.
Lanham • Boulder • New York • Oxford

ROWMAN & LITTLEFIELD PUBLISHERS, INC.

Published in the United States of America
by Rowman & Littlefield Publishers, Inc.
A Member of the Rowman & Littlefield Publishing Group
4501 Forbes Boulevard, Suite 200, Lanham, Maryland 20706
www.rowmanlittlefield.com

P.O. Box 317, Oxford OX2 9RU, United Kingdom

British Library Cataloguing in Publication Information Available

Library of Congress Cataloging-in-Publication Data

Clough, Sharyn, 1965–
    Beyond epistemology : a pragmatist approach to feminist science studies / Sharyn
Clough.
        p. cm.
Includes bibliographical references and index.
    ISBN 0-7425-1464-1 (alk. paper) — ISBN 0-7425-1465-X (pbk. : alk. paper)
    1. Feminism and science. 2. Feminist criticism. I. Title.
    Q130 .C58 2003
    508.2—dc21

                                                            2002015713
Printed in the United States of America

♾™ The paper used in this publication meets the minimum requirements of
American National Standard for Information Sciences—Permanence of Paper
for Printed Library Materials, ANSI/NISO Z39.48-1992.

Contents

Acknowledgments

This project began with my doctoral research at Simon Fraser University. There I was fortunate to work with historian of science Hannah Gay, who agreed to supervise an interdisciplinary dissertation of immense scope. Her careful guidance and direction helped bring the project into focus. Philosopher of science Norman Schwartz and the chair of the women's studies department, Meredith Kimball, rounded out the team of advisers whose commentaries greatly improved my arguments.

A number of fellow graduate students nurtured the ideas that have found their way into this book: Jeff Sugarman and David Hammond, from the philosophy of psychology reading group at Simon Fraser University, introduced me to the work of Richard Rorty and provided me with a space where intellectual vigor and skill were encouraged and expected; Lou Bruno provided engaging philosophical conversation over very good food; Sam (Vanda) Black and Paul Reniers helped me forge links between feminist theory and the real world of labor politics; Edrie Sobstyl contributed, from afar, humor, irony, and intellectual guidance.

I have been fortunate also to have a philosophical mentor and friend in Bjørn Ramberg, whose explication of the work of Donald Davidson and Rorty has been a major influence in my intellectual development.

Over the years, a number of other philosophers have shaped the development of my views on contemporary pragmatism, feminism, and science studies, many of whom provided encouragement through their detailed, incisive reviews of earlier versions of this book. Here I must thank Lynn Hankinson Nelson, Richmond Campbell, and Alison Wylie. A number of anonymous reviewers also contributed helpful commentary.

I want to acknowledge as well the influential writings of Sandra Harding, Helen Longino, and Evelyn Fox Keller. It was only by reading their books that I could begin to explore the links between science, gender, and knowledge that have preoccupied my intellectual horizon ever since.

In the last three years I have been fortunate to be part of the philosophy of science reading group sponsored by the Greater Philadelphia Philosophy Consortium. In particular, I want to thank Miriam Solomon, Hugh Lacey, and Audre Brokes for their indulgence and encouragement.

Finally, I want to thank my two favorite philosophers in the whole world: Donald Davidson, for expressing his pleasant surprise that I'd find an ally in an "old male fogy" like him; and Jonathan Kaplan, for keeping me intellectually challenged, well fed, and smiling.

Sections of this book have appeared previously in different form and are reprinted here with permission: "A Hasty Retreat from Evidence: The Recalcitrance of Relativism in Feminist Epistemology" (1988), *Hypatia* 13 (4): 88–111 and "What Is Menstruation For? On the Projectibility of Functional Predicates in Menstruation Research" (2002), *Studies in the History and Philosophy of the Biological and Biomedical Sciences* 33 (4): 719–32.

Introduction

A century of careful documentation has shown that we can no longer equate Western science with innovation and advance, at least not in any straightforward way. Feminist researchers and other social critics have provided a more complex view by revealing the often negative role that scientific practices have played in the larger social order. Advances in Western medical treatments, for example, have often been purchased at a high cost to the health of the poor women in non-Western countries who have served as test subjects.

Some of the earliest feminist criticisms of science include the work of biologists and psychologists such as Mary Calkins (1896), Helen Thompson Woolley (1910), and Leta Stetter Hollingworth (1914). Together, these scientists addressed the methodological flaws underlying various Darwinian claims, including claims about the inferiority of European women and non-European women and men.

Throughout the mid- to late twentieth century, the number and scope of feminist science critiques increased substantially. Many of these are reviewed by Anne Fausto-Sterling in *Myths of Gender: Biological Theories about Women and Men* (1992 [1985]); Londa Schiebinger in *The Mind Has No Sex? Women in the Origins of Modern Science* (1989); Carol Tavris in *The Mismeasure of Woman* (1992); and Bonnie Spanier in *Im/partial Science: Gender Ideology in Molecular Biology* (1995).

Some of the more contemporary feminist commentaries have begun to address the interlocking sex, race, and class hierarchies that supported the science of Nazi eugenics, American syphilis experiments on black subjects in Tuskegee, nuclear testing on aboriginal lands, and birth control and other pharmaceutical testing on women of the "developing world" (see the essays collected in Sandra Harding's *The "Racial" Economy of Science,* 1993a). It is becoming increasingly clear that science as an institution has often made life more difficult for society's weakest members, no matter how that weakness has been defined.

What is less clear, however, is how best to diagnose the origin of this disturbing pattern and, consequently, how best to treat it. Most of the feminist interventions from the mid-nineteenth and earlier twentieth centuries were directed at the level of empirical research, or methodological critique, attempting on a case-by-case basis to counter faulty sexist and racist practices with more accurate data and methods. However, the late 1970s and 1980s saw feminist scientists and science commentators alike move away from empirical critique and toward more philosophical diagnoses and treatment. It is to this latter philosophical focus that I draw critical attention. I argue that philosophy—in particular, epistemology—is not the most effective focus for feminists engaged in science criticism.

Feminist biologists such as Evelyn Fox Keller (1982, 1983 [1978], 1985) and Ruth Bleier (1984, 1986a, 1986b) formed part of the earliest philosophical turn by diagnosing the oppressive aspects of science at the level of epistemology, in addition to the empirical practices and theories of their fellow scientists. These feminist scientists were supported by feminist philosophers such as Genevieve Lloyd (1984) and Susan Bordo (1987), who had begun to identify sexist gender metaphors in numerous epistemological models from Plato to Descartes. At the same time, other feminist philosophers such as Sandra Harding (1986a, 1986b), Lorraine Code (1981), and Helen Longino (1987, 1990) were investigating why traditional epistemological models consistently failed to account for or even acknowledge the role of sex/gender in either epistemology or science. This failure suggested to them the need for new, more adequate epistemological approaches.

While this shift away from scientific practices and toward the epistemology of science has equipped feminist science studies with a larger range of critical and diagnostic tools, I believe that our investment in an epistemological critique is beginning to yield diminishing returns. It is no longer clear that a philosophical examination of truth, evidence, and/or method helps us identify and address those scientific practices that systematically disadvantage already marginalized peoples. Indeed, I argue that our shift to an epistemological focus has begun to conceptually impede crucial feminist work on the front lines of science studies.

It is important to note that my criticisms are embedded within a commitment to feminist political movement. None of my arguments against feminist work in epistemology of science should be seen as critical of feminism more generally; rather, they address problems in the application of epistemology to feminist science studies. Feminist scholarship has already made important contributions to our understandings of science and society; and it is this body of scholarship that I wish to support and strengthen.

CHAPTER HIGHLIGHTS

In chapter 1, I set the stage for my negative thesis by surveying various approaches within feminist science studies that appeal to epistemological themes, as well as identifying those aspects of epistemological theorizing that make it particularly problematic. On this last point I identify the engagement with skepticism as the primary culprit, and I argue that this engagement is symptomatic of an underlying commitment to a representationalist model of knowers and the world. My articulation of representationalism is inspired by Richard Rorty and Donald Davidson, and their neopragmatic alternatives to representationalism are prescribed in the latter half of the book.

In chapter 2, I make a distinction between problems that seem specific to feminist versions of epistemology and problems that seem to affect epistemology more generally. Of the former I discuss the perennial concerns with essentializing and reifying our categories of analysis, as exemplified in the claim that science (or alternatively, objectivity) is masculine. While essentialism is a well-acknowledged problem within the feminist literature, a solution remains elusive. Of the latter I discuss the relationship between epistemology and representationalism and the self-refuting skepticism that such a relationship fuels. I argue that epistemological arguments are (a) premised on the coherence of a global skepticism, but (b) consistently fail to defeat it. In support of my claims about the relationship between skepticism and epistemology, I outline and augment Davidson's diagnosis of the representationalism underlying Quinean empiricism (a type of empiricism that has inspired numerous feminist epistemological projects in the last decade). With respect to the continuing failure to defeat skepticism, I present a number of arguments, including Wilfred Sellars's arguments about the "Myth of the 'Given,'" Nelson Goodman's "New Riddle of Induction," and Davidson's criticism of correspondence theories.

In chapter 3, I examine the ways in which epistemological theorizing has restricted the effectiveness of a number of influential feminist criticisms of science, focusing on feminist responses to evolutionary research. I begin with the work of Antoinette Brown Blackwell, a feminist contemporary of Charles Darwin. I then discuss the writings of more recent feminist theorists such as Stephanie Shields, Cynthia Russett, Ruth Hubbard, and Bleier. Bleier argues that, historically, the notion of objective epistemic method has been gendered masculine, and that a new, feminine method would be an improvement—she stops short of saying it would be more objective.

The claim that objectivity is gendered masculine is treated further in chapter 4, where I focus on Keller's influential science commentaries (1982, 1983 [1978], 1985, 1987). I trace Keller's arguments from her earliest claims for the increased objectivity associated with feminine gender identity, to her later writings in which increased objectivity is associated with the "not-male." I argue that because her work remains within a representationalist model, it is weakened by skepticism in its relativist guise.

In chapter 5, I discuss Keller's criticisms of objectivity that begin in her 1992 essay collection *Secrets of Life, Secrets of Death*. I also discuss the highly influential writings of Harding (1991, 1993b) and Longino (1987, 1990). Each of these three theorists has continued with more recent work in science studies, but it is the arguments presented in their earlier texts that remain something of a locus classicus for feminist epistemology as it is applied to science.[1]

In these classic texts, Keller, Harding, and Longino each encourage a conceptual midpoint between objectivism and relativism; however, I argue that they remain insufficiently critical of the representationalism that underwrites the debate. Each then struggles with skepticism, in particular with the skepticism that arises from a relativist use of underdetermination theory.

In chapter 6, I focus on my positive thesis by adopting a Rortyan, pragmatist interpretation of Davidson's work. Here I argue that while epistemological arguments about truth and evidence are flawed, they are also unnecessary. The arguments are unnecessary because the fear of skepticism that gave rise to their construction is based on an unnecessary commitment to representationalism. I outline Davidson's philosophy of language as a model of belief and meaning that is *not* premised on the rationality of skepticism. Consequently, his model undermines any epistemological motivation for defeating skepticism.

The positive implications of this Rortyan reading of Davidson are discussed in chapter 7. Specifically, I provide a Davidsonian response to the relativist elements within Longino's use of underdetermination theory. I suggest that if feminist science critics adopt these pragmatist, nonrepresentationalist attitudes toward their own truth claims, we can better avoid the self-refutation of skepticism and its relativist variants.

In the final chapter I provide a pragmatic, nonepistemological response to a more specific case study. Returning to the evolutionary themes with which I began my feminist epistemological survey, I examine debates in the philosophy of biology about the nature of functional traits. Focusing on one functional account in particular, I discuss Margie Profet's research on the function of menstruation, published in the *Quarterly Review of Biology* (Profet 1993). Profet hypothesizes that all internally fertilizing mammals menstruate, and that menstruation functions, she claims, to clean the female reproductive tract of sperm-borne pathogens. Profet argues that the reason scientists have never viewed menstruation as particularly functional is because they have never thought to perform an evolutionary analysis of menstruation. I argue that a number of pragmatic issues must be addressed before Profet's evolutionary analysis can be adequately tested. I conclude that a feminist genealogy of our biological views about menstruation and pregnancy would provide a more complete answer to the question of menstruation's function.

SUMMARY

Throughout the balance of this book I argue that the skepticism invited by the representationalist model can never be answered from within. Once engaged in epistemology, one invites a never-ending struggle with an omnipotent foe. I show that despite feminist criticism of traditional epistemology, our own alternatives still contain representationalist assumptions. I then conclude that the important goals of feminist science studies are best met not by addressing (unanswerable) epistemological problems, but by focusing back on local, empirical research.

The pragmatic model I prescribe encourages the empirical process of decision making in feminist science and science criticism, whereby the truth of our individual beliefs and scientific theories is assigned locally and, of course, fallibly. This sort of empirical assignment is typically ad hoc and dynamic—the criteria are always being adjusted as new information comes in. These features are part of what separates a pragmatist empirical project from a troublesome epistemological one. The latter involves the attempt to identify and apply general normative recipes for truth, or its functional equivalents, in science. As Davidson reminds us, however, "truth is beautifully transparent" (1991a [1983], 122). Because of the interrelationship between truth and meaning, and because we typically know what we mean, truth no longer needs to be seen as the sort of thing about which we need an explanatory theory. Though, certainly, the question of whether our scientific theories are themselves true is itself an important and ongoing project.

More specifically, I want to encourage feminist science critics and scientists alike in the important empirical task of analyzing the causal relations between our theories and the world. However, to the extent that we construct epistemological guidelines for identifying which features of the causal stories indicate truth, we will continually be chasing after new recalcitrant features. The very skepticism the epistemological position was constructed to solve will be reintroduced, leaving us not only to doubt the general reliability of our connections with the world around us but, more particularly, to doubt the reliability of our well-documented accounts of bias and abuse in science.

NOTE

1. Unless otherwise specified, the discussion of these three theorists focuses on Keller (1982, 1983 [1978], 1985, 1987, and 1992a–c), Harding (1986a, 1991, 1993b), and Longino (1987, 1990).

1

Feminist Engagement with Epistemology

EPISTEMOLOGY AND ONTOLOGY

When I claim that epistemology is not the most effective tool for addressing the oppressive aspects of science, I mean also to address a set of ontological issues that are intertwined. Often, epistemological questions of justification and ontological questions of truth are collapsed, because they are so closely related.

Traditionally, epistemological projects have tried to design criteria for discriminating between competing knowledge claims, as well as methods for detecting the degree to which those criteria are met. Typically, however, this project contains an implicit commitment to a certain set of normative, ontological properties that the epistemological criteria are believed to indicate—properties such as truth, or something other than truth, such as "least partiality" or "maximal objectivity."

Contemporary feminist commentators have played an important role by responding critically to the traditional questions regarding epistemology and ontology. In some of Evelyn Fox Keller's earlier work she argues that, historically, normative claims about objectivity have been related to a masculine epistemological method that privileges "detachment" and "control" (Keller 1982, 593–94). She argues that the result is a "parochial, ideologically charged" form of objectivity that needs to be replaced with a more universal or "dynamic" form of objectivity. For Keller, objectivity refers both to an epistemic method and to the normative property that method is used to identify. In her view, then, a scientific theory has the ontological property of being dynamically objective to the extent that it has not been created using epistemic methods that involve masculine notions of detachment from and domination over the object treated by the theory (593–94). Genevieve Lloyd (1984) and Nancy Tuana (1992a) make similar arguments about the historical associations between concepts of masculinity and normative properties such as truth or rationality.

Feminists have also been central in criticizing the nature of the debate between objectivism and relativism—a debate that remains unresolved in the traditional epistemological literature (e.g., Harding 1993b, Longino 1990). In traditional terms, the more objectivist-minded tend to argue that epistemological criteria should appeal to a "permanent, ahistorical matrix or framework," while the more relativistically inclined think the criteria are best understood as "relative to a specific conceptual scheme, theoretical framework, paradigm, form of life, society or culture" (Bernstein 1983, 8).[1]

Richard Bernstein's description of the debate makes clear the close relationship between the specification of normative, ontological properties and the epistemological project of detecting the presence of those properties. Traditionally, the more objectivist-inclined have claimed that the ontological property of truth arises from a correspondence relation between any given knowledge claim and the features of the world described by that claim. Furthermore, an objectivist epistemology that appeals to ahistorical, universal methods is often prescribed for detecting the correspondence relation. Critics of objectivism and the correspondence relation have often specified, instead, a coherence relation, which holds, not between a knowledge claim and the world, but between sets of knowledge claims themselves. These critics typically champion some form of epistemological relativism. For relativists, judgments about the level of coherence between knowledge claims and the choice of which knowledge claims are relevant for comparison are seen as relative to the language scheme, worldview, or culture of the knower in question.

In the face of the continued failure to resolve the objectivist/relativist debate, feminist commentators have argued persuasively against the utility of the inherited dichotomy, attempting instead to carve out a conceptual middle ground. Recognizing the danger of an extreme relativism, Sandra Harding is nonetheless cautious about the possibility of attaining a universal objectivity. She argues that a scientific theory will be "less partial" to the extent that it is supported by "research from women's lives" (Harding 1993b, 56). Helen Longino shares Harding's cautionary approach to objectivity, arguing that our (gendered) background beliefs filter the data used to support any knowledge claim. In the face of this pervasive filtering, she argues, a scientific theory can attain objectivity only by degrees (Longino 1990, chapter 4). In Longino's view, a scientific theory will have the property of being maximally objective to the extent that it has been produced in a scientific community that creates recognized avenues for the criticism of evidence, employs shared standards that critics can invoke, is responsive to criticism, and shares intellectual authority equally among qualified practitioners (Longino 1990, 76).

Feminist engagement with the epistemology of science has brought about numerous other conceptual improvements, in addition to the questioning of the objectivism/relativism dichotomy mentioned previously. For example, while the traditional epistemological model was once motivated by a normative quest for certainty, feminists (among others) argued that this goal needed to be scaled down (e.g., Harding 1991). Many feminists also supported the shift toward naturalistic accounts of knowledge production that focus on the scientific study of social and psychological processes, replacing a priori theorizing about truth and objectivity (e.g., Nelson 1990, 1993; Tuana 1992b; Campbell 1994, 1998). Other improvements suggested by feminists included the development of a more holistic approach to the subjects of epistemological theorizing (e.g., Code 1991). These more "ecological" models focus on human beliefs in lived context, rather than on the abstractions of the traditional epistemological formula "subject S knows that proposition p."

However, I argue that while we have restrained and restructured the traditional quest for certainty, these differences reflect changes in degree more than in kind. Even in feminist versions of epistemology, the project continues to involve the specification of normative criteria—either a priori or through a naturalized, scientific account of human cognition—that would indicate truth, least partiality, or maximal objectivity. Despite the qualifiers, the key similarity is the specification of criteria for detecting normative properties—an epistemic process designed to help us choose between competing knowledge claims.

Linda Alcoff provides a recent feminist endorsement of just this sort of epistemological project when she writes:

> Given a richer and more politically attuned analysis of the production of knowledge, how should we *epistemically* characterize a validity claim? Which criteria should be given priority in demarcating better and worse theoretical claims? (Alcoff 1996, 2–3, italics in the original)

Alcoff also makes clear that these epistemological questions always contain ontological commitments, and that with respect to the latter she favors the nonrelativistic view that "justification requires truth-conduciveness, and that truth is non-reducible to language" (3).

When more naturalistically inclined feminists, such as Lynn Hankinson Nelson and Richmond Campbell, claim that the property at issue is not truth, but "justification by the empirical evidence," their projects still attempt to be philosophically normative and, in any case, as I argue in chapter 2, the truth/justification distinction is difficult to maintain. This latter point is one I share with Alcoff. Also, even though their epistemological criteria are initially based on a naturalized specification of the empirical norms of science, the process involves abstracting those norms from the day-to-day practices of scientists, and knowers more generally, and reapplying them in the form of a template against which to adjudicate new knowledge claims.

In *Illusions of Paradox* (1998), Campbell explains that a scientific hypothesis is objective to the extent that it has been tested using methods that conform to the norms of predictive success, observation independence, and explanatory power (1998, 21). He adds to these the feminist norm of "pursuing the elimination of social bias against women" (22). These criteria are abstracted from the (feminist) scientist's usual array of techniques and prescribed by Campbell as effective indicators of objectivity in hypothesis testing.[2]

In subsequent chapters I provide more detailed support for the claim that feminists engaged in epistemology have retained fairly traditional elements of epistemology, especially the epistemic detection of normative properties. For the moment, however, I would like briefly to explain why I think the retention is a problem.

EPISTEMOLOGY AND SKEPTICISM

While there are now few feminist philosophers, or even traditional philosophers, who would claim that the identification of normative criteria buys us certainty in our beliefs, the search for these criteria continues in a scaled-back form. It is the motivation for this search that concerns me. In every case I have examined to date, the search is motivated by the threat of a global skepticism, more specifically, the threat that our beliefs about the world may be just as they are, and yet the world—and so the truth about the world—may be very different.[3]

Within epistemological approaches to science, skepticism arises as the concern that if philosophers do not, or cannot, identify criteria for detecting normative properties, then scientists, and knowers more generally, will have no way to rationally adjudicate between competing knowledge claims. If, as Longino argues, the evidence for our scientific theories is continually filtered by our gendered background beliefs, then we need epistemology to provide normative guidelines for minimizing the resulting error.

It is important to note that a skeptical claim about the pervasive nature of gendered perceptual filters is distinct from the less metaphysically laden worry that any one of our currently well-supported scientific theories might turn out, some time in the future, to be false. Most scientists, feminist or otherwise, properly entertain this latter sort of doubt about all of their theories. Rorty refers to the acknowledgment of error in this context as "contrite fallibilism" (Rorty 1991c [1987]). Note that, for the fallibilist, detecting error in a particular theory requires exactly the same judgment processes that produced the error-ridden theory in the first place. The fallibilist position simply acknowledges the ongoing nature of scientific investigation.

The skeptic, however, is after a much bigger target. When, at some future time, scientists reconfigure a theory in the face of new evidence, this change will not satisfy skeptical doubt. At this future point the skeptic is no closer to grasping the criteria that would indicate whether the new theory is true, maximally objective, or least partial. For the skeptic, this process must be independent from questions of gathering new evidence, as the nature of evidence is itself the issue of concern. And so, I argue, the skeptical quest becomes self-perpetuating.[4]

This unresolvable skepticism is a problem for anyone who takes epistemological quests seriously, but it is, I believe, especially problematic for feminist science studies. When we embark on the quest for normative ontological properties and the best epistemic methods for their detection, we open up issues of skepticism that can be used against our own well-justified claims about the harms caused by science. When we construe the adjudication of knowledge claims as an epistemic process prior to and independent from the local, empirical justification of those claims, we unnecessarily invite the worry that our claims about the oppression of women, for example, while well supported by empirical evidence, might not meet epistemic criteria conceived as independent of this evidence. This is a skeptical worry that will continue to haunt our claims, no matter how much supportive empirical data we compile.

Again, this global level of doubt is not about whether a particular scientific theory is true or false, whether a particular element of our method is failing to capture the relevant data, or whether a particular set of implicit beliefs has affected our experimental design in ways that inappropriately skew the results. These are all important and appropriate fallibilist worries, and feminists have played a crucial role in investigating these concerns in a number of specific scientific cases. However, as I have argued, within epistemological approaches to science these worries are not the primary focus. For naturalized epistemologists, for example, the concern is not whether a particular scientific theory is objective, but whether we can establish independent tests of the objectivity of the scientifically informed epistemic norms against which the objectivity of individual scientific theories is measured. Indeed, Campbell spends much of his book responding to the circular nature of this skeptical concern (Campbell 1998, especially chapter 5).

It is certainly important to acknowledge that naturalized epistemology, especially when guided by feminism, is an improvement over traditional approaches. The focus on scientific explanations of cognition has properly replaced earlier attempts to respond to global skepticism through more traditional a priori means. However, it is largely the method, not the goal, that has been replaced. As I argue further in chapter 2, naturalized epistemologists bring the experimental methods of science to bear on the same set of skeptical worries as those found in more traditional epistemological approaches from Plato to Descartes.

EPISTEMOLOGY AND REPRESENTATIONALISM

I argue that the skepticism, to which epistemology responds, arises from a continued reliance on a representationalist model of the relationship between knowers and the world. It is the commitment to this model that makes skepticism an ongoing problem. While many of us are familiar with representationalism, especially with the version articulated by Descartes, the details are worth rehearsing as a point of reference.

Within representationalism, beliefs are conceived as representations of their objects. In the most elementary cases, these beliefs are described as the subjective end-product of human sensory processing. The combination and systematization of beliefs/representations produce more complex representations in the form of theories. Sometimes the resulting theory is said to feed back into the perceptual system, so that our allegiance to the theory affects our ability to accurately perceive new data.[5]

Some readers will have encountered representationalism as an empirical model arising out of cognitive science. This is not the sort of representationalism with which I'm concerned. For cognitive scientists, mental representations are no different from pictures, maps, or other "vehicles of meaning"—all convey information only through a process of interpretation (Dennett 1982). There is no privileged "inside" from which a representation's meaning is transparent or "given," even in the case of our own mental images. The point, in the view of many of these cognitive models, is to show that even when we interpret our own mental images, our interpretations are themselves a cognitive product of interpretation. There are no "uninterpreted interpreters"—no homunculi sitting before the grand theater screen in our brains sifting through our representations of the outside world.[6]

I am concerned with representationalism as a philosophical model that does, in the end, invoke an image of knowers as interpreters, collecting data about the empirical world without themselves being part of that world. The problematic features of the model are related to what Davidson refers to as the "scheme/content" distinction. The objects in our physical environment are said to be sensed (this is the sense data or content) and then screened through our subjective perceptual frameworks (the filtering scheme of our political values, worldview, and/or language). On this model we are the uninterpreted interpreters examining the empirical data as they have been filtered and presented to us.

The representational conception of our filtering/interpretational machinery as metaphysically distinct from the natural, empirical world from which the representational data emanates helps explain the skepticism that fuels epistemology. If beliefs are only internal copies or representations of the external world, then it is possible that somewhere in the copying process an error might have occurred, rendering the copy inaccurate. Indeed, all of our representations could be inaccurate because their content has been filtered through the schemes of our perceptual apparatus, language, cultural world-view, and/or theory allegiance. We can never be sure of the fidelity of our representations because we do not have direct access to the empirical world that caused them.

The epistemological search for normative properties arises as a response to this global skepticism. In the ongoing debate between objectivists and relativists, objectivists hope to defeat skepticism with various theories of correspondence, while relativists seem resigned to the skeptical view that the filtering of our beliefs makes truthful representation impossible and coherence between beliefs our only hope.

Most feminist positions articulate a conceptual middle ground whereby maximal objectivity, or least partiality of representations, is viewed as the most reasonable goal. I argue, however, that these middle positions remain geographically—and thereby conceptually—linked to the same unstable territory traversed by the more traditional epistemologists. While feminist theorists have played a critical role in dismantling the representationalist model, our ongoing engagement with skepticism suggests the continued presence of the very Cartesianism we've been criticizing. We need a new perspective on the problem, and, in this respect, I find the contemporary pragmatist approach of Richard Rorty to be particularly compelling.

LESSONS FROM CONTEMPORARY PRAGMATISM

Rorty's concern with Cartesian or representationalist epistemology is inspired by Davidson's philosophy of language (see Rorty 1979, 1991a, 1999 [1994]). Davidson's work is largely unexamined by feminists and, as I've argued elsewhere (Clough 1998), his diagnosis of the epistemological malaise is ripe for feminist appropriation.

Rorty and Davidson are both critical of the epistemological search for normative properties, showing how this search is motivated by the skeptical concern that *all* our knowledge claims might be justified by evidence, but still be completely false. They argue that due to the nature of the representationalist model on which epistemology is based, the battle with such global skepticism is futile (Rorty 1979, 1991a [1986]; 1991b [1988]; Davidson 1990a, 304). And, of course, they suggest that the representationalist model can be set aside.[7]

Davidson's prescriptions are based on the holistic approach of his teacher, W. V. Quine, whose work I discuss in chapter 2. According to Davidson, all our beliefs are interconnected with each other in terms of their content. The resulting "web of belief" is comprised of continual threads that connect beliefs about empirical facts to beliefs about value systems, and back again. Davidson views beliefs about political values, such as feminism, as integral

parts of our interlocking web of belief. This contrasts with the representationalist model, whereby political values are conceived as nonbelief schemes
through which the sensory evidence for our empirically based beliefs is filtered. As I show in chapter 7, Davidson's holism proves to be an important
aid for feminist epistemologists, who sometimes seem resigned to the skeptical view that feminist political values are conceptually separate from questions of empirical evidence.

Davidson also argues that if we view belief, not as a potentially faulty representation of the external world, but as the product of a triangulation between language users and the shared features of their world about which
they are communicating, then we must, in fact, have a number of true beliefs
(Davidson 1989a, 164; 1989b; 1991a [1983]; 1991b, 195). While he admits that
any one of our beliefs may be false, he argues that the detection of false beliefs *requires* that we have a background of true beliefs against which the error of the false beliefs can be measured (Davidson 1984 [1974], 196–97). This
latter claim undercuts the global skeptic who wants to make error a general
concern, that is, who wants to deny or question the existence of norms
against which errors can be measured.

Rorty has been particularly important in articulating what he calls the
"neopragmatist" thrust of Davidson's project (e.g., Rorty 1991a [1986]). Rorty
argues that Davidson's antirepresentationalist approach is best seen not as an
epistemological *response* to skepticism but as a pragmatist shift of the conceptual terrain that effectively *dodges* skepticism. By viewing global skepticism as a nonissue, Davidson's philosophy of language undercuts the epistemological debate about which criteria best answer the skeptic.

This is an important point. The pragmatist, Davidsonian approach I prescribe
is not an alternative epistemology; instead, it is a way of conceiving of knowers
and the world that makes the need for epistemology far less compelling.

While Davidson's account of belief and meaning does not defeat the skeptic on her own terms, he is able to keep the skeptic's case from getting off
the ground. According to him, if one knows a language, then one knows
many things about one's world (Davidson 1989a; 1990a, sec. III). Davidson
does not make the epistemic claim that skepticism can be defeated; that our
language use guarantees that our beliefs accurately represent reality. Instead
he offers a nonrepresentationalist model of belief, from which skepticism is
a nonstarter. I find this suggestion highly attractive.

Returning to the larger Rortyan project from which my appropriation of
Davidson is inspired, I should acknowledge that there are a number of people who find Rorty's pragmatism much less attractive than I do. For example,
there is some concern that Rorty does not remain faithful to the classical
pragmatism of his American forebears.[8] There is also the question whether
Davidson, or anyone else whose work Rorty appropriates, would agree to be
called a "pragmatist" in either the "classical" or the "Rortyan" sense. I am not

particularly concerned with these debates. There are, however, other more substantive points of contention, such as whether Rorty's project (and relatedly, Davidson's) is as successful at escaping representationalist epistemology as it claims. Feminist theorists Nancy Fraser (1989, 1991), Sabina Lovibond (1989, 1992), Seyla Benhabib (1991), and Judith Butler (1991) have all written critically of Rorty's pragmatist program, often interpreting him as a relativist, firmly mired in the representationalism he purports to have escaped.[9] This is a serious charge, related to the claim that I am merely prescribing a new (and perhaps unsuccessful) version of epistemology. I address these concerns more fully in chapter 6.

At this early point, I can say that Rorty's and Davidson's responses to representationalism provide the most satisfactory method I have yet encountered for clearing a path through the epistemological undergrowth of feminist science and science criticism. I use their pragmatist claims largely in negative terms to argue against the utility and coherence of epistemological articulations of truth, maximal objectivity, or least partiality. More specifically, I argue that skepticism about the presence of such normative properties is not a compelling worry, that the ontological and epistemological questions motivated by skepticism do not need answers, and that, historically, any attempts to answer them have resulted in confusion for feminist and traditional philosophers alike.

AN IMPORTANT DISTINCTION:
EMPIRICAL INQUIRY VERSUS EPISTEMOLOGY

While I have argued against the utility of general epistemological questions such as "By which normative criteria might we adjudicate between competing knowledge claims?" I have emphasized that we must still answer local questions about the truth, evidential justification or objectivity, of any *particular* knowledge claim or set of claims. Some might argue that even these more local questions involve themes that are epistemic, more broadly conceived, so, to avoid confusion, I refer to these latter, more local questions as "empirical" rather than "epistemological." Here, "empirical" refers to the uncontroversial view that any investigative project involves a comparison of the knowledge claim in question with our ongoing theories and with our experiences of the world. It is only when we elevate empirical investigation of a specific claim to the prescriptive level of epistemology more generally (e.g., to form the philosophical position called "empiricism") that we encounter the sorts of problems with which I'm concerned.[10]

Compare the concrete nature of the empirical question "Is this scientific theory true?" with the more abstract tone of the philosophical questions "By which epistemic criteria might we adjudicate between competing knowledge claims?"

and "Do these criteria indicate the presence of normative properties such as truth, or something other than truth, such as maximal objectivity or least partiality?" Examinations of the first question are typically dynamic, and often ad hoc, processes of comparing the specific theory in question with an ongoing body of theories and with past and present experiences/data. The assignment of truth, or evidential justification, or maximal objectivity, is site-specific and is adjusted as new information comes in, or as the relevance of previous information is questioned. Importantly, for any given knowledge claim, the assignment of truth (or its functional equivalent) is fallibilistic. That is, the assignment is not immune from revision, nor is such immunity seen as a goal.

Allow me to anticipate two epistemological criticisms that might arise at this point. The first is the skeptical concern that acknowledging the potential for revision at the level of individual theories still means admitting something like radical doubt about the reliability of the local empirical process used to assess the theories in the first place. What Rorty reminds us, however, is that there is no way for us to doubt the veracity of the very ordinary empirical processes I describe, without relying on those very same processes. Our only way to doubt a belief is to check how it fits with our ongoing experiences of the world; the only way to doubt our ongoing experiences is to check how they fit with other experiences; and so on (Rorty 1995). Naturalized epistemologists, feminist or otherwise, might respond in a second way. While they often admit that skepticism is a coherent problem, they are typically confident that we can defeat a certain amount of skepticism if only we elevate our day-to-day empirical processes to the level of epistemological guide. For the naturalized epistemologist, or empiricists more generally, empiricism serves as a methodological recipe for better—that is, well-justified—science. Haack makes this point against Rorty in her book *Evidence and Inquiry* (Haack 1993). Rorty responds by pointing out that the empirical process of testing new theories against our ongoing experiences is as natural a process as breathing. There is nothing to recommend it as a methodological principle, except its ongoing ability to keep us alive. It's a good idea to keep testing new theories against your ongoing experiences, just as it's a good idea to keep breathing, but neither of these would serve as the kind of guide to better living that would satisfy the skeptical seeker of truth (Rorty 1995, 151–52). The lesson from both of these epistemological concerns is that the empirical and fallibilistic assignment of warrant to individual theories cannot involve the prior specification of criteria that could be detected *independently* from the local, empirical process itself, or even, as the naturalized epistemologist prescribes, by the elevation of the local, empirical processes to the role of epistemic norms.

When we move from the more mundane empirical examinations of individual theories to epistemological questions of "truth-indicativeness" or "objectivity-indicativeness" more generally, the philosophical skeptic is made much more welcome to ask, "But how do you *know* that your epistemic criteria *really* signal truth (or objectivity, or evidential justification . . .)?" And the epistemologist is called up once again to respond to the skeptical threat. The more specific empirical examinations at the level of individual theories do not so easily invite skeptical symptoms, so they are less likely to inspire epistemological responses (Rorty 1995, 153).

With respect to more localized, empirical examinations, the most one can reasonably doubt is whether the truth or evidential justification of the theory in question can withstand further testing. If it can't, then we need a new theory, a new test, or a new understanding of the relevant criteria. These are all difficult but ultimately tractable empirical challenges, the same challenges that drive the curious in every population to push inquiry further, the same challenges that conservatives would rather stifle. Feminists are properly champions of these challenges, linking our empirical curiosity with a social vision for a better world. It is what we do best.

As an example, consider the important role feminist criticism has played when we question the relevance of the scientific data against which a new theory is being compared. In the field of social psychology, some feminists asked why it was that a theory about the negative effects of stress was being evaluated only in relation to data on men's psychology. Why, they asked, was it not also compared with data on the psychology of women? After more studies were finally carried out on women, it was found that a number of life events, such as marriage, that had previously been rated positively in the tests on men actually had *negative* stress impacts on women (Muller 1992). Clearly, class and racial identifications will further refine the relevance question. These and numerous other cases where feminists have challenged male-only studies of the "human" body and mind are documented in *The Mismeasure of Woman* (Tavris 1992).

The empirical approach that I am prescribing is also exemplified in the work of feminist scientists and science commentators mentioned previously, such as Schiebinger (1989, 1999), Spanier (1995), and Fausto-Sterling (1992 [1985]). The work of Alison Wylie (1994, 2002), Susan Sperling (1991), and Donna Haraway (1989) is equally illustrative in this respect.[11] In these texts, the very difficult questions of justification that arise from the day-to-day research of feminist scientists are brought to the fore.

Again, it is important to note that a focus on empirical study does not absolve one from the responsibility to question the truth of various claims; to criticize implicit beliefs when they contradict evidence; and to examine the methodology of a study that produces results conflicting with evidence about, for example, the equality of men and women. This sort of work is difficult, both conceptually and practically, and it's also time-consuming. My point, then, is not that empirical work is easier than epistemic study, but that reinterpreting empirical study through the lenses of epistemology, as many feminists have recently done, makes empirical work much more difficult than it would be otherwise. Indeed, I argue, the skepticism invited by the epistemologist's lens makes the problems of empirical justification *intractable.*

As I note in the introduction, the empirical approach documented by Tavris and others continues a tradition of feminist science that can be traced back as early as the late nineteenth and earlier twentieth centuries. The prominence of epistemological discussion is a relatively recent phenomenon in the history of feminist science studies. Feminist scientists from the turn of the twentieth century were concerned almost exclusively with the local, empirical question whether a particular scientific theory was true or false.

In my historical study of this shift, however, I have discovered that despite my dissatisfaction with the current epistemological focus, the motivation for the focus seems reasonable and even compelling. In what follows I both acknowledge and critically address the history that has forged our relatively recent attraction to epistemology.

THE FEMINIST SHIFT FROM EMPIRICAL INQUIRY TO EPISTEMOLOGY

In the history of modern Western science, the late nineteenth and early twentieth centuries saw an increased professionalization among scientists and increased educational opportunities for women (Ainley 1990, 19). Both of these phenomena encouraged more women to break barriers of sexism and racism to become scientists. Many of their stories are documented by Marianne Gosztonyi Ainley (1990), P. G. Abir-Am and D. Outram (1987), and Margaret Rossiter (1982). These histories are still being uncovered, but we know now that many women scientists brought feminist concerns to their research, and they often produced important empirical criticisms of sexist science. The critiques of Darwinian theory provided by Helen Montague and Leta Stetter Hollingworth stand out in this context (Hollingworth 1914; Montague and Hollingworth 1914).

In the late nineteenth century many scientists followed Charles Darwin in claiming that males of most species (including humans) showed greater physiological and mental variability, as a group, than did females (Darwin 1981 [1871]; Ellis 1894, 1903; Patrick Geddes and J. Thomson 1890; James Cattell 1903). Darwin and others claimed that on various physiological scales, such as strength, and various mental scales, such as intelligence, more males than females ranked in the extreme high and low ranges, more females than males in the median ranges. Of course, the fact that more males than females were represented in the lower ranges of many measures was seldom a focus of research; it was the *mediocrity* of females that captured the most attention. It is also important to note that, for Darwin, the greater variability of males was restricted to males of the "higher races."

These and other conceptual wrinkles in the Darwinian project are examined in more detail in chapter 3. The focus for this stage of the discussion is that for Darwin and his supporters, any sex differences in variability were seen to be biologically determined through the cumulative evolutionary effects of the female selection of mates. The potential conflict between the hypothesized choosiness of females and the presumption of universal female passivity was resolved for Darwin upon noting "the well-established fact" that males of any species are more eager to pair up, sexually, than are the females (Darwin 1981 [1871], 272–73). The issue, then, was not about female choosiness, so much as it was a reinforcement of male sexual appetite.

With respect to humans, Darwin conjectured that female mate-choice was probably more prevalent in our early evolutionary history than it was in his own time (Darwin 1981 [1871], 367–68). In any case, he claimed that the female act of choosing had resulted in the evolution of a variety of traits in males from which the females could further choose, cumulatively increasing male variability through biological inheritance (272–73). Despite the highly social nature of humans, the greater variability in the physiology and mental capacity of human males was seldom given a sociological explanation (assuming these differences in variability could indeed be documented).

In response to these evolutionary theories, feminist scientists such as Montague and Hollingworth designed and conducted painstakingly detailed empirical studies that measured physiological variability between the sexes (e.g., Hollingworth 1914; Montague and Hollingworth 1914). In an attempt to control for confounding sociological factors, many of the subjects they tested were infants. Few of the claimed sex differences in physiological variability were supported. Upon careful empirical testing, the biological theory that human males exhibit greater physiological variability was found to be false. With respect to sex differences in mental variability, of the few that could be documented, Montague and Hollingworth found that sociological explanations accounted for the data just as well, if not better, than did biological explanations. Some of the social forces they examined included the restricted educational opportunities for girls and the lower expectations for a girl's success outside the domestic sphere.[12]

Despite the sound empirical challenges to the variability theory and other questionable theories claiming the biologically determined mediocrity of females, such theories continued to be held by many evolutionary biologists and psychologists to the present day, especially in the growing fields of sociobiology and evolutionary psychology.[13] It is completely understandable, then, that some feminist scientists and philosophers of science have chosen an epistemological tack. If more than seventy years of intense empirical examination of the truth or falsity of sexist science have not yet solved the problems about which feminists are justifiably concerned, then perhaps it makes sense to reexamine our philosophical conceptions of truth and falsity.

To be sure, there are many reasons why feminists engage in epistemological study, but I think this particular historical sketch helps explain the rise of epistemology as it appears in feminist science criticism.

The first feminist scientists to have added epistemological commentary to their groundbreaking empirical research include Keller, Bleier, and Ruth Hubbard. Each has publicly expressed similar frustrations at the silence, if not outright resistance, that greets their empirical investigations of sexism in science. This frustration has clearly motivated each to move away from examinations of the empirical question "Is this particular scientific theory true?" and toward examinations of the philosophical questions "By which epistemic criteria might we adjudicate between competing knowledge claims?" and "Do these criteria indicate the presence of normative properties such as truth, or something other than truth, such as maximal objectivity or least partiality?" Each has responded to these latter questions by claiming that our prevailing notions of truth and its detection are affected by sexed/gendered conceptions of rationality. (I discuss the empirical and philosophical work of these three feminist scientists in chapters 3 and 4.)

Within philosophy itself, feminist studies that focus on the epistemology of science produced numerous publications in the 1980s and 1990s.[14] As I have already discussed, this feminist attention has brought about many improvements to the traditional epistemological project, including the recognition of the role of social forces, such as sex/gender, in knowledge production, and the articulation of an epistemological middle ground between objectivity and relativism.

I am entirely sympathetic to the frustration that has often motivated feminist critics of science to focus increasingly on epistemology, and, as my historical sketch of feminist evolutionary biology has shown, I am aware that the sort of empirical criticism I am advocating has not often had immediate, or lasting, positive results within science and science studies (witness the sociobiological hangover). However, such empirical criticism has never, as far as I know, made the situation worse. Not so with our current epistemological focus. Feminist epistemological projects that conceive of political concerns, not as empirical data, but as filters through which empirical data must pass; that search for criteria that signal the truth or maximal objectivity of the resulting representations (ours, it is hoped)—these projects can indeed make things worse, and irredeemably so because they encourage a global skepticism about the objectivity of politicized science critique. At this global level, the skeptical target comes inevitably to include the claim that feminists so engaged in political work cannot possibly produce objective analyses of science.

Elisabeth Lloyd documents exactly this sort of backlash against feminist science studies in her essay "Science and Anti-Science: Objectivity and Its Real Enemies" (Lloyd 1997). It is important to note that Lloyd responds to criticisms of feminist science studies, not by pressing the larger epistemological points made by some feminist scientists-cum-philosophers, but by highlighting the empirical work of feminist scientists. Similarly, in response to the claims of Paul Gross and Norman Levitt (1994) that feminists have failed to find sexism "in the substance of science," Schiebinger notes that Gross and Levitt have focused on feminist historians and philosophers of science and should instead examine the contributions of feminist scientists, contributions she then proceeds to document throughout the rest of her important book *Has Feminism Changed Science?* (Schiebinger 1999, 2).

By questioning the utility and coherence of epistemology, it is my hope that greater numbers of feminists engaged in science studies can shift back to more empirically focused work, assured that our concepts of objectivity and truth are not in need of philosophical reconfiguration; assured also by a variety of experiential and experimental data that our feminist political values have well-established links to beliefs about evidence.

Returning to science with these assurances means returning to the old enemies—working to eradicate the harmful effects of sexism, racism, and other oppressive systems in all aspects of scientific research, laboratory by laboratory, research program by research program. As I have already noted, this empirical undertaking is itself full of conceptual and practical difficulties. In capturing the spirit of my prescription for a feminist refocus on empirical studies, Susan Sperling's essay "Baboons with Briefcases: Feminism, Functionalism, and Sociobiology in the Evolution of Primate Gender" makes the point that these empirical projects will involve an "unbearably messy" and "time-consuming" process (1991, 26). But in the long run, I argue, this empirical process will prove to be more effective and less harmful than our current epistemological focus.

Articulating my empirical prescriptions in terms of existing feminist vocabulary, part of my project involves a return to what Harding calls feminist critiques of "bad science," as distinguished from feminist critiques of "science as usual" or "science at its best" (Harding 1986a, chapter 1). Harding, in contrast, supports the latter critiques. She argues that to identify individual cases of bad science as laden with sexist values and ideology is to miss the larger point that *all* our science, even that produced within the highest of our current evidential standards, is value-laden or ideological (Harding 1986a, beginning on 21–24). Harding suggests instead an epistemological prescription for new evidential standards, which she calls "strong objectivity" (Harding 1991).[15] I argue that we need to take Harding's epistemological route only if we continue to make the representationalist distinction between the "unadulterated" facts, or empirical content available to human sense organs, and the value-laden schemes, worldviews, or cultural filters through which those facts are perceived. This is an example of the epistemological scheme/content distinction that Davidson, in particular, is convinced we should jettison. I spend much of the balance of this book arguing that feminist science studies would be improved if we took his advice.

The large volume of literature combining feminism, science, and epistemology necessitates some selective sampling on my part. I begin by examining the epistemological components of Western feminist responses to, and within, evolutionary biology. The choice of feminist science critiques within the Western tradition reflects my own exposure and training. Within the Western feminist tradition, evolutionary theory is one of the most frequent and familiar targets, and rightly so.

After addressing the epistemological critiques of evolutionary theory, I then discuss the more general epistemological criticisms of science as they appear in classic texts by Keller, Harding, and Longino. Each of these three influential theorists suggests that the oppressive aspects of scientific activity are best addressed, and remedied, by constructing new, feminist conceptions of epistemology.

While I have argued that feminist science studies is not well served by epistemological theory building, I have tried to distinguish this from the claim that feminists don't need to bother with the truth or evidence of individual beliefs. But I continue to take seriously the possibility that these two claims might be conflated. As a result, I spend a great deal of time distinguishing between the local, empirical examination of individual beliefs and the epistemological examination of "truth-indicativeness" or normative properties more generally, and even more time cataloging the problems encountered by feminist scientists and science critics who have engaged in epistemological theory building. It is my hope that by documenting a number of examples of how epistemology has failed us, I can shift the burden of proof to those in science studies who argue in favor of continuing with an epistemological focus. I devote three full chapters arguing this negative portion of my thesis (chapters 3, 4, and 5). Readers might want to focus on one or two of these chapters. The positive aspects of my thesis begin in chapter 6 with an examination of Davidson's work.

NOTES

1. In Bernstein's characterization of the debate (*Beyond Objectivism and Relativism* 1983), he blends the standard "objectivism vs. subjectivism" and "absolutism vs. relativism" distinctions to pick out their epistemological and ontological strengths. He argues that few philosophers currently support either absolutism or subjectivism, whereas some forms of objectivism and relativism continue to be debated (Bernstein 1983, 8–12). I make reference to his objectivist/relativist distinction throughout this book, but I use the distinction for purposes of which he would not generally approve. In particular, I champion Richard Rorty's work against both objectivism *and* relativism, while Bernstein argues that Rorty is a relativist (Bernstein 1983, 9). My arguments against a relativist interpretation of Rorty begin in chapter 6.

2. While he makes clear that these are not the only norms to which scientists appeal (and to which they sometimes fail to appeal), he writes, "It is arguable that they

play a central role in guiding the construction and evaluation of scientific tests" (Campbell 1998, 22).

3. This definition of skepticism comes from Davidson (1990a, 298).

4. In his book *The Significance of Philosophical Skepticism* (1984), Barry Stroud offers a similar analysis of the pervasiveness and power of skeptical doubt, though he sees skepticism as part of the natural human condition, while I see it as arising out of a particular (and unnecessary) model in epistemology.

5. Alessandra Tanesini provides a helpful description of representationalism in her book *An Introduction to Feminist Epistemologies* (1999, 10). Tanesini argues that feminist epistemologies have moved beyond representationalism in a number of ways, including the articulation of knowledge as a social process, rather than as an exchange between individual representers and the world (12). I argue that the move to a social account does not adequately address the problems of skepticism invited by representationalism.

6. For more on the empirical use of representational language as it appears in cognitive science, see Daniel Dennett (1982).

7. Michael Williams's work parallels Rorty's arguments against Stroud and others who see skepticism as a natural human condition (Williams, *Unnatural Doubts*, 1991). Williams argues that skepticism arises out of epistemological realism. On the Rortyan analysis I recommend, realism would be one part of a larger representationalist commitment, making my analysis more general than, but still largely sympathetic to, that offered by Williams. See Rorty (1998) for a detailed discussion of the differences between Rorty, Davidson, and Williams.

8. Susan Haack has been a major critic on this front (e.g., Haack 1997). In "Truth without Correspondence to Reality" (Rorty 1999 [1994], especially 35–36), Rorty outlines what he sees as the main differences between the original pragmatists, such as Dewey, and the neopragmatists he champions, such as Davidson. Some feminist philosophers have begun to examine connections between feminism and classical pragmatism (see, for example, the summer 1993 special issue of *Hypatia*, edited by Charlene Haddock Seigfried, devoted to the topic, and also more recent work such as Seigfried [1996, 2001]), but it is the contemporary pragmatic themes of Rorty, Davidson, and, to a lesser extent, Quine, that interest me here.

9. Other points of difference between Rorty and Fraser, in particular, concern the degree of radicalness of Rorty's politics. Fraser argues that Rorty's pragmatist philosophy leads to a political agenda that is not radical enough. However, Bjørn Ramberg has argued, successfully, I believe, that it is possible to support Rorty's antirepresentationalism without supporting his "bourgeois liberalism"; that, as Rorty himself says, no philosophical position necessarily underwrites any one particular political agenda in any detail (Ramberg, "Strategies for Radical Rorty," 1993a). The differences between Rorty and Fraser on this point are discussed further in "Thinking with Fraser about Rorty, Feminism, and Pragmatism" (J. M. Fritzman 1993). I agree with Fritzman's assessment that, increasingly, the differences between feminists and Rorty can be regarded as "a tension within feminism itself" (1993, 113). Certainly, my feminist championing of Rorty could be construed as an example of this tension. Finally, Rorty has written an essay on the parallels between pragmatism and feminism (Rorty 1991f), although he does not touch on the representationalist concerns within feminism that I address here.

10. My articulation of the difference between empirical and epistemological questions is a blending of the arguments of Ramberg (1989, 9) and Rorty (1995, 148–53).

11. Haraway's analysis of evolutionary theory and primatology is not as straightforwardly empirical as the other science commentaries just cited. However, while Haraway's literary approach does not focus on the empirical question whether various primatological theories are true, neither does she attempt to construct epistemological responses to those theories. Her work has the virtue of analyzing evolutionary and primatological theories as texts, in all their historical and cultural specificity, thereby avoiding the epistemological problems I have described previously and providing a good foundation for future empirical work. The importance of Haraway's work is revisited in chapter 8.

12. For more details of these studies, see Hollingworth (1914); Montague and Hollingworth (1914); Helen Thompson Woolley (1910, 1914); and Mary Calkins (1896).

13. For a historical discussion of the problem, see Stephanie Shields (1982). Doreen Kimura's "Sex Differences in the Brain" (1992) is a good example of more recent claims about the biologically determined nature of behavioral sex differences. Kimura uses hormonal and evolutionary evidence to support the claim that human males are better at mathematical and spatial abilities than are females. For a thorough, empirical criticism of the evidence she uses, see Jeffrey Foss (1996). Foss notes with some discouragement that these same criticisms have been leveled by feminists, and others, many times in the past (Foss 1996, 24), but they have obviously failed to persuade scientists like Kimura. See also Hilary Rose and Steven Rose (2000), which contains a number of empirical criticisms made by feminist scientists against evolutionary psychology.

14. A sample of the more recent literature not already cited includes Jane Duran's *Philosophies of Science/Feminist Theories* (1998); the collection edited by Lynn Hankinson Nelson and Jack Nelson, titled *Feminism, Science, and the Philosophy of Science* (1997); "Women, Gender, and Science" (1997), edited by Sally Gregory Kohlstedt and Helen Longino; a number of essays from *Engendering Rationalities* (2001), edited by Nancy Tuana and Sandra Morgen; *Women, Knowledge, and Reality: Explorations in Feminist Philosophy* (1996 [1989]), edited by Ann Garry and Marilyn Pearsall; *Feminist Epistemologies* (1993), edited by Linda Alcoff and Elizabeth Potter; *A Mind of One's Own: Feminist Essays on Reason and Objectivity* (1993), edited by Louise Antony and Charlotte Witt; and *Feminism/Postmodernism*, edited by Linda Nicholson (1990). Earlier examples include essays from *Feminism and Science* (Nancy Tuana 1989); *Sex and Scientific Inquiry* (Sandra Harding and Jean F. O'Barr 1987); *Feminism and Methodology* (Harding 1987); *Science, Morality, and Feminist Theory* (Marsha Hanen and Kai Nielsen 1987); and *(Dis)covering Reality: Feminist Perspectives on Epistemology, Metaphysics, and Philosophy of Science* (Sandra Harding and Merrill B. Hintikka 1983).

15. Louise Antony suggests a different prescription for addressing what she calls "the bias paradox" in feminist epistemology. Her alternative is an epistemology naturalized, which is modeled after Quine (Antony 1993). Feminist approaches to naturalized epistemology are discussed in more detail in chapter 2.

2

Epistemology in Feminist Science Studies: Causes for Concern

After a century of producing well-documented examinations of abuse and bias in science, many researchers engaged in feminist science studies have begun to shift away from local, empirical responses and toward more general epistemological examinations of scientific method, objectivity, and truth. I have introduced arguments suggesting that, with respect to addressing the oppressive features of science, this epistemic shift is not the most effective direction to maintain. My main concern is that epistemology is based on a Cartesian or representationalist model that invites an unanswerable, global skepticism about our ability to know the world around us, including our ability to make well-founded criticisms of scientific theories and practices. While feminist epistemologists have been instrumental in dismantling the traditional Cartesian project, I argue that the deconstructive task is incomplete and that elements of our representationalist inheritance remain. Until we are fully free from this tradition, skepticism will remain an omnipotent foe.

I believe that the futile but ongoing responses to skepticism are necessary features of feminist (or any other) engagement with epistemology, as I have defined it here. However, before I go further, I want briefly to explore a number of difficulties that, while not necessary features of feminist epistemology, seem to be ubiquitous historically. These are the problems of abstraction and the overgeneralizations that often inform our categories of analysis. With the benefit of hindsight it has become apparent that these difficulties, too, have restricted the usefulness of feminist epistemology as it is applied to critical science studies.

THE PROBLEMS OF ABSTRACTION AND ESSENTIALISM

Much of the feminist epistemology applied to science studies is too abstract to meet what remain our most urgent political needs. Increasingly, our epistemic criticisms and prescriptions have focused on the general institution of science and/or scientific method, as exemplified in Keller's question "Is the nature of scientific method masculine?" By working at this level of abstraction, we are less able to contribute to more immediate and concrete feminist goals, such as the identification and censure of the individual funding agents, scientists, and laboratories responsible for endangering lives.[1]

It is true that there are many feminist scientists/epistemologists who focus critical attention on their own particular fields of scientific study. Ruth Hubbard, Ruth Bleier, and Evelyn Fox Keller focus compelling and critical empirical attention on various biases and abuses in biology. However, at some point in the text of their arguments they each move away from specific empirical questions such as "Is the evolutionary theory of women's lesser variability true?" and toward a more general and abstract set of epistemological questions, including: "Which epistemic criteria have we been trained to use in our adjudication of competing knowledge claims?"; "What is the role of gender in those criteria?"; and "If the role has been significant, can we then say the criteria indicate normative properties such as truth?"

As I argue further in chapters 3 and 4, the abstract level at which these references to gender, truth, and objectivity are pitched disengages the reader from the more concrete discussions of bias in science raised earlier in these texts. This is a problem for Bleier's and Keller's discussions in particular, as both scientists add one further level of abstraction in the form of psychoanalytic theory. Neither theorist provides enough details to connect these abstract discussions back to the empirical examples with which they were initially concerned. And, of course, my particular worry is that these abstract, epistemological discussions invite dangerous levels of skepticism about all the important empirical claims of bias and abuse in science that were established earlier in their arguments.

Further doubts about the utility of this epistemological focus concern not just the abstract level at which we end up working, but also about the content of those abstractions. I return here to the metaphorical labeling of science as "masculine." It is becoming clear that characterizing science or scientific method as masculine has the rhetorical effect of forcing young women to choose between feminism or science. It seems that no matter how much we try to avoid it, when our diagnosis of sexism in science is pitched at this level of abstraction, two messages are sent: Science is not for any woman who would call herself a feminist; and women scientists are, by definition, antifeminist, or worse, masculine. Georgina Feldberg has documented this phenomenon in her study of undergraduates in feminist courses on gender and science (Feldberg 1992). She found that the feminist women students who were not scientists interpreted the claim that science is male or masculine to mean that science had no relevance in their lives. They also viewed women scientists as having compromised their feminist integrity in order to succeed at science.[2]

Aside from issues of rhetorical utility, the level of abstraction in our epistemological projects has required generalizations about science that have been difficult to support empirically. Some of our feminist epistemological projects make references to science as if it were a monolithic, homogenous institution. But, of course, "science" names a multiplicity of disciplines with a wide range of practitioners and normative practices that have varied under the usual pressures of changing historical periods and cross-cultural exchange.[3] Keller's (and others') suggestion that our conceptions of truth, objectivity, and science are gendered masculine is difficult to support in the face of this multiplicity.

Assuming that this latter problem is one of execution, rather than of conception—in other words, assuming that if we are sufficiently careful with the historical and cultural details, we can indeed draw some general conclusions about science as an institution (which I think can be done)—and assuming that such abstractions are useful to feminist projects at this particular moment (something of which I am less certain), the next problem concerns the limitations of our existing categories of analysis.

As with "science," the categories "women"/"feminine"/"female" and "men"/"masculine"/"male" don't often serve the purposes for which they are enlisted within feminist epistemology. As antiracist and postcolonialist writers have long pointed out, the generalizations about men and women embedded in some versions of feminist standpoint theories, for example, often ignore important distinctions among women and among men, assuming that the experiences of a dominant group of women are the experiences of all women (Spelman 1988). Also obscured are important similarities between women and men who have a common experience as oppressors or as victims of oppression (hooks 1989). These problems of inadequate categorization mirror those encountered by Marxist theories of class that ignored race and sex/gender, and antiracist theorizing that ignored sex/gender and class, to name the three systems of oppression that have been the most closely examined, to date.

While this problem of feminist essentialism is now well recognized, we don't seem to be able to move much beyond the recognition, and few concrete proposals for change have been suggested or embraced. I wonder if the lack of progress on this point doesn't support a change of focus away from big epistemological questions that require big, and often inaccurate, generalizations. Moving toward more local, empirical examinations of science and other social institutions might allow for more sensitive and fine-grained analyses of the roles of sex/gender, race, and class. I find support for this suggestion in the examinations of feminist essentialism provided by Judith Butler (1992) and Cressida Heyes (2000).[4] Heyes, in particular, provides a helpful discussion of the linguistic essentialism that occurs not just at the level of biological sex categories, but also at the level of socially constructed gender categories, as, for example, when we use the term "woman" to refer to "people united by the socially constructed aspects of their femininity" (2000, 37). That oppressive, essentialist elements can remain even within social, as opposed to biological, categories is an important point to which I return in my discussion of Keller in chapter 4. Heyes responds to linguistic essentialism by prescribing a local, empirical approach to our categories of analysis, based on a Wittgensteinian "family resemblances" model.[5] Her prescriptions overlap well with my own pragmatist approach.

The problems of abstraction and essentialism are revisited throughout the balance of this book. Some pragmatist solutions are offered in chapter 7.

THE PROBLEM OF SKEPTICISM

Abstraction and essentialism are difficult problems, and assuming we wanted to continue with our current epistemological focus, they could perhaps be overcome. However, as the history of epistemology has shown us, the problems arising from skepticism are not just difficult, but quite possibly intractable. (This latter generalization about epistemology serves an important reminder: The problem of essentialism, for example, is not due to the fact that generalizations are involved—we could not do without these—but that the generalizations are often empirically inadequate, that is, *over*generalized. My job throughout this book will be to offer as much empirical support as possible for my generalizations about epistemology in feminist science studies. My hope, of course, is that any exceptions I might overlook will be those that prove the rule.)

So far, I have argued that we only need answer questions such as "By which epistemic criteria might we adjudicate between competing knowledge claims?" if we are convinced that global skepticism is a rational concern. The epistemological worry is that our theories might be justified by the evidence, but still not have that special elusive relationship with truth (or a functional equivalent). Again, this is not a healthy, contrite fallibilism that acknowledges that any one of our current theories might turn out to be wrong. It is a global worry that *all* of our knowledge of the external world might be wrong, and, worse, that we might never even be aware of it.

At one end of the epistemological continuum, objectivists attempt to answer global skepticism by suggesting that truth *can* be recognized if one is sufficiently objective in establishing a correspondence relation, for example.

Relativists, at the other end of the continuum, are critical of objectivist attempts and resign themselves to accepting some level of skepticism in its relativistic guise. For relativists, the global worry that all our knowledge of the external world might be wrong becomes the global worry that there is no way to adjudicate between theories about the external world that are produced from within our own internal frameworks. Coherence *between* a collection of subjective theories is the only criterion left for the relativist. The well-known problem with this sort of relativism is that it robs the relativist of any epistemological bite when she attempts to promote one theory over another (even her theory of relativism). As I explain below, skepticism remains a motivating factor even for intermediate epistemological positions, such as empiricism or instrumentalism, which fall somewhere between the objectivism/relativism poles.

In a debate that has been alive since Plato, if not earlier, neither objectivists, instrumentalists, nor relativists have succeeded in persuading each other that they have identified once and for all the normative property that would answer skepticism. Feminist criticisms of science that make use of any of these epistemological approaches are weakened by the global skepticism that these theoretical avenues invite but then leave unanswered. If we attempt to address the oppressive elements of science at the level of epistemology, then the global skepticism toward which epistemology is directed can be used against our own well-justified claims about the instances of scientific bias and abuse. When skepticism takes the shape of relativist resignation, we are similarly vulnerable. We have argued that the bias and abuse in science must stop, but the truth of this argument is not to be taken as relative to a subjective feminist worldview. It is true *simpliciter.*

People are being harmed by various scientific practices, theories, and methods. Some women and men have been oppressively excluded from practicing science on the basis of irrelevant criteria such as sex and race. They have also been described as subjects of biased scientific theorizing in ways that justify their continued exclusion from science and other arenas of "rational inquiry," further restricting their opportunities and freedoms. We know, too, that many people have been physically harmed or killed by scientific products that have been inadequately tested. We need to combat any number of skeptical responses to these claims.

As I noted in chapter 1, I have found Richard Rorty's pragmatist project to be very helpful in combating the very idea of skepticism. His project provides a basis for criticizing the debate between objectivists and relativists, by showing that the skepticism they both try to answer arises from a questionable representationalist model of knowers and the world (Rorty 1991a [1986], 1991b [1988]). Rorty uses Donald Davidson's philosophy of language as a nonrepresentational model of meaning and language use that makes skepticism a nonissue. I believe this model to be a useful one for feminists. In this

next section I examine more closely how Rorty and Davidson view the relationship between epistemology, representationalism, and skepticism.

SYMPTOM: SKEPTICISM; DIAGNOSIS: REPRESENTATIONALISM

Rorty argues that epistemological questions such as "By which epistemic criteria might we adjudicate between competing knowledge claims?" assume
the very coherence of the skepticism they are meant to combat. He identifies
the epistemological reliance on representationalism as the primary culprit
(e.g., Rorty 1991b [1988], 151–61). However, whereas Rorty focuses on the
representationalism inherent in the objectivist side of the debate, I discuss
the problem as it affects the entire continuum of positions from objectivism
to relativism.

Advocates from either end of the continuum view beliefs, sentences, or
theories as representing the world. Both sides claim, in some form, that we
acquire these representations through a filtering process. According to
Davidson's diagnosis, this representationalist commitment conceives of our
language scheme, worldview, or culture as a subjective interpretive medium,
metaphysically distinct from the empirical content, sense data, or facts of the
external world for which the medium serves as a filter (Davidson 1984).

The concern I share with Rorty and Davidson is that, by invoking this filtering process, the representationalist invokes a metaphysical gap between
the inner, subjective, end-product of belief and the external, objective reality
the belief is about—a gap between the non-natural (supernatural?) "inner
space" of the uninterpreted interpreter and the facts given to the interpreter
by the natural world.[6] While some might protest that only a naive few continue to conceive of the external world as simply "given," it is important to
make a distinction between believing (a) that the given data of the world are
out there, but that our *access* to that data is filtered (many feminist theorists
have argued this point); and believing (b) that the internal filter/external data
model is incoherent (not as many have made this stronger point or followed
out its implications). I sketch out this distinction in detail in chapter 6.

Epistemology is a required response, given these representationalist metaphysics. The metaphysical independence or gap between the inner subjective stuff of mind and the external objective reality makes coherent the worry
that the two worlds might not be bridgeable—*all* of our subjective theories
about external reality "might be just as they are and yet reality—and so the
truth about reality—be very different" (Davidson 1990a, 298). When one
conceives of such a gap between representations and the world represented,
there is always the possibility of massive error in the representations—that
is, it becomes conceivable that all of our bridgework could be completely
undependable. This is the worry of global skepticism, so clearly articulated

by the protorepresentationalist Descartes in his theory of mind/body dualism. Epistemology arises as a necessary but futile response to this skepticism, even, I argue, within feminist traditions long critical of Cartesian dualism.

While the three principle responses to skepticism—namely, objectivism, empiricism/instrumentalism, and relativism—are well known, the representationalist commitments that accompany each position are less familiar. I believe that the representationalist problems accompanying each of these positions are prototypical and can be generalized to any number of epistemological positions that have been articulated elsewhere. In chapters 3, 4, and 5, I identify a number of feminist responses to skepticism that do not fit neatly into the objectivist, relativist, or instrumentalist camps, but that are consistently weakened, nonetheless, by their reliance on representationalism.

Objectivism

In representationalist terms, the objectivist makes the assurance that skepticism about the truth of our representations can be defeated—that we can delineate a priori the criteria for judging whether our representations have the requisite normative properties. In other words, the claim goes, we can tell if and when the bridgework between our subjective inner space and the objective outer reality is dependable. While "objectivity" names a normative property, it also describes an epistemic method for detecting such properties. If we are objective, if we stand apart from the filters of all our subjective theories, if we enlist the help of other objective observers similarly placed, then we can open the bridgeway between our sensory receptors and the causal forces of the empirical data. The clarity of this bridgeway between theory and world is often articulated in terms of a correspondence relation with the natural facts given up by the world the theory purports to describe.

C. I. Lewis prescribes a version of objectivism in his book *Mind and the World Order* (1956 [1929]). He explains that "the two elements to be distinguished in knowledge are the concept, which is the product of the activity of thought [such as the forming of a hypothesis or a theory], and the sensuously [empirically] given, which is independent of such activity" (Lewis 1956, 37). For Lewis, the "given" of experience is "what remains unaltered, no matter what our interests, no matter how we think or conceive" (Lewis, 52). This is what Davidson refers to as the "content." Our conceptualization of the given is the imposing of a filter or "scheme" over the content.

For Lewis, the sense data and our subjective filtering of that data must, *in principle,* be capable of separate analysis. The intuited experience of the given is error-free; error arises only from our filtered conceptualizations of the given (Lewis, 121). Objective knowledge of the empirically given data results when a conceptualization of the given holds up to empirical test over time, and the probability of error produced by the subjective filters decreases

(Lewis, 37), or, in other words, when the gap between our inner conceptual space and the outer world is successfully bridged.

Instrumentalism/Empiricism

Instrumentalists and empiricists take these objectivist views to be generally coherent, but false for a specified range of claims. More specifically, they disagree with the traditional objectivist view about the possibility of identifying correspondence relations that would hold *directly* between the theoretical or unobservable elements of any given theory and the external world the theory represents. But they typically agree with the objectivist that a normative identification of relational features is possible and necessary, as long as the focus is restricted to the observable or otherwise empirically accessible elements of the theory.

For example, Bas van Fraassen's constructive empiricism maintains that we can have objective access to the truth about *observable* entities only. He explains that "to accept a theory is (for us) to believe that it is empirically adequate—that what the theory says about *what is observable* (by us) is true" (van Fraassen 1980, 18; italics in the original). When a theory makes reference to unobservable entities, we cannot have such knowledge. He argues that theories that contain unobservables can be "empirically adequate" but not true or false as a whole (18). Theories about microparticles, for example, cannot be true or false as a whole (17). More traditional instrumentalists, such as the positivists, deny the existence of unobservables outright, rather than remaining agnostic as van Fraassen does. Willard Van Orman Quine's naturalized version of empiricism and feminist responses to it are discussed in the next section.

Relativism

Extending the Rortyan/Davidsonian diagnosis, I argue that relativism, too, can be shown to have representationalist underpinnings, evidenced in the relationship between relativism and skepticism. Those who have moved away from the objectivist end of the epistemological continuum end up approaching skepticism in its relativistic guise—a relativism that resigns them to doubt, at a very general level, the existence of any firm causal relationships between their theories and the world. Their tacit claim is that if we are critical of the objectivist notion of correspondence relations linking our representations and the world, then we are left with the position that links can be made only between representations themselves. Our subjective filtering of the external world is so opaque that our criteria for adjudicating between representations— criteria that would signal the presence of truth or objectivity—can only be said to be relative to our interests, our politics, our worldviews, and not to the world. Hubbard presents such a relativist view when she claims that "every theory is a self-fulfilling prophecy that orders experience into the framework it provides" (Hubbard 1983 [1979], 47). At best, we can attain "maximal" objectivity or "least partiality." Bleier doubts that we can have even this. Both of these responses are discussed further in chapter 3.

As I've shown, the questionable metaphysics of the representationalist model make skepticism a coherent concern for any number of positions on the epistemological continuum. In the absence of any consensus that skepticism has been defeated, feminist critics of science who enter the epistemological debate invite skepticism with no guarantee that it will not be used against their own critiques. A more detailed examination of this problem, in terms of Quinean empiricism, follows.

QUINE'S FAILURE TO DEFEAT SKEPTICISM

Quinean empiricism has become an increasingly popular epistemological model for feminists (e.g., Nelson 1990, 1993; Antony 1993; Campbell 1994, 1998; Alcoff 1996). But it, too, is haunted by skepticism in ways that reveal a reliance on representationalism. Recall that for empiricists, generally, the relational bridge between our subjective linguistic entities (theories, sentences, beliefs) and the objective world can be known to be reliable, at least for those entities that have empirical content. If we are sufficiently objective observers, then we can open the bridgeway between our inner subjective world and the causal forces of the observable data from the external world that impinge on our sensory receptors. The reliability of knowledge about theories with observable content is said to provide a foundation for knowledge about theories with more abstract, unobservable content. We can be fairly sure of the reliability of theories that have little or no observable content if we can link them to the epistemic foundations provided by more stable observable theories.

Quine's early writings mark one of the most sophisticated versions of empiricism in the literature (see, for example, the first two chapters of *Word and Object* [Quine 1960]). The sophistication, by my antirepresentationalist criteria, results partly from the fact that Quine does not identify correspondence as an epistemic relationship between two metaphysically distinct entities. He attempts to naturalize the inner "subjective" side of the subject/object gap, making the subject *part of* the external world treated by empirical science, rather than part of some metaphysically separate supernatural order. So far, so good.

Quine also takes a holistic approach to meaning and truth. Unlike the reductionistic views of his positivist colleagues, views to be found in Rudolf Carnap's early work, for example (Carnap 1939), Quine argues that only sentences, not individual terms, can be said to have meaning and that this meaning comes from the sentence's role in the larger theory of which it is a part. He is also much more holistic about the division between sentences with observational content and sentences without, than is, say, van Fraassen. That is, for the most part, he views the division as a continuum. The criterion for whether a sentence is "observational" or "nonobservational" is relative to the placement of that sentence in the web of sentences from which it derives its meaning.

However, Quine argues that the division between sentences with observable content and those without is still an epistemologically crucial division. For example, in the chapters of *Word and Object* cited previously, he argues that what makes a sentence (or theory) true is its relation to sensory stimulation. Here it is clear that he retains an interest in the epistemological question "By which epistemic criteria might we adjudicate between competing knowledge claims?" As I argue in the discussion that follows, his sophisticated answer nevertheless fails to defeat skepticism.

Quine calls those sentences that have a close relation to sensory stimulation "observation sentences." Observation sentences, such as "There's a cat on the mat," "prompt the assent" of any number of people receiving the same visual stimulus (Quine 1960, 43). Quine writes that observation sentences "suggest the datum sentences of science," that is, the *evidence* (44).[7]

Not all sentences have this close link to sensory stimulation, however. Some sentences will *not* prompt assent from different speakers similarly placed, especially if the sentences contain words that get their meaning from relation to other words, as opposed to acquiring meaning through more-or-less direct ostension. Quine gives as an example "[He is] a bachelor" (45). According to Quine, the sentences of our various theories of the world stand in a weblike relation to each other, with observation sentences ("There's a cat on the mat") at the periphery, well anchored to the sensory stimulation of the outside world. Nonobservation sentences ("He is a bachelor") are found in the webbing of the center.

Now, to be sure, Quine approaches the distinction holistically; there are no hard and fast boundaries between words that get their meaning from observation and those that get their meaning from their relation to other words. Indeed, the holism suggested by the fine grading off between observation and nonobservation sentences makes it look as if the meanings (and, relatedly, the truth, or evidential justification) of the sentences of any theory are always, to some extent, *relative* to their place in the web of the "containing theory," rather than being objective and definitive. Quine uses the concept of "stimulus meaning" to respond to this relativistic worry. "The stimulus meaning of a sentence for a subject sums up his disposition to assent or to dissent from the sentence in response to present stimulation" (Quine 1960, 34). He continues,

> If a sentence is one that (like "Red" and "Rabbit") is inculcated mostly by something like direct ostension, the uniformity [of the language] will lie at the surface and there will be little variation in stimulus meaning; the sentence will be highly observational. If it is one that (like "Bachelor") is inculcated through connections

with other sentences, linking up thus indirectly with past stimulations of other sorts than those that serve directly to prompt present assent to the sentence, then its stimulus meaning will vary with the speakers' pasts, and the sentence will count as very unobservational. (1960, 45)

The stimulus meaning of any sentence can be examined in isolation from the sentence's relation to other sentences. Quine explains how this responds to worries about relativism:

> We may well have begun . . . to wonder whether meanings even of whole sentences (let alone shorter expressions) could reasonably be talked of at all, except relative to the other sentences of an inclusive theory. Such relativity would be awkward, since, conversely, the individual component sentences offer the only way into the theory. Now the notion of stimulus meaning partially resolves the predicament. It isolates a sort of net empirical import of each of various single sentences without regard to the containing theory, even though without loss of what the sentence owes to that containing theory. It is a device, as far as it goes, for exploring the fabric of interlocking sentences, a sentence at a time. (Quine 1960, 34–35)

According to Quine, then, if the stimulus meaning of a sentence varies greatly from speaker to speaker, then the meaning is related less to direct sensory stimulation and more to other sentences. Observation sentences with stimulus meanings that are more uniformly shared by speakers are candidates for objective knowledge because they acquire their meaning through their relation to sensory stimulation from the external world.

According to Davidson, this argument shows that for the Quine who wrote *Word and Object,* observation sentences play a normative, justificatory role. In other words, Quine wants "to anchor at least some words or sentences [the observation sentences] to non-verbal rocks" (Davidson 1991a [1983], 126). Davidson describes Quine's view further:

> Whatever there is to meaning must be traced back somehow to experience, the given, or patterns of sensory stimulation, something intermediate between belief and the usual objects our beliefs are about. (Davidson 1991a, 126)

Unfortunately, as with all epistemological projects, this "something intermediate" leaves conceptual space for skepticism. Injecting intermediaries between the meaning of our beliefs and that which would make our beliefs true or well justified encourages skepticism, because we don't know if these intermediaries are supplying us with correct information. How could we ever step outside the process to check? (Davidson 1986). Davidson argues that "no such confrontation makes sense,"

> for of course we can't get outside our skins to find out what is causing the internal happenings of which we are aware. Introducing intermediate steps or entities into the causal chain, like sensations or observations, serves only to make

the epistemological problem more obvious. For if the intermediaries are merely causes, they don't justify the beliefs they cause, while if they deliver information, they may be lying. (1991a, 125)

Davidson understands why sensations, for example, have been thought to play an epistemological role. We are aware of our sensations in a way that gives them salience in the causal process of belief acquisition. However, this awareness is simply another belief. He explains,

> Emphasis on sensation or perception in matters epistemological springs from the obvious thought: sensations are what connect the world and our beliefs, and they are candidates for justifiers because we often are aware of them. The trouble we have been running into is that the justification seems to depend on the awareness, which is just another belief. (1991a, 124)

Here, meaningful understanding of the external world is made a function of an epistemic intermediary. Of the resulting skepticism Davidson writes, "It is ironical. Trying to make meaning accessible has made truth inaccessible" (1991a, 126).

A further problem results from the fact that there is no way to tell at what point the sensation of the "uninterpreted world" ends and our subjective interpretation or perception begins. This is the representationalist problem of the scheme/content distinction. One of the more well-known examples of Quine's early adherence to the scheme/content distinction follows:

> We cannot strip away the conceptual trappings sentence by sentence and leave a description of the objective world; *but* we can investigate the world, and man as a part of it, and thus find out what cues he could have of what goes on around him. *Subtracting his cues from his world view, we get man's net contribution as the difference.* This difference marks the extent of man's conceptual sovereignty—the domain within which he can revise the theory while saving the data. (Quine 1960, 5; emphasis mine)

Here, Quine still makes the questionable assumption that there is a meaningful epistemological distinction between unanalyzed sensory cues and one's worldview or analysis of those cues, even though his naturalism toward the subject that produces the worldview gives him little conceptual apparatus for making the distinction.

Few feminists who champion Quine make mention of these conceptual weaknesses. Harding provides the first major feminist treatment of Quine in *The Science Question in Feminism* (1986a). Harding did her doctoral work on Quine, and it is clear from her discussion that she is generally sympathetic to his arguments, especially those that set him against logical positivists. However, Quinean debates with Davidson and Rorty are not part of her focus.

Harding is supportive of Quine's holism and his criticism of the analytic/synthetic distinction, but she writes against his empiricist epistemology, and against feminist versions of empiricism in particular. Harding describes feminist empiricism as the view "that sexism and androcentrism are social biases correctable by stricter adherence to the existing methodological norms of scientific inquiry" (1986a, 24). Stricter adherence to the norms, says Harding, involves the claim that science is or should be value-free. But, Harding points out, feminist values were *needed* in order for cases of sexist science to be recognized. Here Harding begins to articulate a conception of values as conceptually distinct from empirical data.

Unlike the anti-epistemology route taken by Davidson and Rorty, Harding moves from her criticism of empiricism to a prescription for a better epistemology. She argues that some sort of epistemology, some sort of philosophical justificatory scheme for our beliefs, is still required—appeals to empirical data are not enough. In later writings, "strong objectivity" is offered as a new epistemological prescription (Harding 1991). We reach stronger levels of objectivity, she claims, when feminist biases and values are used as the standpoint from which we filter scientific evidence. According to Harding, the level of objectivity attained is relative to the scheme through which the data pass. Harding's concept of strong objectivity is discussed in detail in chapter 5.

Lynn Hankinson Nelson is critical of Harding's description of empiricism and her suggestions that a feminist standpoint would provide a strengthened objectivity. Like Harding, she did her doctoral work on Quine, and her dissertation became the book *Who Knows? From Quine to a Feminist Empiricism* (1990). After her work a number of feminist philosophers, including Nancy Tuana (who also did her dissertation on Quine) and Campbell, published critiques of the relativism implied in Harding's suggestions for strong objectivity and reexamined the feminist case for some version of empiricism (Tuana 1992a; Campbell 1994). However, Nelson continues to come the closest to engaging with the important concerns about skepticism and relativism raised between Quine, Davidson, and Rorty.

While she makes no direct mention of Davidson's concerns about Quine, Nelson does include a brief discussion of the possibility that Quine's view implies a scheme/content dualism (Nelson 1990, 25). However, her defense of Quine on this point is not a focus of her project and receives only brief, so not entirely satisfactory, treatment. Nelson also tries to defend Quine from the charge that he is an epistemological foundationalist (Nelson 1990, 23), despite the fact that observation sentences do play something like a foundational normative role in his theory, however holistic and relative to a community that foundation is described (a point she acknowledges later in the book on pages 110–11).

Quine himself acknowledges his foundationalism in a number of places. For example, in his contribution to a collection of essays devoted to Rorty's

Philosophy and the Mirror of Nature, Quine notes that he differs from Rorty "on the score of observation sentences, which do have the 'special epistemological status' of being keyed directly to sensory stimulation and thus linking theory with outer reality" (Quine 1990c, 119). Quine also approves of Susan Haack's description of his position as a blend between coherentism and foundationalism (Quine 1990b, 128). Attempts to reconcile Quinean foundationalism with the needs of feminist empiricism figure as ongoing challenges.

Finally, Nelson argues that skepticism is not a problem for Quine (Nelson 1990, 27), insofar as Quine's is a theory of evidence rather than a theory of truth. Because Davidson's criticisms on this point are not central to her discussion, I find it difficult to evaluate her claim. However, I suspect that the difference between a theory of evidence and a theory of truth, in much of Quine's writings, is a difference without a difference.

Support for my suspicion comes from Campbell's work that brings Quine's naturalized, empiricist epistemology to bear on feminist science studies and moral theory. In his paper "The Virtues of Feminist Empiricism" (1994) and his book *Illusions of Paradox: A Feminist Epistemology Naturalized* (1998), Campbell's defense of feminist empiricism responds to skepticism in fairly typical ways, despite Nelson's arguments that such responses are obviated by the Quinean focus on evidence over truth.

In his introductory remarks, Campbell admits, "As long as we allow that epistemology is about how knowledge and the justification of belief are possible, it will be important to understand how naturalized epistemology can recognize the challenge of skepticism as a problem, *whether or not it is able to solve it*" (1998, 6, emphasis mine). One particular skeptical concern informs at least two chapters of his book (chapter 3 on realism and chapter 5 on normativity). In both cases Campbell defends his project from variants of the skeptical charge that by relying on empirical norms to argue for the importance of empirical norms, he is assuming a foundation for which he has no independent rationale. As I discuss earlier, this is exactly the skeptical problem diagnosed by Rorty in his response to Haack (Rorty 1995, 153). Rorty argues that these skeptical concerns would be avoided if local empirical methods were not elevated to the level of epistemological guide.

Despite the energy Campbell devotes to defending against skepticism, the holism of his Quinean project closes all but a very few of the usual entry points for skeptical worry. One of the few remaining entry points concerns Campbell's articulation of the role of feminist norms. Recall that Davidson's holism challenges the scheme/content dualism in some of Quine's earlier views that distinguished empirical content from the conceptual schemes through which the content is filtered. I find a similar dualism lingering in Campbell's conception of feminist norms as separate from the empirical data of science. One of Campbell's main theses is that if we base our hypothesis testing simply on the local empirical process of evidence gathering, then we might miss data we'd otherwise catch if we added feminist norms to our empirical method (e.g., Campbell 1998, chapter 3). By *adding* feminist norms/values, not as data, but as epistemic method, we increase our objectivity.

Compare this view of the role of norms and values with Davidson's view. As I explain in more detail in chapter 6, for Davidson, and less so, Quine, every belief gets its meaning from its place in a holistic web, a placement based on connections firm, or not so firm, to beliefs about the empirical world. Feminist norms, as with any other value set, are *themselves* beliefs. Though beliefs about norms are geographically remote from beliefs about empirical observations, the fact that feminist norms have any meaning at all shows that they have connections to beliefs about empirical data. If we conceive of feminist norms as something conceptually separate from empirical data—as something to be added to the empirical process—then we invite skepticism about the relationship between feminist norms and empirical evidence. However, the very reason feminist norms are valuable arises from our sense that they have firm connections to the empirical data that is our everyday experience. If feminist norms are properly viewed as a set of empirical claims, then stricter adherence to local empiricist examinations of evidence will show feminist versions of scientific hypotheses to be an improvement over sexist versions in every relevant case. Failure to do so will result in shoddy science, as so much good feminist criticism of science has shown.

In later chapters of *Illusions of Paradox,* Campbell returns to a more consistent holism, arguing that norms and empirical data are holistically of a piece—for example, that feminist norms are empirically defensible. He explains, "The cognitive and normative import of any terms is to be determined holistically by reference to their place within an evolving theory that is itself embedded within an evolving language" (1998, 153–54).

At these later points, it is not clear to me that Campbell's naturalist project must, of necessity, suffer from the epistemic malaise as I've outlined it. Having shown that we can articulate our feminist norms as beliefs about politics that have a strong relationship to beliefs about empirical evidence, any further epistemic analysis seems unnecessary. However, Campbell makes clear that, for him, epistemic analysis remains an important step for the naturalist. He uses the holistic links between evidence and feminist norms to support what he calls a "realist" epistemic interpretation of those norms (1998, chapter 8). The addition of the realist interpretation is needed, he argues, to guard against the skeptical view of norms as subjective and mind-dependent. Stated positively, we need epistemic realism to guarantee that our norms are objective features of the mind-independent world. As the review of Davidson's critique of Quine shows us, battling skepticism in this way often invites as many problems as it solves. In chapter 7, I offer a Davidsonian account of the objectivity of our norms that does not arise from epistemic responses to skepticism.

In sum, while I agree that Quine's naturalized epistemology is a sophisticated version of empiricism, his project still includes attempts to address
skepticism that meet with questionable success—a fate shared by a number
of the feminist science commentators who base their work on Quine. It is my
hope that a more thoroughgoing examination of Davidson will invite feminist empiricists to reassess their allegiance to Quine and, of course, to epistemology more generally.[8]

WEIGHING IN WITH SELLARS AND GOODMAN

I have argued that despite Quine's holistic approach to epistemology, his
views still make use of a questionable distinction between the content of unanalyzed sensory cues and the scheme or filters of our worldviews, culture,
or language—a representationalist distinction of which Davidson is suspi-
cious. In *Science, Perception, and Reality* Wilfred Sellars further criticizes the
notion of unanalyzed sensory cues, or what he calls the "myth of the given"
of sensory information (Sellars 1963). Providing a historical overview of the
use of the "given" in the empiricist tradition, Sellars writes that

> classical sense-datum philosophers have . . . taken givenness to be a fact which
> presupposes no learning, no forming of associations, no setting up of stimulus–
> response connections. In short, they have tended to equate *sensing sense contents*
> with *being conscious*, as a person who has been hit on the head is *not* conscious,
> whereas a new-born babe, alive and kicking, *is* conscious. (1963, 131)

Sellars argues against this view, explaining that perceiving even the most
"primitive" sense datum requires all kinds of previous abilities, such as the
ability to discriminate the one sense datum from others. Therefore, knowledge of the particular sensation in question cannot be epistemologically
foundational. Of the knowledge required *before* a particular sensory datum
can be perceived, he writes,

> Observational knowledge of any particular fact, e.g., that this is green, presup-
> poses that one knows general facts of the form *X is a reliable symptom of Y*. And
> to admit this requires an abandonment of the traditional empiricist idea that ob-
> servational knowledge "stands on its own feet." (1963, 168)

Presupposing objective criteria for distinguishing between the categories X
and Y also proves to be difficult. Here, Nelson Goodman casts a critical eye over
our certainty about the categories nature objectively "supplies" and to which
our true hypotheses "correspond" (Goodman 1955). He begins, famously, with
the category or predicate "green" that we use, for example, in the hypothesis
"All emeralds are green." We assume that every time we observe another green
emerald, this is empirical evidence in favor of the hypothesis. But what if,

Goodman asks, "green" was the wrong category? What if there was another category, "grue"? ("A colour which applies to all things examined before [January 1, 3009] just in case they are green but to other things just in case they are blue" [1955, 74]). If we were observing "green" emeralds before January 1, 3009, it might just be that this observation does *not* confirm the hypothesis "All emeralds are green," but instead, or likewise, confirms the hypothesis "All emeralds are grue." Goodman's "riddle" is a problem for both objectivists and empiricists, that is, for anyone who wants to use sensory reports as objective foundations for knowledge. Goodman's critique shows that the epistemologist can never be sure that even her most straightforward sensory reports of nature's "given" categories provide objective evidence for her theories about those categories. Problems with skepticism seem only to multiply here.

To review to this point, elements of Quine's earlier writings showed an empiricist attempt to "harness" sensation in the service of epistemological justification (Ramberg 1989, 13). Quine argued that those beliefs expressed in sentences that arise from direct links to sensations (e.g., observation sentences) provide the foundations for those sentences and beliefs not so directly linked (e.g., Quine 1960, 42). However, Davidson reminds us that sensory stimulations, while causally related to belief, "cannot, without confusion, be considered to be evidence, or a source of justification, for the stimulated beliefs" (1991a [1983], 132). And Goodman's riddle reminds us that we have no epistemologically objective criteria for choosing some categories as empirical evidence over others.

So what epistemological role is left then for objectivist empirical intermediaries? None, according to Davidson and Sellars. However, Sellars reminds his readers that his analysis still leaves an important, though *nonepistemological,* role for empirical sensation of the outside world. It is this nonepistemic notion of empirical sensation that I want to promote.

Notice that for there to be any empirical sensations at all, there must be a world causing those sensations. While Sellars argues against the claim that sensations provide epistemic justification, he harbors no idealist doubts about the existence of an objective reality (Sellars 1963, 161). Paralleling Sellars on this point, Davidson writes, "No doubt meaning and knowledge depend on experience, and experience ultimately on sensation. But this is the 'depend' of causality, not of evidence or justification" (1991a [1983], 127). Davidson concludes,

> The moral is obvious. Since we can't swear intermediaries [such as sensations] to truthfulness, we should allow no intermediaries between our beliefs and their objects in the world. Of course there are causal intermediaries. What we must guard against are epistemic intermediaries. (Davidson 1991a, 125)

Contrary, then, to what many objectivists and empiricists have argued, the detection of empirical entities cannot be conceptually rallied for the purposes of warding off skepticism. Relativists fare no better, as they simply use this weakness to show the futility of attempts to construct a correspondence bridge that is free from the filters of our subjective conceptual schemes. Better to invoke the coherence of one theory with another, they suggest, rather than trying in vain to bridge the metaphysical gap between subjective, scheme-riddled theories and the content of the objective, external world. But, of course, the claim that relativism is itself a true description of our relation between our theories and the world cannot be defended from skepticism. No epistemological escape from skepticism appears in sight.

However, some epistemologists continue to see this failure as one of execution, rather than of conception—putting renewed energy into bridging the correspondence gap by attempting to rebuild on the failed foundations of previous epistemological theories. While the traditional correspondence theory of truth has fallen from favor, the metaphysics underlying the theory are still prevalent in many current representationalist responses to skepticism. Davidson's antirepresentationalism provides a useful response to this lingering epistemological commitment. He predicts problems for the building of correspondence bridges, not simply because previous bridge designs have been flawed, but because the concept of truth as correspondence is itself incoherent.

ANOTHER LOOK AT CORRESPONDENCE

Davidson mounts numerous criticisms of the idea of truth as correspondence (e.g., in Davidson 1984 [1974], 1990a). According to the representationalist conception of correspondence, a sentence or theory "fits our sensory promptings, successfully faces the tribunal of experience, predicts future experience, or copes with the pattern of our surface irritations, provided it is borne out by the evidence" (Davidson 1984, 193). But as Rorty points out, comparing a theory to the available evidence is just what we *all* do when we examine whether the theory is true, maximally objective, or least partial. Here the skeptic typically responds that because our theories could be wrong in the future, correspondence with *available* evidence is not enough. Truth, she claims, must be correspondence with all *possible* evidence, past, present, and future (Davidson 1984, 193). However, the skeptic has still not told us anything new about truth; she's just added more of the criteria with which we're already familiar. Future criticism of our current theories will continue to be made on the basis of new evidence. As Davidson argues, to say that a theory corresponds with the totality of evidence past, present, and future "adds nothing intelligible to the simple concept of being true" (193). That is, truth-as-correspondence is not a new property against which we can test our theories (194). As one Davidson commentator writes, "To say that 'x is true' means 'x corresponds to the facts' provides no elucidation of the predicate 'is true.' Correspondence is just another way of talking about truth, and not a way of telling us what truth is" (Malpas 1992, 241).

Examining the claim that true theories correspond to the totality of the evidence also shows us that there is nothing "interesting or instructive" to which these theories can be said to correspond (Davidson 1990a, 303). If all true theories correspond to the totality of evidence, then they all correspond to the same thing (303). Trivializing correspondence in this way removes the individually "given" facts to which our true theories are said to correspond. And if the individually given facts cannot be provided, then we lose the notion of our beliefs, sentences, or theories as *representations* of those facts because "there is nothing for them to represent" (304). Losing the reified notion of "facts" given up naturally and objectively by the external world, and losing the notion of our theories as subjective, internal representations of those facts, are major steps toward losing our skeptical fear that there is a metaphysical gap between our theories and the world those theories describe.

According to Davidson's criticisms, reality is not divided into ontologically given facts to which our true theories correspond. Our true theories correspond to the totality of evidence as a whole. Furthermore, we cannot rely on detecting correspondence relations to tell us if our theories about the world are true, no matter how holistically we conceive of "the totality of evidence." This is because detecting correspondence presupposes a notion of truth; it doesn't explain truth. Davidson argues that viewing correspondence as a bridge across the representationalist gap is a conceptual confusion. Furthermore, he argues, the confusion is telling—there *is* no representationalist gap to bridge.

SUMMARY

I begin this chapter by examining a number of concerns that seem specific to feminist epistemology especially when applied to science studies. First, I discuss my concern that when feminist epistemology addresses the general institution of science and/or scientific method, the characterizations are often overgeneralized and empirically unsupported. However, even if this general focus was more accurately portrayed, I questioned its utility. The general focus on science as an institution distracts from the crucial issue of pinpointing specific agents responsible for harming people. I then argue that when feminist epistemologists do include more specific scientific examples of bias and abuse, the more general epistemological analyses that accompany their local empirical analyses typically introduce skepticism about knowledge claims in general, and the veracity of their local science reportage in particular. Second, I note that the level of abstraction in our discussions of science is often matched by an overgeneral, that is, linguistically essentialist, characterization of sex/gender categories that exaggerates the similarities among women and ignores similarities between women and men. Assuming that we *can* make important and useful generalizations about science, women, and men—that is, assuming that these concepts are coherent, which, I think, at some carefully articulated level is true—then we need to be much more careful with how we give content to these concepts. (I follow up this suggestion in chapter 7.)

The balance of my argument is devoted to problems with epistemology more generally. Specifically, I argue that the representationalist model underlying epistemology makes global skepticism an intractable problem. Given this problem, I argue that engagement in the epistemological debate was no longer the most fruitful approach for feminist science studies, again, worried primarily that once global skepticism is introduced by the debate, there is nothing to keep it from being used against important, well-documented feminist claims. Introducing global skepticism calls into question the very notion of empirical documentation. In support of my arguments, I offer a Rortyan/Davidsonian explanation of the metaphysical mechanisms that relate representationalism, skepticism, and epistemology, focusing on a Davidsonian response to Quine and to various feminist versions of Quinean epistemology. I hinted that Rortyan pragmatism provides good reasons to think that choosing representationalism (and engaging in epistemology) is optional because there is a nonrepresentational perspective from which skepticism is a nonissue. If global skepticism is a nonstarter, then the epistemological debate becomes radically unmotivated.

I introduce this nonrepresentationalist perspective in chapter 6. In the next three chapters I continue my negative thesis by documenting the conceptual problems that result when feminist critics of science adopt an epistemological framework. In particular, I show how, often, these feminist science commentaries become caught between objectivism and relativism. In the end, most feminist critics are satisfied with neither epistemic position, but because their dissatisfaction does not fully address the problems with the representationalist model on which both objectivism and relativism rest, the epistemological continuum continues to define the limits of the debate and skepticism continues to haunt their claims.

NOTES

1. My thanks to Edrie Sobstyl for stressing the importance of this point to me.
2. My thanks to Jodi Jensen for drawing these concerns and this study to my attention.
3. See Peter Galison and David Stump, eds., *The Disunity of Science: Boundaries, Contexts, and Power* (1996), for a philosophical response to the heterogeneity of the sciences.

4. Judith Grant makes some helpful points about essentialism in feminist episte-mology in her book *Fundamental Feminism* (1993).

5. Linda Nicholson uses Wittgensteinian analyses to similar effect in her book *The Play of Reason: From the Modern to the Postmodern* (1999). See also Ann Clark's es-say "The Quest for Certainty in Feminist Thought," which prescribes Dewey's classi-cal pragmatism to address the problems with essentialism in feminism (Clark 1993).

6. My thanks to Bjørn Ramberg for suggesting this characterization.

7. There are debates about whether it is the public assent to the sensory stimulus or the reception of the stimulus itself that Quine *ultimately* considers to be the evi-dence for a sentence's truth (e.g., Davidson 1990b, and Quine's response in the same volume [Quine 1990a]), but, certainly, there are clear passages where Quine gives the evidentiary role to the physical reception, and my discussion focuses on these.

8. Other recent feminist attention to Quine includes Alcoff's book *Real Knowing: New Versions of the Coherence Theory* (1996). Alcoff views both Quine and David-son as coherence theorists. I argue at length in chapter 6 that while Quine has co-herentist moments (precisely those moments where he tries, but fails, to address skepticism) Davidson's project is best seen as falling outside the epistemological tra-dition of which coherence is a part.

3

Feminist Epistemology and Evolutionary Theory

One of the most common and appropriate targets of Western feminist science criticism has been evolutionary biology—in particular, Darwinian theories of sexual selection. Charles Darwin's foray into the world of sex difference began tentatively in *The Origin of Species by Means of Natural Selection* (Darwin 1962 [1859]), but it is in *The Descent of Man and Selection in Relation to Sex* (Darwin 1981 [1871]) that he focused on these differences more explicitly. Darwin postulated his theory of sexual selection to account for the evolution of secondary sexual characteristics—sex-specific characteristics not directly related to reproduction, such as the "extravagant plumage" of the peacock. The fact that both the peacock and peahen survive and procreate while unequally endowed meant that, strictly speaking, the plumage isn't necessary for survival (Darwin 1981, vol. 1, 258). Expanding his theory of natural selection to include sexual selection, Darwin hypothesized that secondary sexual characteristics do indeed have a biological function because they better enable the individual to attract a mate, fend off competitors for that mate (vol. 1, 258), and/or provide for the care of offspring. In the next section I provide a few details of his theory, followed by some feminist epistemological responses both to the Darwinian theory and to the work of contemporary sociobiologists.

THE DARWINIAN THEORY OF SEXUAL SELECTION

In his examination of the nature of the differences between secondary sexual characteristics in males and females, Darwin observed that it is usually the adult male of any species who is more modified with respect to secondary sexual characteristics (vol. 1, 272). Within any given species, he observed, adult females and the young of both sexes tend to look more similar to each other than do males (272). In the case of humans, he noted that secondary sexual characteristics tend not to be as spectacular as those of the plumes of the peacock, but, he claimed, both physical and mental sex differences are readily apparent.

Of the physical differences, Darwin identified adult human males as taller; heavier; stronger, with more angular shoulders and more plainly pronounced muscles; hairier, especially on the face; and deeper in voice than adult females and children of either sex (vol. 2, 316). Among Europeans, he noted that women have more "brightly coloured" skin than adult men (vol. 2, 316). Women, generally, were also observed to have rounder faces and broader pelvises than adult men (vol. 2, 317). While these observations about women might contradict the claim that men are more varied, Darwin noted, instead, that most of these adult female physical traits are shared also by children, male or female (vol. 2, 317), and, he claimed, male and female children more closely resemble each other, even across races (317). Darwin did allow women something of a distinct identity "intermediate between the child and the man" with respect to certain features such as skull shape (317).

Darwin believed that these physical differences between the sexes are accompanied by mental differences. He wrote, "Man is more courageous, pugnacious and energetic than woman, and has more inventive genius" (vol. 2, 316). Furthermore,

> The chief distinction in the intellectual powers of the two sexes is shown by man's attaining to a higher eminence, in whatever he takes up, than can woman . . . whether requiring deep thought, reason, or imagination, or merely the use of the senses and hands. (vol. 2, 327)

Some positive mental characteristics were observed to be "more strongly marked" in women, such as intuition, rapid perception, and imitation, but Darwin is quick to point out that "some, at least, of these faculties are characteristic of the lower races, and therefore of a past and lower state of civilization" (vol. 2, 326–27).

Comments about the "lower races" show that Darwin's Victorian sexism was often complicated by racism. He explained that "all the secondary sexual characters of man are highly variable, even within the limits of the same race; and they differ much in the several races" (vol. 2, 320). He seldom wrote of "human" sex differences unless he had first cataloged various instances of the differences within the "races" or "subspecies" of humans. For example, only after a survey of various races did he conclude that "women in all races are less hairy than men" (vol. 2, 319). Often, however, he found he had to qualify such generalizations between races. He noted fewer sex

differences in amount of hair and general physique among "American abo-
rigines" than among the "negroes" and the "higher races" (vol. 2, 323). He
also cited Carl Vogt's observation that sex differences in cranial cavity "increase with the development of the [human] race so that the male European
excels much more than the female, than the negro [excels with respect to]
the negress" (Vogt 1864, quoted in Darwin, vol. 2, 329–30, footnote). In a discussion of sex differences in "voice and musical powers," Darwin wrote that
"natives of China" do not exhibit the sex differences found in other races
(vol. 2, 330). Aside from these scattered observations, Darwin devoted an entire section to the discussion of race differences in sexual selection, entitled
"On the Causes which Prevent or Check the Action of Sexual Selection with
Savages," where he gave examples of the lower levels of sexual difference
in "primitive" and "barbarian" tribes of his own time (vol. 2, 358–67).

Often, then, a woman had to be of "civilised" European ancestry before
she would qualify for the particular brand of sexism inherent in Darwinian
discussions of sex differences. Otherwise, her psychology and physiology
were relegated to discussions of the "lower races," where, it was claimed,
"progressive" sex differentiation was not as evolved.[1]

As I discuss briefly in chapter 1, Darwin ascribed the superiority of male
secondary sexual characteristics to "greater male variability" (vol. 1, 275).
Across species, more males than females were thought to rank in the extreme high (and extreme low) ranges in measures of physical and mental
prowess. Darwin argued that greater male variability was due to the greater
sexual "eagerness" of males (vol. 1, 272). He explained that "the female . . .
with the rarest exceptions, is less eager than the male. . . . She generally 'requires to be courted'; she is coy, and may often be seen endeavoring for a
long time to escape from the male" (vol. 1, 273). Regarding female mate-
choice, Darwin's characteristically keen powers of observation afforded him
the view that a female typically accepts "not the male which is the most attractive to her, but the one which is the least distasteful" (273). Regardless of
the details, he concluded that "the exertion of some choice on the part of the
female seems a law almost as general as the eagerness of the male" (273). Female selection of male mates, would, over time, encourage more variability
in males to satisfy choosy female tastes.

In those instances of species where the female has the more pronounced
secondary sexual characteristics, or where there are no such differences between the two sexes at all, Darwin suggested that perhaps there has been
mutual selection, where the males "have selected the most attractive females, and the latter the more attractive males" (vol. 1, 277). However, in the
next passage he discarded this view, writing that "from what we know of
the habits of animals, this . . . is hardly probable, for the male is generally eager to pair with any female" (277). It is more probable, he continued, that the
female traits were acquired by the male and transmitted to and developed in

the female, perhaps during periods when there were greater numbers of females than males. Under such circumstances, males might have become uncharacteristically choosy about their mates (277).

With respect to humans, in particular, the fact that some variation is inherited by both males and females required special consideration (vol. 2, 328). Making a virtue out of necessity, Darwin concluded that if women did not at least benefit by inheriting some of the sexually selected superiority of men (though only in small amounts, if he had to concede any at all), then "it is probable that man would have become as superior in mental endowment to women, as the peacock is in ornamental plumage to the peahen" (vol. 2, 328–29).

For the most part, however, Darwin expressed a great deal of equivocation about whether and how secondary sexual characteristics are inherited. In those cases where he was sure that only males exhibit the trait, he offered the following explanation (vol. 1, 280). Employing a pangenetic theory that anticipates modern hormonal theories, Darwin hypothesized that "gemmules" or "undeveloped atoms," derived originally from the male tissue that produced the male secondary sexual characteristic, are passed to offspring of both sexes. However, he argued, these gemmules remain undeveloped until after puberty in the male and forever undeveloped in the female. After puberty, the adult male body produces newly modified cells for which the gemmules have an affinity. In the presence of the appropriately modified cells, the gemmules unite and develop, forming new tissue to reproduce the male secondary sexual characteristic. In the case of the less-modified adult females and the young of either sex, the appropriately modified cells are absent, so the gemmules of the male secondary sexual characteristic don't develop. Darwin admitted, though, that "why certain characters should be inherited by both sexes, and other characters by one sex alone, namely by that sex in which the character first appeared, is in most cases quite unknown" (vol. 1, 285).

Undaunted, Darwin concluded that the superior secondary sexual characteristics of the ("civilised") human male have the biological function of helping the male attract females and subsequently support and maintain a wife and family (vol. 2, 327–28). The time when these superior physical and mental characteristics are most needed and developed is during maturity, and hence these characteristics will be passed on mostly to the male offspring to be manifest at their maturity (vol. 2, 328).

Evolutionary views about the sexes had a number of harmful effects on women. The claim that women varied less on measures of intelligence, for example, led many (male) scientists and scholars of the time to argue against the utility of educating girls and women, especially in the fields of math and science. Granville Stanley Hall made similar arguments in his two-volume work *Adolescence* (1904). Hall wrote extensively on the negative influence of women's menstrual cycle on their abilities at school and in life more generally (vol. 1, 490–94). He asserted that women are less reliable because they are "slaves" to the fluctuations of their hormones. Ironically, this lack of reliability was claimed to be indicative of women's more generic (less-varied) nature. He wrote, "Everyday of the 28 [days in her cycle] she is a different being . . . [which] reveals her as a more generic creature than man" (494). And "to know one [woman] more involves knowing all" (505). Evolutionary arguments were also used in appeals to restrict women's political influence, in favor of keeping women in the domestic sphere (see, for example, Herbert Spencer 1969 [1873], 340–42).

As I discuss in chapter 1, there were a number of women scientists working at the turn of the century who were critical of the evolutionary theories of Darwin and his colleagues. Among these were Mary Calkins (1896), Helen Montague and Leta Stetten Hollingworth (1914), and Helen Thompson Woolley (1910, 1914). These scientists criticized the observations of mental and physical sex differences and constructed new research designs to test sex differences.[2] Montague and Hollingworth, in particular, used research designs that included subjects from a wide variety of races and classes (Montague and Hollingworth 1914). When sex differences *were* in evidence, these women criticized the biological variability explanation, suggesting social factors instead.

Recall, for example, that the theory of greater male variability predicts that more males than females will be found at *both* extremes of any particular physical or mental scale. Some evolutionary theorists, such as Havelock Ellis (1894), argued that the variability theory accounted for the higher numbers of males than females in mental institutions. Hollingworth responded by noting first, that the higher number of males is found only for those under the age of sixteen. She argued that "feebleminded" girls under sixteen were more likely to be "absorbed" quietly into the isolation of menial family chores, whereas the "deficient" boy who leads a more public life at school, and so forth, is more quickly found out and brought to the attention of the medical community. From this research she concluded that the lower numbers of women in institutions did not necessarily prove the biological determinism of the variability hypothesis (Hollingworth 1914, 515).[3]

In these early stages of feminist criticism of evolutionary theory, most of the work was empirical in focus. In particular, these feminist scientists focused on examining the truth of theories of women's lesser variability and intelligence, and the harmful implications these theories would have on pedagogical, legal, and political reform for women and girls (e.g., Hollingworth 1914, 510–11). Concerns that this empirical focus was not proving to be effective did not typically arise until the "second wave" of Western feminism in the middle of the twentieth century, and so the more troublesome epistemological themes that develop out of this concern were rare in the earlier writings. However, the criticisms of evolutionary theory by one early feminist, Antoinette Brown Blackwell, stand out for their prescient introduction of epistemological issues. Blackwell herself was not a scientist.

BLACKWELL: THE SEXES THROUGHOUT NATURE

Blackwell was a feminist contemporary of Darwin and the first woman in the United States to be ordained as a minister (Newman 1985, 8). She responded to Darwin's theory of sexual selection in her book *The Sexes throughout Nature* (1875). Blackwell agreed with Darwin that there are biologically based differences in the mental capacities of men and women, but she argued against Darwin's view that the "feminine" instincts and tendencies are inferior to the "masculine." Rather, she viewed the feminine and masculine mental capacities as different but equivalent in quality and importance. And she eloquently, if somewhat naively, argued that this "different but equal" status can be measured empirically:

> If the special class of feminine instincts and tendencies is a fair offset in every grade of life to corresponding masculine traits, this is a subject of direct scientific investigation. It is a question of pure quantity; of comparing unlike but strictly measurable terms. In time it can be experimentally decided, and settled by rigid mathematical tests. We do not weigh lead and sunbeams in the same balance [but we can still] estimate their equivalent forces. (Blackwell 1875, 11)

In this passage Blackwell reveals some methodological assumptions about, for example, the empirical accessibility of sex differences. However, a conflict soon arises between her belief that the facts of sex difference can be straightforwardly accessed and her belief that bias *filters* our access. Blackwell claimed that Darwin's theory of the inferiority of feminine traits was not based on objective empirical measurement, but was biased by his "extra-empirical" evolutionary commitments. And, she claimed, this relativist problem will arise for any "positive thinker" (a reference to the positivism of Auguste Comte):

> Any positive thinker is compelled to see everything in the light of his own convictions. The more active and dominant one's opinions, the more liable they must be to modify his rendering of related facts—roping them inadvertently in to the undue service of his theories. (1875, 13)

The inconsistency of Blackwell's position is certainly a problem—are facts about sex difference directly accessible or are they masked by our convictions? But it is the representationalist tone of her writings that has me more concerned. The representationalist diagnosis needs to be made with care. Certainly, her admonishments concerning all "positive thinkers" could be interpreted simply as a cautionary methodological note, reminding us to keep our minds as open as possible when examining data. However, Blackwell highlights what seems to be a *conceptual* distinction between the empirical content of the data or facts and the extra-empirical organizing schemes or opinions of the investigator. Employing the scheme/content distinction characteristic of the representationalist model, Blackwell argues that the objective content or facts of the world are "modified" through the filter of the investigator's conceptual schemes, ideologies, or worldviews. Note the parallels with the early Willard Van Orman Quine, who suggested that the facts or cues available to the scientist are conceptually distinct from her worldview (Quine 1960, 5).

My main point in making the representationalist diagnosis is my worry about the invitation of skepticism that the scheme/content distinction invites. If Blackwell is indeed invoking this distinction, then her next step would be to recognize and respond to the skeptical question "What is the guarantee that the content or facts can ever be accessed directly, unfiltered by our conceptual schemes?" More specifically, she would need to answer why, in the face of the pervasive filtering of the facts about female evolution, we should be persuaded by her *own* subjective rendering of the facts.

Tellingly, Blackwell responds directly to this skeptical concern. She claims that despite the inherently biased filtering of *all* our representations, her particular bias, accrued by virtue of her experience as a woman, bridges the gap between her subjective views and the objective "facts of womanhood." She writes,

> However superior [the men's] powers, their opportunities, their established scientific positions, yet in this field of inquiry *pertaining to the normal powers and functions of woman*, it is they who are at a disadvantage. Whatever else women may not venture to study and explain with authority, on this topic they are more than peers of the wisest men in Christendom. Experience must have more weight than any amount of outside observation. We [women] are clearly entitled, on this subject, to a respectful hearing. (1875, 6–7; emphasis in the original)

This response to the skeptic's question is weakened, however, by yet another instance of inconsistency between an objectivist claim about the epistemic privilege of women's experience and the earlier, more relativistic claim that worldviews and experience filter and *bias* the facts. Her response is also troublesome insofar as it relies on a fairly monolithic conception of women and their "normal powers and functions."

As I argue in chapter 2, overgeneralizations about the categories "women" and "men" often accompany feminist epistemological claims of the sort Blackwell is making. With respect to her claim that there are "facts of womanhood" about which she has the authority to speak, two aspects of the essentialism problem are in evidence. First, Blackwell's argument entails the questionable essentialist conception that there are experiences that all women share, namely, those experiences "pertaining to the normal powers and functions of woman." Second, she assumes that her own experiences are representative and that, with respect to claims about women, these experiences provide her with a generic female epistemic authority over all males. With the perspective provided by late-twentieth-century criticisms of feminist essentialism, we can see more clearly that Blackwell's experiences were not generic; rather, they were highly specific. She was not a generic "woman"; she was educated, American, and white.

While her essentialism is a weakness in itself, it also weakens the important empirical elements of her arguments, such as her argument that Darwin failed to apply his principles of evolution consistently in the area of sex differences (e.g., Blackwell 1875, 16). Here, she notes that if Darwin is right that selective pressure adds only to the male's endowment, then the inequality between the sexes, unless met with "a check in some unknown law" would continue to increase "to a degree which it is startling to contemplate!" (Blackwell, 19). Blackwell concludes that some checks will evolve in the future to prevent "too great an inequality between the sexes, [and therefore] it cannot be too preposterous to suppose that, in the past and in the present, similar natural checks always have been, and still are, in active operation" (19). Recall, however, that Darwin acknowledged that in humans most traits are passed to both sexes, especially in the case of the "lower races," where, he claimed, less sex differentiation had evolved. Unfortunately, Blackwell continues to make overgeneralizations about Darwin's analysis, discussing the "various structural modifications" that must have evolved as checks to maintain "a virtual equivalence of the sexes" (20), without taking into consideration any of Darwin's differential claims regarding race.

As I note in chapter 2, such overgeneralizations about sex/gender categories are not necessary aspects of feminist epistemology, but I do think there are contexts in which they seem to be conceptually intertwined with epistemological claims. For example, Blackwell initially invoked an essentialized concept of "woman" (and "man") as a foundationalist response to skepticism—that is, she justified her epistemic challenge to Darwin by appealing to the fact that she was a woman and therefore in possession of a privileged epistemic standpoint. This response was required in the face of the relativism she invited by invoking a representationalist scheme/content distinction ("any positive thinker is compelled to see everything in the light of his own convictions").

However, her essentialist approach to sex categories is related to her representationalist commitments in other more direct ways, as well. When Blackwell continues to impose her own overgeneralizations about the categories "men" and "women" onto Darwin's more fine-grained and racist theories of "barbarian" men, and women of the "civilised 'races,'" Blackwell evinces a certain ontological rigidity; a tendency to view the categories "men" and "women" as naturally "given." This rigidity in categorization is often shared by epistemologists of an objectivist and/or empiricist stripe. Both positions require a link between inner, conceptual representations and naturally categorized chunks of the empirical world. It is this reified view of our observational categories that is criticized so effectively by Davidson, Sellars, and Goodman.

While Darwin's sex/race categories were just as reified as Blackwell's, her failure to acknowledge the greater complexity of his categorization is a telling epistemological weakness. If she had an empirical argument about the equivalence of the races that told against Darwin's racist claims about race differences, then this argument needed to be provided, and it would have been welcome. Instead, she invokes the essentialist assumption that women of different races all share the same experiences "pertaining to the normal powers and functions of woman" (namely, her own experiences). This essentialism results in the same sort of racism we find in Darwin's work, when he assumed that women of different races had *different* experiences. Blackwell's criticism of Darwin's theory could have been much stronger if she had shown a greater ontological flexibility about her categories of analysis.

SECOND-WAVE EPISTEMOLOGISTS

In the hundred years after the publication of Blackwell's critique of Darwin, there is little epistemological commentary to be found in the largely empirical criticisms of evolution offered by feminists and other advocates for social justice. However, in the mid-1970s, the work of Stephanie Shields marks a return to epistemological arguments and the problems with which such arguments are associated. In "Functionalism, Darwinism, and the Psychology of Women" (1975) and "The Variability Hypothesis: The History of a Biological Model of Sex Differences in Intelligence" (1982), Shields documents the relationship between the scientific facts of variability and the cultural/political context within which those facts were "discovered." As a feminist and a psychologist she begins by making important empirical criticisms of the way evolutionary theory has been used to explain human intelligence. She focuses her criticism on claims that males exhibit greater variability in intelligence, while females exhibit greater mediocrity. However, she also makes epistemological claims that invoke a conceptual splitting of the evidence and the political values through which the evidence is screened. The resulting problem is twofold.

The first, and least serious, problem is that her writings contain conflicts and inconsistencies similar to those in Blackwell's book. That is, she makes appeals to both relativism and objectivism. On the relativist side, she argues that the reception of Darwin's theory of sexual selection and greater male variability was filtered by the sexist ideology of Victorian culture (Shields 1975, 753; 1982, 771). On the objectivist side, her more positive portraits of Victorian critics of Darwin, such as Karl Pearson (1897) and a number of feminist scientists, including Woolley, Hollingworth, and Calkins, suggest that some scientists were able to remove their cultural filters and get the scientific facts of variability right (Shields 1982, 776–77, 783–89). Another parallel with Blackwell is that Shields, too, leaves unexamined the fact that the "sexist" variability question in humans was also, for Darwin and his colleagues, a "race" question about the extent to which European men and women were different from men and women of "the lower races."

The second, and most serious, problem, conceptually, occurs when Shields tackles the charge of inconsistency head on and confines herself to the relativist option, applied consistently both to Darwinian research *and* to the research of those she thinks have it right, including, presumably, her own. At the end of her 1975 essay, for example, she writes of Darwinian science— "That science played a handmaiden to social values cannot be denied. Whether a parallel situation exists in today's study of sex differences is open to question" (Shields 1975, 753). Here she is confronted by the self-directed skepticism that inevitably results from making a conceptual split between the scientific facts (of evolution) and the social values (of both Victorian sensibilities and late-twentieth-century sexual politics).

After the well-documented empirical critique she has just presented, Shields is entitled to a conclusion that speaks more confidently about the accuracy of her own study of the sex-difference literature, but her representationalist language robs her of that confidence. Unlike Blackwell, who made a defensive, though unsuccessful, move against this sort of self-directed skepticism, Shields admits that skepticism is a coherent concern—for all we know, we might be blinkered by the filters of our own politics and culture, in such a way that we can never be confident even about our own feminist critiques of the sex-difference literature. Remember that this sort of worry is not just that we might need to improve our critiques in the future—because, of course, we will—it is a worry that any notion of "improvement" is bankrupt because of the unbridgeable gulf between our subjective feminist politics and the objective world of sex differences.

There are a number of other critiques by the second wave of Western feminist scientists-cum-philosophers that are more self-conscious about the existence of these epistemological concerns, though they do not fully acknowledge the representational model that fuels them. The influential essays of Ruth Hubbard, Cynthia Eagle Russett, and Ruth Bleier are discussed in this regard.

Hubbard's essay "Have Only Men Evolved?" parallels Shields's critique and focuses on both Darwinian and more recent sociobiological evolutionary theories (Hubbard 1983 [1979]). A certain amount of ontological rigidity about the distinctness of sex categories and race categories appears early in the introduction to her essay, when she explains that she will focus on the androcentrism of Darwinian accounts of sex differences, as opposed to his ethnocentrism. Here, she explains that "the ethnocentric bias of Darwinism is widely acknowledged," while its "androcentrism is rarely mentioned" (52).

However, as Darwin himself made clear, his theory of sexual selection in humans was often applied differentially among the human "races." We cannot coherently analyze his androcentrism and ethnocentrism as separate phenomena. The continued insistence that they can and should be separated hints at an objectivist or empiricist need for observational categories that are firm or reified enough to support epistemological bridges.

Confirmation of this concern arises when Hubbard invokes an epistemic scheme/content distinction in her description of the constructed nature of scientific knowledge (Hubbard 1983, 46). She explains, "every theory is a self-fulfilling prophecy that orders experience into the framework it provides. Therefore, it should be no surprise that almost any theory, however absurd it may seem to some, has its supporters" (1983, 47). She writes further, "There is no such thing as objective, value-free science" (47).

Unfortunately, without the accompaniment of a thoroughgoing critique of representationalism, these criticisms of objectivity tend only to undercut the persuasiveness of the latter half of her paper. In this latter half she provides a local, empirical analysis that presents powerful evidence against Darwinian and sociobiological claims about women. However, given her earlier argument that "every theory is a self-fulfilling prophecy," the skeptic is invited to question her arguments against Darwin.

Taking a cue from Blackwell, rather than from Shields, Hubbard defends herself from these skeptical worries. She argues that despite the relativist filtering of biases and worldviews, women scientists can make moves toward objectivity by "recogniz[ing] an androcentric myth when they see one," by "think[ing] beyond it," and by "com[ing] up with ways of seeing the facts and of interpreting them" (66). Furthermore, women scientists "can sift carefully the few available facts by paring away the mythology and getting as close to the raw data as possible" (66).

Unlike Blackwell and Shields, Hubbard is conscious of the paradox she invokes here; she recognizes the two rhetorical options forced by the epistemological model. One option is simply to accept the charge of inconsistency by both acknowledging the relativist filter of sexism, while, at the same time, suggesting that somehow women, or nonsexists, have an objective edge. This is the option Blackwell chose, and, in the previous quote, it seems that Hubbard does as well. In an attempt to be more consistent, however, the other option is to admit that women do not have an objective edge because "women's" experience is as likely to filter the data as is "men's." This is the option that Shields took at the end of her 1975 essay. With this latter option, consistency is paid for with the high price of introducing skepticism about knowledge claims in general, but about feminist criticisms of Darwin in particular.

In the next passage Hubbard, herself, moves closer to the second option. She acknowledges that "paring away the mythology" will be difficult because "women scientists tend to hail from the same socially privileged families and be educated in the same elite universities as our male colleagues," that is, the biases and worldviews of these women will be similar to those of the men (66). However, she claims that because she and her women scientist colleagues are at least "marginal to the mainstream," this should make it easier to "watch ourselves push the bus in which we are riding" (66).

I am not convinced that merely invoking this quasi-Neurathian metaphor resolves either the skepticism invited by the second option or the inconsistency of the first. In my view, Hubbard does not fully acknowledge the seriousness of the representationalist problem, and again, the reader is left with a level of methodological skepticism that undercuts the important content of her claims against Darwinian and sociobiological theory.

This same representationalist pattern arises in Cynthia Eagle Russett's book *Sexual Science: The Victorian Construction of Womanhood* (Russett 1989). Here, Russett presents a careful historical analysis of the early, Western psychology of sex differences. Unlike the other feminist critiques surveyed, Russett's writing more fully acknowledges the racism of this science, though, like Hubbard, she tries to separate the race categories from the sex categories and then justifies dealing exclusively with the latter. Russett begins by acknowledging that racism influenced science and scientists:

> Race was a burning social issue in England and America. Abolitionist movements agitated the issue of black emancipation with increasing stridency. In this atmosphere science became a weapon, its findings useful as they legitimated or discountenanced the claims of black people to political and social equity. (1989, 7)

However, according to Russett, the "women's movement" was even more challenging, and she uses this challenge to justify her focus on sexism:

> It even dared broach the subject of equality in personal, and especially matrimonial, relationships. Such assertiveness was more unsettling than the racial threat because it was more intimate and immediate: few white men lived with blacks, but most lived with women. Scientists responded to this unrest with a detailed and sustained examination of the differences between men and women that justified their differing social roles. (1989, 10)

What she most likely means by this is that few white men lived with black men or women, but most lived with white women. By using the term "women" instead of the term "white women," it appears that the term "blacks" refers only to black *men*.[4] It is also important to note that the "women's movement" Russett refers to was largely by and for white, middle-class women, and the response from evolutionary science was to highlight the sex differences between white men and white women, not between men and women of the "lower races."

Russett continues her discussion of women and the sex differences between women and men, speaking generically, without making any of these important distinctions. For example, she describes the racism and sexism of evolutionists as resulting from a need to maintain some kind of hierarchy *within* the human species, given that they no longer believed in a strict hierarchy that placed humans *apart* from other species. She writes that "women and the 'lesser races' served to buffer Victorian gentlemen from a too-threatening intimacy with the brutes" (14). In other words, when evolutionists placed "'women' and the 'lesser races'" midway between "Victorian gentlemen" and apes, this eased the evolutionists' message about the ignoble nature of human origins. However, while certain Victorian gentlemen might have conflated the terms "women" and "Victorian women" Darwin, often, did not. Either way, feminist critics of Darwin and his contemporaries need to provide a more careful, nuanced discussion of the women and men affected by sexist and racist science, lest the use of more general categories appear ontologically rigid and essentialist.

While her use of overgeneral sex and race categories appears to reflect an epistemologically objectivist or empiricist approach, Russett's methodological criticisms of Victorian science begin with a straightforward and important empirical critique of the sort I've been encouraging. She characterizes the Victorian science of sex differences as "bad science" that does not live up to the standards of scientific method required for today (11). Furthermore, and more important, she explains how, in many ways, it did not even live up to the scientific standards circulating among scientists at the time (182–88). She writes that eventually, however, "the Victorian paradigm [of sex differences] erodes" due to improvements in scientific understanding:

> Together, genetics and endocrinology made some of the headier 19th-century theories of sex difference no longer tenable. Woman was not a lesser man. She was not man arrested short of developmental perfection. She did not stand midway between the child and the man. (1989, 161)

Russett self-consciously rejects the relativist claim that scientific improvements regarding women's status were exclusively a result of "extra-empirical" circumstances. According to Russett, this more constructionist view of scientific change, described by Hubbard previously, leaves insufficient room "for [the effects] of alterations in the scientific evidence, for factual or interpretive disproof, correction, and emendation" (Russett 1989, 178).

While this rejection of the relativist elements of representationalism helps her avoid the problems of inconsistency found in the other feminist writings, her rejection, and thus her avoidance of the problems, is only partial. She concludes that although Victorian science was biased and flawed, it is actually not fair to expect anything more because science and ideology, "far from being polar opposites, are part and parcel of one another. Scientists cannot help but bring cultural beliefs and interests in to the construction of their theories" (188). However, she then argues that despite the filtering effects of these ideological preconceptions, "good scientific practice, in the late 19th century as now, should not have permitted those preconceptions to distort the scientists' vision, to blinker them in such a way as to predetermine their conclusions" (Russett 1989, 189). Following the representationalist model, Russett begins to make epistemological characterizations of politics, worldviews, and culture as "extra-empirical" filters through which bad science sifts the empirical evidence. The sorts of inconsistencies I have highlighted, previously, are the inevitable result.

Returning briefly to Donald Davidson's prescriptions, I suggest that we view political beliefs as members of the same holistic web of evidence occupied by empirical beliefs, rather than as nonbelief filters through which the data of the empirical beliefs pass. It is this latter representationalist view of evidence that guides the work of the feminist epistemologists I have been surveying. The problem with the representationalist split between politics, on the one hand, and the empirical data, on the other, is that it makes it conceptually impossible for feminists to document the strong relationship between our empirical, factual beliefs and our politically motivated beliefs.

Returning to Russett's work, her readers are left with the view that there is the objective evidence, facts about "men" and "women" given up by nature, and there is our subjective rendering of the facts. If we follow some a priori notion of "good scientific practice" (about which Russett provides little detail), we can lessen the effects of our subjective filters and be sure that the gap between the evidence and our theories has been sufficiently bridged. But the "inseparability" of scientific facts from the filters of subjective, value-laden ideology means we can never *eliminate* the filters, allowing skepticism about knowledge seeking once again to make an unwelcome appearance.

Skepticism becomes a major factor in Ruth Bleier's arguments in *Science and Gender: A Critique of Biology and Its Theories on Women* (Bleier 1984). Her main target is the biological determinism entailed in evolutionary and sociobiological theories of sex differences in mind and behavior. Her empirical criticisms are insightful and important. Unfortunately, they are sandwiched between lengthy introductory and concluding essays on "patriarchal science" and issues in feminist method and epistemology. Here, she self-consciously addresses the conflicts between objectivism and relativism that I have been highlighting throughout this chapter. She begins with the characteristically relativist claim that scientific facts are constructed by those in power (13). Consistently, at least, she notes that her own critique of sociobiology involves offering "counter facts" that are no less free of values and interests (13). In the face of the relativism she believes is inherent even in her own work, Bleier argues that the only justificatory criterion to which she can consistently appeal is whether or not her criticisms disrupt the status quo. Her explanation is worth quoting at length:

> I would argue that the nature of my own worldview, as it influences my approach in this book, is its own justification. That is, while biological determinists—in the face of overwhelming contradictions—assert the genetic, hormonal, and evolutionary determinism of human nature and our behaviors, it is my aim to describe all those myriad contradictions that make such theories totally inadequate as explanations of behaviors and forms of social relationships. Even if some of the "facts" I cite in support of my arguments are disputable, I will have made the case—and I hope convincingly so—that there is no simple "truth" as Sociobiologists and other supporters of the status quo would have us believe. (1984, 13)

Here I think Bleier's representationalism has unnecessarily weakened her project. While I agree that there is no "simple truth" as understood by objectivists—that correspondence doesn't bridge the gap between subjective theory and objective reality, as some epistemologists might have hoped—this doesn't mean that we have to be resigned to Bleier's level of skepticism about the justification of our feminist claims. Rather, it adds fuel to Rorty's contention that we should choose a nonrepresentationalist alternative to the subject/object gap.

In a later chapter, "Patriarchal Science, Feminist Visions," Bleier reinforces the relativist version of skepticism introduced previously. Again I quote a passage at length, as in it she articulates better than even Richard Rorty or Davidson how the representationalist metaphor of an unbridgeable gap invites skepticism about our most basic beliefs. Unlike Rorty or Davidson, Bleier feels that such skepticism is inevitable. She writes,

> Scientific ideas and theories represent efforts to describe and explain the natural world; that is, reality. That reality, in the form of our perceptions and interpretations of it, is like the rest of our culture, a product of human thought. Yet it is perceived as objective reality, which becomes incorporated, in its various forms, into our early and developing consciousness. That consciousness is the medium through which we perceive and interpret the "objective realities" of the external world, learn our individual location within it, and form a worldview. That consciousness and its worldview provide a framework for ordering and interpreting our experiences, *which come to confirm the worldview of which they are, in part, the products.* (1984, 193; emphasis mine)

Bleier's thesis is now firmly, and unnecessarily, mired in the relativist variants of skepticism with which I am concerned. How, if her own framework orders her experiences, can she persuade her readers of the truth of her claims? Bleier's response in this regard is a startling one that, in concert with similar themes in the early writings of Evelyn Fox Keller, has left a lasting stamp on the field of feminist critiques of science. Bleier does not make Blackwell's claim that women are simply more objective in their studies of women; rather, she suggests that truth and objectivity are *themselves* patriarchal concepts that require feminist (or female) reconfiguration.

At this point in her thesis she asks a more self-consciously epistemological question, "Which normative criteria have we been trained to use in our adjudication of competing knowledge claims?" and argues that our traditional concepts of truth and objective method have been produced by a biased patriarchal discourse. Her discussion at this point exemplifies the abstract and overgeneral approach to science found in many feminist epistemological projects. The prescriptions for science and scientific method that result from her epistemic analysis are exceedingly vague, and it is difficult to see how they might be applied to actual scientific settings, including her own empirical work as a biologist. I discuss these concerns further in the next section.

SCIENCE, OBJECTIVITY, AND MASCULINITY

Bleier begins her discussion of scientific method by reviewing the evolutionist claim that the male mind is objective and detached—the seat of Reason—whereas the female mind is subjective, emotional, and inferior. She then notes that the allegiance of science to objectivity and detachment means that science "has defined itself" as "*the* expression of the male mind" (196; emphasis in the original). Scientific "truth or its perception is contingent on being male" (196).

There are a number of problems with this conception of science as a masculine monolith. For example, her claim about the male nature of science is an overgeneralization of the claims made by the individual scientists involved. Bleier's analysis doesn't take into consideration the fact that many of the nineteenth-century evolutionary theories of sexual selection assign the "male" privilege of rational objectivity and detachment only to certain sorts of male minds, namely, white/European males. If any sex-related characterizations of this heterogeneous institution of science can be made, then perhaps we might say that science is the expression of the white or European male mind. But then this more specific characterization flies in the face of centuries of science produced by indigenous Asian, African, and other non-European cultures. We have no evidence to suggest that the science produced by these cultures proceeds with less rationality, less objectivity than does science produced in the West. We need to be careful that a feminist characterization of science as "white" and "male" does not reinforce Darwinian evolutionary claims about the lesser rational abilities of nonwhites or non-Europeans.

Bleier encounters exactly this problem when she qualifies her discussion quite suddenly and explains that we associate science with the male mind because a highly specific group of men in "western industrial class culture" has been trained to think a certain way—they have been trained to be in control. She provides no evidence for this claim, but continues, writing, "to know, to be certain, is part of being in control" (202). She further explains the relationship between knowledge and control by arguing that "it is important to know causes for events and phenomena, for without that 'knowledge' one cannot know how to intervene effectively in order to remain or be in control" (202).

Women from Western cultures, she claims, have been trained differently. They have been socialized not to gain control, but to be attentive to "context," "interaction," "process," and "nondualistic" modes of thinking. Very little in the way of careful description is provided for any of these terms. And then, speaking generically again, she asserts that "for women in general, control has been a non-issue" (202–3). She explains,

> Just as men were not taught or expected to think about parenting as a relevant issue for their lives or their self-definition before the contemporary women's movement, the question of being in control (of anything or anyone, including their own selves) was never part of women's frame of reference for conceptualizing or realizing their own relationships to others or to nature. (202)

The three-way, overgeneralized association between men from Western industrial class culture, their training to be "in control," and the control required for knowledge in science is said to explain the association between science and the male mind. In chapter 4, I review arguments that complicate this essentialist view, referring to some of the research about the control many women, as mothers, have over children and the control many white women have had and continue to have over black people, both women and men.

While Bleier's discussion suggests an ontological rigidity about categories such as "men" and "women," she makes it clear that she does not believe that sex differences regarding control are biologically determined. She invokes the psychoanalytic theories of H. Hein (1981) to explain that these essential differences between women and men arise not from differences in biology but from different patterns of socialization (Bleier, 202). Whether psychoanalytic theory escapes its own biological determinism is a question I examine in the next chapter.

Bleier claims that women have been socialized with a female style of thought that is nondualistic (201). She explains that male thought, in contrast, continually invokes dualisms such as "subject–object, culture–nature, thought–feeling, active–passive" (198) and that women find the opposite, "fluid" mode of thought more "easy" because they are attentive to context, interaction, and process (201). She provides no evidence for these overgeneral claims, though she occasionally mentions the psychoanalytic "suggestions" of feminist theorists Hein (1981), Elizabeth Fee (1982), and Mary O'Brien (1981).

She argues, furthermore, that the female epistemic style provides clues for preserving a concept of knowledge and objectivity that is not filtered by the patriarchal worldview (Bleier, 201). The dualistic thinking associated with males obscures the "flux, change, and interaction" of "life and matter"; and male reasoning styles of control, detachment, and dualistic thinking weaken what would otherwise be good scientific practice (201). She argues further that using a nondualistic women's reasoning style would improve the situation. She explains,

> While women certainly are . . . educable to male-defined rules, they are more attuned to the fluidity of life, and acceptance of change, fusion, and interaction. Such experiencing of life more easily generates a sense of inclusiveness and contextuality as cognitive frameworks and modes of perceiving and understanding the world. (Bleier 1984, 201)

Again, she does not explain how she has arrived at these exceedingly obscure and overgeneral characterizations of a female epistemic style. What is clear is that she believes a better science would result if scientists modeled the female style, "put aside" preconceived male notions of static dualities, and allowed the flux and change of nature to "speak" to the scientist (206). However, she provides no concrete examples of how such a science would proceed. The well-researched, local, epistemological criticisms of evolutionary theory from her earlier chapters are unconnected from and superseded by these overgeneral epistemological accounts of science, men, and women.

In summary, Bleier uses psychoanalytic theories of the difference between female and male minds in order to construct a new epistemological approach. This new approach is based on a female concept of cognition that will somehow, without inconsistency, both acknowledge the relativism of our socialized worldviews and provide an improved methodological foundation from which to justify feminist theory and science criticism. It is a complicated project that I am not convinced will work, largely because it remains firmly in the representationalist mode. However, in order to do justice to the complexity of the psychoanalytic claims on which her epistemic theory is based, I now turn from feminist critiques of evolutionary theory to the more general science critiques found in the highly influential writings of Evelyn Fox Keller. It is in Keller's work that psychoanalytic theories receive the most attention.

NOTES

1. American evolutionary theorist Edward Drinker Cope is one of the most explicit theorists in this regard (see Cope 1974 [1887], 280–90).

2. A number of turn-of-the-century debates about evolutionary claims of sex and race differences can be found in the pages of *Popular Science Monthly*. Louise Newman has edited a collection of pertinent articles from *Popular Science,* entitled *Men's Ideas/Women's Realities: Popular Science 1870–1915* (Newman 1985).

3. My thanks to Meredith Kimball for helping me articulate the details of Hollingworth's argument.

4. The problems associated with this particular type of feminist essentialism are well recognized, though still pervasive. For a groundbreaking critique, see *All the Women Are White, All the Blacks Are Men, But Some of Us Are Brave* (Hull, Scott, and Smith 1982).

4

Keller's Epistemological Reflections on Gender and Science

In her role as a philosopher and historian of science, biologist Evelyn Fox Keller has been one of the most influential feminist proponents of using psychoanalytic theory to explain how, in her view, our very understandings of objectivity and truth have become filtered by a male or, alternatively, masculine worldview (Keller 1982, 1983 [1978], 1985). That is, our understandings of truth and objectivity have been made relative to a gendered conceptual scheme. Keller attempts a way out of this relativism by conceiving of the existence of a more universal, dynamic concept of objectivity to which feminists can then appeal when justifying their own claims. However, like Bleier, Keller's alternative succeeds only in replacing masculine filters with feminine (or nonmale) filters. As a result, elements of relativism remain in Keller's prescriptions.[1]

It is important to acknowledge that Keller's work has provided many of the central themes within feminist science studies, and she has inspired an entire generation of feminist scholars of which I am a part. Because she is a leader in the field of feminist science studies, her theories have already been the focus of intense critical scrutiny, both from within feminism and without. My own motivation for revisiting her epistemic work, in particular, is to draw attention to those elements of her project that are insufficiently critical of the representationalist model underlying epistemology. The problems that Keller's project encounters in this respect are probably some of the best illustrations of why I think we feminists engaged in science studies should abandon our current epistemological focus.

KELLER'S EARLY FEMINIST WORK

In one of her earlier essays on feminism and science, Keller discusses and supports what I have characterized as the feminist move from local, empirical criticism to epistemology (Keller 1982). She writes that feminist criticism of unwarranted inferences from data to theory, sloppy methodology, and other empirical concerns typically affects the truth of theories only in the "'soft' sciences," such as evolutionary biology (1982, 593). Keller is after a more "radical" epistemological critique that would detect "androcentric bias even in the 'hard' sciences, indeed in scientific ideology itself" (1982, 593). Her feminist criticisms of traditional epistemology question the gendered nature of the normative criteria historically used to adjudicate between competing knowledge claims, and she prescribes new criteria to address these gendered shortcomings. She prescribes a twofold epistemological task to this effect.

First, she writes, it is necessary for feminists to "distinguish that which is parochial from that which is universal in the scientific impulse, reclaiming for women what has historically been denied to them" (1982, 593–94). That which is parochial is the association of objectivity with masculinity, domination, and control (594). Women, she argues, have typically been denied any association with objectivity, parochial or otherwise (594).

Second, feminists have to "legitimate those elements of scientific culture that have been denied precisely because they are defined as female" (594). This point is less clear. The male associations with science receive more attention in her essay than do female associations. But she does give brief mention to three "repressed" elements of scientific culture that are associated with the female and need to be legitimated by feminists. Her descriptions of these female elements make use of psychoanalytic concepts that are poorly defined. (I draw out the details of Keller's psychoanalytic project shortly.)

The first of these repressed elements is female "subjectivity" (594); another is the cultural association between feminine gender identity and "ego merging" (a psychoanalytic term used in contrast to masculine "ego autonomy"); and, although she doesn't label it "female," the reader is to infer an association between females and the "erotic impulse," another psychoanalytic concept that she associates with "union" or "merging" (598). The relation between ego-merging, the erotic-impulse, and scientific *method* is similarly vague, but she does write that the erotic impulse can be contrasted with the aggressive impulse that we associate, in science, with masculinity, power, and control over the objects of study (598).

Keller's thesis, then, is that in science the universal ideal of objectivity has been confused with a "parochial" version that associates objectivity with masculine aggression and the detachment from and domination over the object of scientific study. Furthermore, science has devalued alternative elements of the universal objective ideal that are associated with females, such as subjectivity and identification and union with the object of study (1982, 593–94). She argues that if we become conscious of the sexist ideology that fuels these mistaken conceptions of objectivity, then we can choose to reject what has been associated with the male and embrace what has been associated with the female (1982, 598). As with Bleier, Keller refers to objectivity as both an epistemic method and a normative property that the method helps identify. Feminists, says Keller, must not let objectivity lose its "*intrinsic meaning*" (593; emphasis mine), but must work to "transform" the traditional understandings of objectivity (603) in order to create a truly objective science that is freed of its patriarchal moorings. The representationalist element in her appeal to this ideal notion of objectivity becomes apparent when she argues that straying from the objective ideal would invite skepticism in its relativist guise (e.g., Keller 1982, 593). She writes,

> Feminist relativism is just the kind of radical move that transforms the political spectrum into a circle. By rejecting objectivity as a masculine ideal [relativism] simply lends its voice to an enemy chorus and dooms women to residing outside of the Realpolitik modern culture; it exacerbates the very problem it wishes to solve. (Keller 1982, 593)

For Keller, it is crucial that feminists keep the ideal of objective science apart from the sexed associations of males with objectivity and females with subjectivity. Otherwise, she writes, feminist criticism of the association between objectivity and male domination, for example, could mistakenly be construed as a criticism of objectivity *simpliciter*. And, as we've seen, Keller believes that a criticism of this sort necessarily involves a move toward relativism, a move she rightly recognizes as disastrous for feminism. She argues that we need a nonrelativized concept of objective knowledge to defeat skepticism and to give normative force to our important political claims (Keller 1982, 593). But, as I argue in chapter 6, we don't need objectivist epistemology to provide this normative force. Indeed, as I've attempted to show, adopting any position on the epistemological continuum only makes our way more difficult.

Keller argues that the relativized male concept of objectivity is merely an *ideology* of objectivity that is "linked with autonomy and masculinity, and in turn, the goals of science with power and domination" (1982, 594). Her alternative is *dynamic* objectivity, the universal ideal of objectivity that represents "the quintessentially human effort to understand the world in rational terms" (1982, 594).

Keller's work contains many examples of my concerns with feminist entry into the epistemological debate. First, as was found with Bleier's arguments, Keller's critique moves away from examinations of specific scientific theories and toward a much more general target—the monolithic conception of science as male (midway through her essay Keller begins referring to "western" science [598]). As I have argued, however, even if this target is conceptually co-herent, it is probably not the most useful focus for the already-constrained re-sources of feminist scholars. Second, as with all of the feminist epistemologists discussed in chapter 3, Keller makes extensive use of overgeneralized cate-gories such as "male" and "female." In response to criticisms of the essentialism such categories support, Keller defends their explanatory efficacy (see Keller 1987, 1992b). I believe that Keller's support of these more ontologically rigid categories of analysis is connected to her discussion of ideal objectivity. And it is this connection that reveals an insufficiently critical reliance on representa-tionalist epistemology. I highlight each of these concerns throughout my dis-cussion of Keller's work, beginning with her use of psychoanalytic theory.

KELLER AND PSYCHOANALYTIC OBJECT RELATIONS THEORY

Keller writes that the twofold task of feminist science criticism is aided by a psychoanalytic study of various psychological processes affecting the char-acter of scientists and science itself (Keller 1982, 595). She argues that the sex symbolism of science is explained by a psychoanalytic account of the child-hood development of individual scientists. The psychoanalytic view Keller prescribes is object relations theory. She refers to the work of psychoanalyst D. Winnicott (1971) and two feminists who make extensive use of the the-ory, Nancy Chodorow (1978) and Dorothy Dinnerstein (1976).

Within much North American psychology and psychiatry, the validity of observations made in the case study reports of psychoanalysts has long been questioned. Philosophers, too, have engaged the validity question (e.g., Popper 1962, 1974; and Grünbaum 1984). Karl Popper, famously, argued that psychoanalytic theory was not a science because its hypotheses could never be falsified: "It [is] practically impossible to describe any human be-haviour that might not be claimed to be a verification of these theories" (Pop-per 1962, 36). Adolf Grünbaum agrees that psychoanalytic method is "epis-temically flawed," although he disagrees with Popper about its lack of falsifiability (Grünbaum 1984, 124). For the purposes of this chapter I leave aside the question of the validity of psychoanalytic observations—for exam-ple, observations of differing cognitive styles between male and female chil-dren. I confine my criticisms instead to the biological determinism inherent in the psychoanalytic *explanations* of those observations. While most of us are now familiar with psychoanalytic object relations theory, it is worth re-viewing the basic points as a reference for the critical analysis that follows.

Briefly, object relations theory predicts that when females are the primary caregivers, the girls and boys in their care will differ in their patterns of gen-der, cognitive, and emotional development. These different patterns result from the different ways that children have of *relating* to the *objects* (including people) in their world—hence "object relations."

Feminists who make use of object relations theory retain a number of parallels with Freud's original theory of psychosexual development, but typically they focus on the social and relational, rather than the instinctual, life of developing children. For example, Nancy Chodorow argues that from a relational, rather than an instinctual, standpoint, pre-oedipal and oedipal children need to turn to a father because he is a "non-mother" primary figure (Chodorow 1978, chapter 6). Connection with a nonmother provides relief for their fragile developing egos as they strive to differentiate themselves from the all-encompassing mother (Chodorow, chapter 6). She argues that a boy has a lessened need to turn to the father at this stage because the mother sets the boy apart as an object of her (hetero)sexual desire, allowing the boy to develop a sense of himself apart from his mother. Furthermore, his male identity is enhanced by turning away from the female mother and the feminine in himself. Girls are not set apart in this way and often feel overwhelmed by their mothers, especially if their mothers identify with their daughters as similar selves (Chodorow, chapter 6). (One of the first overgeneralizations required by object relations theory is the assumption that all mothers have a feminine gender identity and are heterosexual.)

Like Freud, Chodorow hypothesizes that girls, more than boys, will turn to the father as a result of penis envy. For Chodorow, penis envy enters the clinical picture because the boy's independence is embodied in his penis, the site of difference from the mother. The daughter has no such site of difference. Thus the penis is envied as the daughter longs for independence and liberation from her mother. The penis functions as a symbol of power and independence (Chodorow 1978, 123–25).

Unlike Freud, Chodorow highlights the importance of the girl's continued relationship with her mother, and highlights the social, rather than instinctual, elements of the girl's motivation. For example, Chodorow suggests that the girl's envy of the penis may also be a result of her realization of the preferential treatment her mother gives to those who have a penis. The girl discovers that her mother desires and prefers those people with penises. The girl "comes to want a penis, then, in order to win her mother's love" (Chodorow 1978, 125).

OBJECT RELATIONS, OBJECTIVITY, AND SCIENCE

These differences in psychosexual development are said to have parallels in cognitive development, or "ways of knowing." Recall the claim that male children learn a masculine gender identity by relating to their female mother in behavioral opposition to her and all that is feminine. The mother encourages this by setting the male child apart as an object of her (hetero)sexual desire. This masculine pattern of coming to know the world by distancing, and being distanced, from the primary object in one's world is different from the learning pattern that accompanies a female's feminine gender formation. Female children learn their feminine gender identity by closely modeling their behavior after their mother, which she encourages. A female child's pattern of coming to know the world involves empathetic understanding, modeling, and identification. This difference in the gender socialization of children is said to be the first step in the association between males, masculine gender development, and a way of knowing marked as "objective"—an epistemic style that puts distance between the knower and the known. Females, in turn, come to be associated with feminine gender development and a subjective, relational process of knowing.

In the following passage, Keller describes the link that feminist work in object relations theory suggests between cognitive, emotional, and gender development:

> Our cognitive ideals . . . [are] subject to the same psychological influences as our emotional and gender ideals. Along with autonomy, the very act of separating subject from object—objectivity itself—comes to be associated with masculinity. The combined psychological and cultural pressures lead all three ideals—affective, gender, and cognitive—to a mutually reinforcing process of exaggeration and rigidification. The net result is the entrenchment of an objectivist ideology and a correlative devaluation of (female) subjectivity. (Keller 1982, 595–96)

Feminist object relations theorists claim that for some male children, the objective cognitive style can develop from the normal need for autonomy (the differentiation of "self" from "other") to an exaggerated need to dominate "others." This is the same masculine, objectivist ideology that Keller sees in science. She writes,

> I invoke psychoanalytic theory to help illuminate the forms of expression that [the] impulse [to dominate] finds in science as a whole, and its relation to objectification in particular. The same questions I asked about the child I can also ask about science. Under what circumstances is scientific knowledge sought for the pleasures of knowing, for the increased competence it grants us . . . and under what circumstances is it fair to say that science seeks actually to dominate nature? (Keller 1982, 597)

Continuing with this linking between the masculine gender development of male children and the masculine gender development of science, Keller explains that the male child/science comes to define his/its self as "not female," as *different from* mother/nature. Furthermore, the child/science is not immune from the disdain with which the larger social context treats any feminine associations, such as that of empathetic, relational knowing. From Keller's viewpoint, then, it is hardly surprising that a feminine, subjective process of knowing is devalued in science, at the expense of more masculine, objective modes of knowing (1982, 596).

Keller provides a contrast to masculine, objectivist domination in her concept of "dynamic objectivity," which involves the more feminine idea of "letting the material speak to you." The endorsement of such a naive view of induction seems odd coming from Keller, given that she makes numerous criticisms of Bacon, himself a champion of a similarly naive inductive approach.

Augmenting her psychoanalytic thesis with a historical account of the link between science, objectivity, and masculinity, Keller argues that Bacon's inductivism involved "subduing the feminine" aspects of nature (Keller 1982, 598–99). Her use of Bacon has been effectively criticized by Edrie Sobstyl, who challenges feminist overgeneralizations about the historical relationship between scientific method and masculinity (Sobstyl, "Gender and Knowledge: Some Disquiet about the Masculine Mind of Science," unpublished manuscript). Sobstyl compares Susan Bordo's claims that René Descartes was "fleeing the feminine" in himself (Bordo 1987), with Keller's claims that Bacon was subduing the feminine. Given that Descartes and Bacon arrived at completely opposite understandings of what constitutes "scientific method," one championing deduction and rationalism, the other induction and empiricism, how, Sobstyl asks, can we use patriarchal domination to explain both? The only way we can do this, she argues, is by making overgeneralizations about the history of science that gloss over crucial details of their work and the reception of their work by their peers and later generations of scientists.

Leaving aside the coherence of Keller's analysis of the masculinity of Bacon's inductive method, we are left with the somewhat inconsistent championing of this inductive approach in the work of geneticist Barbara McClintock. Keller writes that McClintock's "major criticism of contemporary research is based on what she sees as an inadequate humility" (Keller 1985, 162). McClintock reports that "much of the work done [by others] is done because one wants to impose an answer on it," when, for her, the most successful approach is to "just let the material tell you" (McClintock, in Keller 1985, 162). Keller despairs that while most scientists *observe* their object of study, they do not "encounter the object as such, in its own fullness" (166). The "feeling for the organism" of study is missing with many scientists (Keller 1982, 599). Here the contrast with Bacon becomes a little clearer—while he wrote about "gaping open-mouthed at nature," he was not necessarily known for promoting anything like a "feeling for the organism."

In these passages from Keller and McClintock, we are presented with a fairly straightforward version of the representationalist view. The material of study is described as offering itself up, if only the scientist is willing to be truly objective, relinquishing her desire to impose her subjective ideological filters over the otherwise "natural" data, clearing the bridge between the objective world and the inner subjective mind. When she is more free from her dominating impositions, the scientist, it is claimed, can better empathize and identify with the data. While Keller sees this alternative, feminine approach embodied in McClintock—

a woman—she tries to de-emphasize the biological determinism of psychoanalytic theory. She argues that McClintock's approach can be, and is, practiced by both men and women, because "neither science nor individuals are totally bound by ideology" (1982, 599). In the next section I argue that Keller's attempt to downplay the biological determinism is inconsistent with the larger psychoanalytic model to which she is committed.

Keller also argues that just as the processes or modes of acquiring knowledge have been gendered, so, too, have the products—that is, the theories and models. She explains, "Individuals drawn by a particular ideology will tend to select themes consistent with that ideology" and, conversely, reject themes inconsistent with that ideology (1982, 600). Keller provides an example of the favoring of "master molecule" models over interactionist models, in cellular biology. The former models assume a hierarchical approach, whether it involves claims that the nucleus operates in a top-down fashion over the rest of the cell or that genes provide information for the rest of the cytoplasm, with no two-way interaction between them. Interactionist models, such as the one McClintock used in her research, are more complex and allow for feedback between components of the genetic material in a non-hierarchical fashion. Keller argues that one of the reasons McClintock's work was not initially accepted by her masculine science colleagues was because the favored master molecule models are more easily aligned with masculine symbolism of domination and control, than are the interactionist models that McClintock used (1982, 601).

There is, in this latter argument of Keller's, the same vagueness and overgeneral approach to terminology that I noted in the epistemological writings of Bleier. While Keller's claims that "ideology plays a role in the choice of theory" make sense, especially, I will argue, if we view ideological beliefs as holistically related to more straightforwardly empirical beliefs, we still need to be precise about our characterization of the ideology in question. As Popper would remind us, arguing, as Keller does, at this overgeneral level, almost *any* phenomenon can be read as symbolic of "masculine domination and control."

A MIDPOINT REVIEW

Keller's 1982 essay encourages feminist analysis of the psychoanalytic factors at work in the masculine gendering of male scientists and science itself, at the same time that she champions alternative methods and theories that have been historically downplayed because of their association with the feminine gendering of females. For Keller, the utility of analyzing the masculine gendering of male scientists and science results from her belief that neither male scientists nor science are slaves to gender. She believes that revealing the unnecessary relationship between the ideology of objectivity, masculine symbolism, domination, and control will allow scientists to see that they have a choice to abandon this relationship and embrace feminine modes of knowing, to produce a more universal, less-parochial, dynamic objectivity (1982, 598).

> I will suggest that we might . . . use feminist thought to illuminate and clarify part of the substructure of science (which may have been historically conditioned into distortion) in order to preserve the things that science has taught us, in order to be more objective. (589)

Recall that Keller wants to salvage a dynamic notion of objectivity, in order to avoid the relativism of claims that objectivity *itself* is relative to masculine gender identity. Dynamic objectivity, she claims, does not necessarily have this "parochial" connection with gender—anyone can develop the more feminine, cognitive style—so it can provide a universal, nonrelative foundation for justifying our good science.

It would seem from this that Keller, like Bleier, is relying on the important feminist distinction between biological sex and socialized gender roles. One of the implications of the sex/gender distinction is that gender is not necessarily determined by sex—one can be male without being masculine, for example. Any scientist, no matter what his or her sex, can, and should, develop the more feminine dynamic objectivity.

Unfortunately, Keller's use of psychoanalytic theory restricts this case for individual gender flexibility. No matter how much she writes of our individual freedom from "gendered ideology," object relations theory is, at bottom, an account of how the *anatomical* similarity and difference between the child and the child's primary caregiver explain the cognitive capacities of boys and girls, *as grouped by sex,* not as gendered individuals. Boys with female primary caregivers (these mothers are seen as feminine by definition) will develop the capacity for the ideologically charged autonomous objectivism; there is no explanation given for how they might deviate from this development. Girls with female primary caregivers will develop the capacity for the preferred dynamic objectivity, and it seems impossible that they could develop the more negative autonomous objectivism. According to Keller's use of object relations theory, then, only females are able to develop dynamic objectivity (though certainly many do not exercise this capacity). Dynamic objectivity is the method available to one half of humanity (at the most) and does not provide Keller with a neutral or "universal, human" foundation to which she can appeal to ward off relativism.

ACCEPTING BIOLOGICAL DETERMINISM AT WHAT COST?

In later writings (*Reflections on Gender and Science,* 1985; "The Gender/ Science System," 1987), Keller acknowledges the biological determinism of object relations theory, namely, that masculine gender development is causally reducible to the interplay between the male child and the female mother, while feminine gender development is causally reducible to the interplay between the female child and the female mother. In chapter 4 of *Reflections on Gender and Science,* she notes that the development of objective, autonomous cognitive styles, though "relevant for children of both sexes," will come to be associated with only one sex, if children of both sexes have a female as a primary caregiver (1985, 85). And, relatedly,

> it is important to recognize that, although children of both sexes must learn equally to distinguish self from other and have essentially the same need for autonomy, to the extent that boys rest their sexual identity on an opposition to what is both experienced and defined as feminine, the development of their gender identity is likely to accentuate the processes of separation. (1985, 88)

She explains later that "the relevance of gender to science is (a) a socially constructed relevance [brought about by parenting patterns], but (b) *carried* by the sex of its participants" (1987, 43; emphasis in the original).

In this passage she explicitly supports the usefulness of generalizations about human cognitive capacities that are based on membership in the categories "male" or "female." While her acknowledgment of the deterministic relationship between sex and gender increases the consistency between her use of psychoanalytic theory and her writings about the associations between gender and science, this consistency is purchased at the expense of explanatory power. Again, assuming that omnipresent female caregivers are the statistical norm for most of the cultures that have produced modern scientists, Keller's theory is unable to explain the development of dynamic objectivity in male scientists, something she clearly wants to do (see, for example, Keller 1985, 175). In the case of Barbara McClintock—Keller's prototypical example of dynamic objectivity in action—the problem of explanation is reversed. Keller acknowledges that although McClintock exhibits dynamic objectivity, McClintock did not have an omnipresent mother, and she has never been a mother herself. Keller attempts to redescribe what looks to be a lack of fit between theory and evidence by explaining that "'however atypical (McClintock) is as a woman, what she is *not*, is a man'—and hence under no obligation to prove her masculinity (i.e., she does not have to enforce her autonomy by separation from her subject of study)" (Keller 1987, 42; emphasis in the original).

What Keller is left with, then, is a modified version of dynamic objectivity that discourages dominating male objectivism while encouraging nonmale (no longer necessarily female) relational and nurturing approaches to objectivity. However, even this modified version fails to defeat relativism, insofar as dynamic objectivity is still relative to the cognitive capacities of only one category of persons—nonmales. Because Keller's theory requires the use of these overgeneralizations about nonmales and males, her representationalist attempts to champion objectivity and defeat relativism continue to be unsuccessful, and her thesis is considerably weakened as a result.

Keller's use of these overgeneralizations is related to representationalism in other ways as well. Her theory of the psychosexual relationship between cognitive capacity and sex/gender proceeds as if the categories "male" and "female" were uncomplicated and natural. Her theory requires that sex/gender categories be uncomplicated by race, culture, and class, for example. Keller continues to defend the conceptual priority of sex/gender categories in her later writings (e.g., Keller 1987, 1992b). However, it is not obvious that sex/gender categories (even if they were not collapsed together) are isolatable from other well-documented features of human identity, nor is it obvious that they mark the only, or even the primary, difference in cognitive capacity (assuming again that psychoanalysts have indeed documented such differences).

COMPLICATING SEX/GENDER

Elizabeth Spelman's response to the questionable essentialism of object relations theory is as well known as object relations theory itself, and equally worth reviewing here. It is important to note that while many feminists have found Spelman's deconstruction of sex/gender categories to be helpful, many continue to be concerned that she invites a relativist approach to the very categories around which feminism is focused and, therefore, a dangerously relativist approach to feminism itself (e.g., Stoljar 1995; Okin 1994). With Cressida Heyes (2000), I believe these particular worries can be assuaged by approaching our analytic categories from a pragmatist (for Heyes, a Wittgensteinian) perspective. In what follows I review Spelman's critique of essentialism, taking up a pragmatist antidote to the problem in chapter 7.

In chapter 4 of her book *Inessential Woman: Problems of Exclusion in Feminist Thought* Spelman discusses problems with essentialism as they arise in the work of feminist object-relations theorists such as Chodorow (Spelman 1988). Spelman argues that while Chodorow is critical of much of Freud's psychoanalytic theory, she still retains his universalist, overgeneral views about the parent–child relationship. Chodorow portrays women's experiences as mothers and daughters, and men's experiences as fathers and sons, as uniform and monolithic. Chodorow is, of course, aware of differences within the categories "woman" and "man," such as "white" and "Chinese," "working class" and "middle class." She argues, however, that these differences are secondary to the primary similarities between women as mothers and daughters, and men as fathers and sons (e.g., Chodorow 1978, 77, 137, 175). While Chodorow doesn't speak of the essential characteristics of all women and men throughout history, she still sets her arguments within less-than-nuanced historical and cultural contexts (e.g., she often refers to mothering in "industrial late-capitalist society" [1978, 32], or "western industrial society" [57]).

Spelman hypothesizes that for feminists, like her and me, who are white and whose education provides an economic privilege, sex/gender may indeed be our only or main site of difference from the male oppressor, who is also typically privileged and white. But Spelman argues that it would be a mistake to generalize this particular experience of masculine oppression to the experience of oppression of all women, even within the modern, industrialized West (Spelman 1988, 97–100).

Marilyn Frye makes a similar point in her book *The Politics of Reality:* "Because we white women have been able to think of ourselves as looking just at *women* and *men* when really we were looking at white women and white men, we have generally interpreted our connections with these men solely in terms of gender, sexism and male dominance" (Frye 1983, 124).

What this means, of course, is that *even if* sex/gender is the only or main site of difference for white, middle-class women, race and class still operate in their experience of oppression. To have sex/gender as the only site of one's oppression *requires* that one be of a certain race, class, sexual orientation, age, linguistic grouping, and so forth (Spelman 1988, 104–6). In this way it is difficult, and questionable, to try to conceptually isolate the effects of sex/gender from that of the other prominent features that mark the human experience of oppression. Even acknowledging other experiences of oppression by "adding" them on, for example, by adding the experience of white supremacy to a black woman's experience of patriarchy, still treats these experiences as discrete and isolable variables of a woman's life. Against this, many black women and other women of color have spoken of their difficulty in isolating the sexist or racist elements of a particular experience of oppression (e.g., hooks 1981, 12–13). Further complications for sex/gender categories come from writings by and about transgendered persons and transsexuals, who feel part of neither the female nor the male world and refuse to be classified one way or the other (see Rothblatt 1995; Herdt 1994; Bornstein 1994).

Returning to object relations theory, we have to ask whether it is conceivable that boys and girls relate to their mothers only or even primarily on a discrete sex/gender dimension. It would seem more likely that the sex/gender dimension is complicated by the child's and the parent's sense of where they fit in the larger human context of racism and classism, for example, *as well as* sexism. Boys and girls don't grow up to be "generic" men and women, but as specific men and women (and, for some transgendered persons and transsexuals, for example, even this more specific sex categorization remains ambiguous). Spelman rightly questions how this specificity is accounted for by object relations theory (Spelman 1988, 97).

Again, while these problems of essentialism have long been recognized, oversimple categories continue to inform our thinking. For example, the linking of science and reason with masculinity, *simpliciter*, still figures prominently in feminist science studies. In Alessandra Tanesini's review of feminist epistemology (1999), she provides a nuanced discussion of essentialism in feminist standpoint theory (152–55), but then later notes that

> the most innovative contribution of feminism to the critique of reason resides in the examination of the connections between reason and masculinity. There is no doubt that during the last few centuries women, on the whole, have been seen as emotional creatures. Instead, men have been taken to be capable of engaging in scientific reasoning. Nobody, I believe, would contest these claims. (214)

As we have seen, Darwin and his colleagues, as well as any number of scientists advocating racialized theories of intelligence, would argue that only certain men are capable of engaging scientifically. For Darwin, males and females of the "lower races" hardly qualified as men and women, let alone as rational men and emotional women. While it is true, then, that our feminist studies of science have involved concerted attempts to move beyond essentialism, a comprehensive critical response to the sexism and racism of scientists like Darwin requires that we further refine our categories of analysis. It is my hope that by promoting a pragmatist approach, the problems of essentialism can be even more effectively diagnosed and treated. I present this alternative in chapter 7. In the section that follows I continue my analysis of the historical link between essentialism and epistemology, particularly within feminist standpoint theory.

OBJECT RELATIONS AND FEMINIST STANDPOINT THEORIES

Keller's use of object relations theory to articulate the difference between male and nonmale approaches to knowledge is modeled on a Hegelian/Marxist view of epistemology. Both Hegel and Marx argued that in hierarchical social worlds, one's material position in the hierarchy affects the extent of one's knowledge or, more radically, affects one's ability to recognize truth itself (see Marx and Engels 1964). Many feminist theorists have modeled this materialist approach to epistemology explicitly, using object relations theory, or variants, to describe a feminist or woman's standpoint (e.g., Hartsock 1985, 1987 [1983]). Nancy Hartsock argues that in a social hierarchy divided by sex, what men can know is partial or distorted, and what women or feminists can know is epistemically superior or more objective (1985, 1987).

Unfortunately, as in Keller's work, the conceptual problems with object relations theory can also be found in these feminist standpoint accounts. For example, in her chapter entitled "The Feminist Standpoint: Toward a Specifically Feminist Historical Materialism," Hartsock uses object relations theory to focus on women, generally, as mothers and daughters (Hartsock 1985, chapter 10). She explains, "In addressing the institutionalized sexual division of labor, I propose to lay aside the important differences among women and instead search for central commonalities across race and class boundaries" (Hartsock 1985, 233).

Aside from the problem of isolating the effects of race and class, Spelman notes that the decision to "lay aside important differences among women" does not typically involve the general problem of deciding whether to focus on the similarities among or differences between women. Instead, the problem, as she and many others have pointed out, is typically that of conflating the conditions of white, heterosexual, able-bodied, middle-class women with the conditions of all women. What becomes apparent is that any problematic differences between women are actually the differences between the first group of women and all others. Spelman explains,

> The focus on women "as women" has addressed only one group of women— namely, white, middle-class women of western industrialised countries. So the solution has not been to talk about what women have in common, as women; it has been to conflate the condition of one group with the condition of all and to treat the differences of white middle-class women from all other women as if they were not differences. (Spelman, 1988, 3)

I rehearse these problems with essentialist views of sex/gender because I believe they are related to the epistemological problems of relativism found in Keller's work. For Hartsock, there is an objective or epistemically privileged vantage point for gaining the truth about power relations (Hartsock's particular interest), but her account of this "more adequate" view becomes relativized to the lived experience of women (or feminists). Hartsock writes,

> Whereas Marx relocated power on to the empirical ground of production, I argue that women's lives provide a related but more adequate empirical terrain for understanding power. Women's different understanding of power provides suggestive evidence that women's experience of power relations, and thus their understanding, may be importantly and structurally different from the lives and therefore the theories of men. I suggest that, like the lives of the proletarians vis-à-vis capital, women's lives make available a particular and privileged vantage point not only of the power relations between men and women but on power relations more generally. (Hartsock 1985, 151)

One final concern with those feminist standpoints derived from object relations theory is that often masculine gender development is equated with dominating and objectifying others, in a way that makes sexism the *model* for other sorts of oppression (e.g., by "adapting" male domination over females to explain whites dominating blacks, capitalists dominating workers, or science dominating nature) (Spelman 1988, 85). Sexism is also often described as the *cause* of these other sorts of oppression. Chodorow defends both these claims in an essay replying to criticisms of her book (Chodorow 1981).

Hartsock writes that using object relations, "one might then turn to the question whether capitalism rests on and is a consequence of male supremacy" (1985, 262). The claim here, says Spelman, is that "if men weren't so insecure about their sense of self vis-à-vis their mothers, they wouldn't need to define anyone else as Other" (Spelman 1988, 85). However, this equation between masculine identity and the development of classism or racism makes it difficult, if not impossible, to understand the development of these features in women, unless these women have absent mothers and omnipresent fathers. But surely the population of classist and/or racist women is larger than these unusual parental configurations would allow.

bell hooks also voices concern about the equation of masculine gender development with the development of racism and classism, in her book *Talking Back: Thinking Feminist, Thinking Black* (hooks 1989, chapter 4). She points out that this equation allows women to mask their own role in oppression and domination. She writes, "Women can and do participate in politics of domination, as perpetrators as well as victims" (hooks 1989, 20). Women can be racist and homophobic, for example. Similarly, Biddy Martin and Chandra Mohanty (1986) highlight how white, privileged daughters participate in oppressive systems because they *share* race and class with *both* their parents. The similarity in experience between daughters and fathers is undertheorized in object relations theory (Martin and Mohanty 1986, 204). hooks examines the ways in which women, despite the predictions of object relations theory, participate in oppressive relationships, particularly *as* mothers (e.g., 1989, 20). She writes,

> Even as I speak, women who are ourselves exploited, victimized, are dominating children. It is necessary for us to remember, as we think critically about domination, that we all have the capacity to act in ways that oppress, dominate, wound. (hooks 1989, 21)

Bat-Ami Bar On (1993, 92–93) is also critical of the romanticizing of mother–child relationships that necessarily neglects the unequal power dynamic involved. These theorists each speak against feminist arguments about the unique relationship between masculine cognitive styles and (scientific) domination and control.

REPRESENTATIONALISM CONTINUED IN "THE GENDER/SCIENCE SYSTEM"

In the paper "The Gender/Science System," Keller continues with her representationalist arguments for the importance of objectivity in science (Keller 1987). More specifically, she argues that abandoning objectivism can lead only to relativism; that skepticism is a coherent but unassailable problem; and that sex/gender is a primary, isolable, natural kind.

With respect to the first feature, Keller argues that science is a "maximally reliable (even if not faithful) representation of nature" (46). This sounds fair enough (invoking the word "representation," in itself, raises no flags). But she then reports that to think otherwise about science is to embrace a "postmodern" relativist alternative—the view that what counts as true in science will depend not on nature, but will instead be relative to the politics of various scientists (48). This invocation of relativism reveals the continuing influence of the representationalist model. If one stays within representationalism, then any criticisms of an objectivist view of science will inevitably involve concessions to skepticism in its relativist guise.

That Keller believes skepticism to be a rational concern is motivated by the view that there is a gap between the scientist as subjective representer and the objective world as the data represented. As I have argued, this gap invites the unnecessarily skeptical view that while our scientific representations must be faithful to be true, the representations are metaphysically separate from the external world so their fidelity can never be guaranteed. Keller has a certain amount of faith in the accuracy of scientific representations (they can be "maximally reliable," even if not faithful). And, against the extreme relativist, she argues that nature *does* exist. However, she claims, we must acknowledge the skeptic's point that "nature" is "ultimately unrepresentable" (48).

It appears from these passages that she is aware that no objectivist argument can satisfactorily explain how it is, on the representationalist model, that we can get completely outside our subjective skins to accurately represent the outside world of nature. But, for Keller, this is a more satisfactory level of skepticism than that found in the relativist claim that the truth of the outside world is somehow constructed by us. However, as I argue in chapter 6, neither of these representationalist options needs to be satisfactory for feminists, because there is a nonrepresentationalist option available.

Finally, in response to the essentialist debates about the priority of gender to race and class, Keller criticizes the view that gender is "infinitely plastic" (1987, 38). According to Keller, feminists need to acknowledge the important relationship between gender and sex—we can't ignore the "recalcitrance of sex" (1987, 48). She writes that feminist theorists who concentrate on the "proliferation of difference" between women of different races and classes, for example, are humbled in the face of the sameness that is our sex (1987, 48). And again she offers a skeptic's warning: "Neither nature nor sex *can* be named out of existence. Both persist, *beyond theory*, as humbling reminders of our mortality" (1987, 48; first emphasis in the original; second emphasis, mine).

In this passage, our mortal, sexed natures are viewed as fixed givens beyond which we cannot and should not stretch our feminist theories about the plasticity of gender. Again, Keller's view is confined by the representationalist model. While she is critical of the objectivist view that scientific method provides a direct or infallible correspondence between our theories and nature (nature and sex, she says, exist beyond theory), she is also concerned about a radical relativism where the truth about nature is relative to our conceptual schemes. In the end her position approaches that of a disillusioned objectivist. She accepts skepticism: Nature, like sex, must exist out there somehow; but both remain "ultimately unrepresentable." This disillusioned view of the powers of human investigation weakens the feminist project of investigating and eliminating the oppressive features of science. As we know, many feminist investigations of oppression in science have been found to be accurate and reliable (including many examples provided by Keller herself). There is no mystery to the phenomenon of oppression—only a fallibilist's sense that we still have more to investigate. By imposing epistemological limitations on the scope of scientific investigation, Keller's criticisms undercut the progress of the very feminist projects she seeks to support.

Keller continues her discussions of gender and science in her 1992 collection of essays *Secrets of Life, Secrets of Death*. Here, her defense of the priority of gender over other categories within race and class is not necessarily based on the biologically determined relationship between gender and "recalcitrant sex," but rather on the fact that in science, at least, everyone is typically white and economically advantaged, so race and class can be "bracketed" from the discussion (e.g., "Gender and Science: An Update," 1992b, note on p. 17). She does note that the conception of gender bracketed in this way is necessarily specific "to a particular subset of western culture" (17), which is, of course, also true of her conception of science. However, she then defends the importance of gender categories, generally, to discussions of science, generally, with the following:

> Gender and gender norms come to be seen as silent organizers of the mental and discursive maps of the social and natural worlds we simultaneously inhabit and construct—*even of those worlds that women never enter* [i.e., most of science]. (17; emphasis in the original)

But by the same token, these worlds are also not inhabited by certain sorts of men (indeed *most* men), so I remain unconvinced of Keller's arguments for the natural priority of sex/gender categories as uncomplicated givens, especially when discussing as complex an institution as science.

I return to this collection of Keller's essays in the next chapter. There I discuss how, in these more recent writings, Keller's writing takes a decided turn away from objectivist epistemology, but because she remains in a representationalist framework, her work ends up making concessions to relativism. She is joined in this troublesome move toward relativism by the arguments of two other important feminist science critics, Sandra Harding (1991, 1993b) and Helen Longino (1987, 1990).

NOTE

1. While I will be analyzing those arguments of Keller's that have been the most influential within feminist science studies, she has, of course, continued to publish important analyses of biology, beyond those I discuss here (e.g., Keller 2000, 2002). In *Making Sense of Life: Explaining Biological Development with Models, Metaphors, and Machines* (2002), Keller moves away from her earlier interest in psychoanalytic explanations of science by examining epistemic issues in biology at the level of "local, and historically specific, disciplinary culture[s]" (x). This sounds exactly like the sort of project that is needed in feminist science studies; however, Keller has also moved away from her previous interests in the effects of sexism and gender bias in science. Reapplying Keller's most recent methodological shift to the outstanding questions of bias and abuse in science remains an open research project.

5

From Objectivism to Relativism in Feminist Science Studies

In the introduction to *Secrets of Life, Secrets of Death,* Evelyn Fox Keller rejects some of her earlier views about objective method, "non-male" or otherwise (1992a, 4). She explains that she no longer believes that objective method is that which distinguishes theories based on "ideology" or myth from theories based on "fact." She describes this more critical view of objectivity as "my linguistic turn," which, she continues,

> represents a shift from my earlier preoccupation with the frailties of description, and in one respect at least, a departure from my initial confidence in the possibility of identifying certain beliefs as "myth-like," as distinct from other beliefs that are, by implication, "myth-free." Such a notion now seems to me suspiciously reminiscent of the old demarcation between "truth" and "ideology," or between "good science" and "value-laden science," demarcations that are themselves residues of the copy theory of truth. (1992a, 4–5)

Putting this change in representationalist terms, Keller is now critical of the claim that objective method involves distinguishing between those theories that have the requisite normative relational property and those that are based merely on ideology. In another essay in the collection, "Critical Silences in Scientific Discourses," she writes of "abandoning the hope for a one-to-one correspondence with the real" (1992c, 73).

My concern throughout these essays is that Keller's abandonment of objectivity is based on a perceived failure, not of conception, but of execution. In Keller's view, correspondence is indeed the sort of relation we need to bridge the metaphysical gap between us and the world, but we are consistently thwarted in our bridge construction because our bridges are always blocked by the influence of cultural conceptual schemes. She explains,

"Since nature is only accessible to us through representations and since representations are necessarily structured by language (and hence, by culture), no representation can ever 'correspond' to reality" (1992a, 5). Again, on the representationalist model, this criticism of objectivism inevitably leads to skepticism in a relativist form. The only alternative to objective correspondence is to view our representations as filtered products of our subjective language scheme or culture.

However, as we've seen, this alternative invites a skeptical epistemic query: "By what normative criteria should we adjudicate between competing subjective representations, given that none has the objective relational property of one-to-one correspondence with the external world?" Keller replies that we should choose those representations that facilitate certain "interventions," to use Ian Hacking's phrase (Hacking 1983). Specifically, we should choose those interventions that best suit our political goals. In the following passage Keller explains the options she believes this sort of conceptual relativism leaves for feminists:

> Since it is demonstrably possible to envision different kinds of representations, we need now to ask what different possibilities of change might be entailed by these different kinds of representation? For this, we need to understand the enmeshing of representing and intervening, how particular representations are already committed to particular kinds of interventions. Is there, for instance, a sense in which we might say that the program of modern genetics already has, written into its very structure, a blueprint for eugenics? Or that nuclear weapons are prebuilt into the program of nuclear physics? And if so, what kinds of theories of the natural world would enable us to act on the world differently? (Keller 1992c, 76)

In this quotation, Keller makes the representationalist acknowledgment that subjective linguistic schemes or filters play an instrumental role in our choice of theories. However, she is still concerned to acknowledge the flipside of the scheme/content coin, namely, the role of the "non-linguistic" realm—the objective reality or content the theories describe. In her essay "Gender and Science: An Update," Keller writes that for feminist critics who take the objective success of science seriously, the new task is to answer the question "How do 'nature' and 'culture' interact in the production of scientific knowledge?" (1992b, 36). But discovering how these two metaphysically distinct realms interact becomes as much of a problem for Keller as it was for Descartes. Despite her switch from objectivist searches for truth to instrumentalist searches for success, the representationalist underpinnings remain, as does the skepticism. In the next section, I argue that the epistemological theories of Sandra Harding and Helen Longino encounter similar problems. While both Harding and Longino have made crucial contributions to the deconstruction of the objectivism/relativism polarity, their deconstruction of the representationalist model on which the polarity is based remains incomplete.

HARDING ON OBJECTIVITY

Harding has been one of the most effective commentators on the futility of the objectivism/relativism polarity as it is constructed by Cartesian or representationalist models in epistemology (e.g., Harding 1986a, Harding 1991, 1993b).[1] Recognizing both the incoherence of objectivism and the dangers of relativism, Harding has tried to carve out a conceptual middle ground. Paralleling Keller's views in the 1992 collection, Harding's influential work on feminist standpoint theory is particularly critical of the claim that objective method consists in detecting a one-to-one correspondence between true representations and the world. However, I argue that Harding, like Keller, does not place adequate critical focus on representationalism itself. She places most of her energy on criticizing the clarity of correspondence relations.

Harding argues that certain aspects of culture—namely, the social standpoint of the representer—filter the correspondence between any one representation and the world represented. As with Hartsock, this is Harding's version of the Marxist claim that one's lived reality, one's social standpoint, will "organize and set limits" on one's understanding of the world (Harding 1993b, 54). In "Rethinking Standpoint Epistemology: What Is 'Strong Objectivity'?" (1993b), Harding explains her commitment to the general tenets of standpoint theory:

> The starting point of standpoint theory—and its claim that is most often misread—is that in societies stratified by race, ethnicity, class, gender, sexuality, or some other such politics shaping the very structure of a society, the activities of those at the top both organize and set limits on what persons who perform such activities can understand about themselves and the world around them. . . . In contrast, the activities of those at the bottom of such social hierarchies can provide starting points for thought—for *everyone's* research and scholarship—from which humans' relations with each other and the natural world can become visible. This is because the experience and lives of marginalized peoples, as they understand them, provide particularly significant *problems to be explained* or research agendas. (1993b, 54; emphasis in the original)

Before I discuss the lingering elements of a scheme/content distinction at work in Harding's standpoint theory, I want to draw attention to her careful use of sex/gender and other categories of analysis. Earlier I had argued that some feminist epistemologies seem to require the treatment of sex/gender as a natural and primary observational category. Such treatment, I argued, was related to an objectivist or empiricist need for the sorts of natural kind categories that are firm enough to support the relational bridge building required by epistemological metaphysics. In Harding's theory, however, there is a welcome move away from the overgeneral categories of sex/gender that were found in Keller's arguments, for example. Harding discusses, instead, the complex ways in which many oppressive forces shape the lives of marginalized peoples.

Her justification for the value of hearing from marginalized peoples seems also to be free of the inconsistent objectivist claims found in Keller's earlier work. Harding does not rely on claims about the different and/or more objective cognitive *style* of marginalized peoples; rather, she makes the less problematic claim that starting scientific inquiry from their lived experience would introduce different, and long-neglected, *content* for scientific examination ("problems to be explained").

Unfortunately, Harding goes on to make a number of claims about sex/gender categories that conflict with those in the previously quoted passage, evincing an ambivalence about how best to address the problem of essentialism. Right after her statement about "the lives of those at the bottom of social hierarchies," she returns to a more overgeneral prescription of starting science from "women's" lives, borrowing from the standpoint theory of Dorothy Smith (Smith 1987a, 1987b). According to Smith and Harding, *all* women share the common work of "caring for bodies" (Harding 1993b, 55). In a footnote, Harding acknowledges that grouping women together like this might be inappropriate, because wealthy women, for example, don't have to care for bodies as much as poor women do. But, she claims, wealthy women still have to care for bodies more than do their wealthy brothers (footnote, p. 55). However, a number of poor and/or nonwhite men do participate in caring for bodies, and it might be that on this particular labor axis, these men and their impoverished sisters share a standpoint more closely than do wealthy women and poor women. At other times Harding reduces her detailed descriptions of science from "western, bourgeois, homophobic, white, [and] sexist" to oversimplified descriptions such as the "male bias" of the "most fundamental categories of scientific thought" (both quotes are from Harding 1986b, 652).[2]

Harding's continued ambivalence about the notion that science is simply "gendered" or "sexed" and that sex/gender categories are primary and/or given by nature is evidenced in subtle ways, more recently in her introduction to her edited collection *The "Racial" Economy of Science* (Harding 1993a). Referring to the title of the book, she explains that "racial" is put in scare quotes to denote the constructed, contested nature of race and the racism of science (Harding 1993a, 2 [footnote]), which seems right. However, she doesn't use scare quotes in discussions of sex/gender and the sexed/gendered nature of science (e.g., in the same text she uses the phrase "'race' and gender" [11]). While Harding properly questions the ontological naturalness or primacy of race categories, sex/gender categories receive less consistent deconstruction.

As with Ruth Hubbard, Ruth Bleier, and Keller, Harding's struggle to conceptualize the primacy of sex/gender is related to problems with the representationalism that continues to influence her epistemology. For example, Harding writes that "starting off research from women's lives will generate less partial and distorted accounts not only of women's lives but also of men's lives and of the whole social order" (Harding 1993b, 56). That "starting off research from women's lives" might produce different (more appropriate?) scientific research about women is a claim that needs a lot more detail and documentation than she provides, but it is, I think, defensible. That starting research from women's lives might produce increased objectivity or decreased distortion in scientific studies about women might also be defensible on a case-by-case basis, presumably by showing that most women scientists have fewer biases about women than do most men scientists. However, the claim that research started from women's lives will provide increased objectivity about "men's lives and the whole social order" is a much more problematic claim that encounters precisely the same representationalist conflicts found with the standpoint views of Nancy Hartsock and the early Keller.

Translating Harding's claim in terms of its representationalist underpinnings is to say that while different degrees of opacity accrue to different social standpoint filters, not all social standpoints generate equally partial representations or beliefs. In *Whose Science? Whose Knowledge? Thinking from Women's Lives* (1991) Harding argues that the social standpoints of women, or feminists with "maximally liberatory social interests," for example, "have generated less partial and distorted beliefs than others" (Harding 1991, 144, 148). She explains,

> The history of science shows that research directed by maximally liberatory social interests and values tends to be better equipped to identify partial claims and distorting assumptions, even though the credibility of the scientists who do it may not be enhanced during the short run. After all, anti-liberatory interests and values are invested in the natural inferiority of just the groups of humans who, if given real equal access (not just the formally equal access that is liberalism's goal) to public voice, would most strongly contest claims about their purported natural inferiority. Anti-liberatory interests and values silence and destroy the most likely sources of evidence against their own claims. That is what makes them rational for elites. (148–49)

Because she argues that *all* beliefs have a social filter, Harding disavows the claim that the standpoints of women or feminists will produce "true beliefs"— just less partial, less distorted ones than those produced by "anti-liberatory interests" (1991, 185, 149). Paralleling the problems encountered by Hubbard on this point, Harding purchases some consistency by claiming that all knowledge is somehow distorted, but this skeptical claim robs her of the foundation she then needs to argue that the knowledge produced from some standpoints is less distorted, generally, than that produced from others. The skeptic is immediately invited to ask whether this latter claim is similarly distorted. Harding needs to be able to answer in the negative, but her relativist point that subjective filters affect all our knowledge claims precludes this answer.

Also, the overgeneral nature of some of the standpoints she invokes begins to reappear as a conceptual difficulty. While there are certainly areas
about which some people have more objectivity than others, her claim that
women, or feminists, as a group have more objectivity about the whole social order than do men, or nonfeminists, as a group is empirically unsupported. In her essay "Marginality and Epistemic Privilege" (1993) Bat-Ami Bar
On adds some important conceptual criticisms in this regard.

Bar On argues that the existence of multiple systems of marginalization
(e.g., within groups of women, and within groups of men) problematizes
claims of the empirical privileging of any one marginalized group. "Is any
one of these groups more epistemically privileged than the other, and if that
is not so—if they are equally epistemically privileged—does epistemic privilege matter?" (1993, 89). Clearly, she thinks it does not, and I agree. If every
marginalized social status can produce epistemic privilege, the claim to priority of any one sort of status loses its bite. And, in any case, along with the
increase in awareness of the multiple axes on which any one person might
be materially disadvantaged, there is a decreased focus on the relationship
between any one axis and the day-to-day practices of scientists. Again, diagnosing the oppression resulting from these day-to-day practices needs to remain a focus for feminist critics of science.

To review, Harding argues that even with the less partial view provided by
the standpoint of women or feminists, *objective, true* knowledge is impossible to attain. This does not mean, however, that objectivity has no place in
Harding's project. Just as Keller reconfigured scientific method, Harding re-
configures objectivity, to give it a new role.

In *Whose Science? Whose Knowledge?* Harding rightly criticizes the traditional view of objectivity that she calls "objectivism." Objectivism results in
a "semi-science" that "turns away from the task of critically identifying all
those broad, historical, social desires, interests, and values that have
shaped the agendas, contents, and results of the sciences much as they
shape the rest of human affairs" (1991, 143). Unfortunately, by my nonrepresentationalist criteria, she puts a new epistemological position in its
stead. As an improved epistemic method for adjudicating knowledge
claims, Harding critiques objectivism and substitutes "strong objectivity"—
a position that extends the idea of scientific research "to include systematic
examination of . . . powerful background beliefs," thereby "maximising objectivity" (149). By using strong objectivity, our theories are more likely to
have the normative property of being maximally objective or least partial.
Again, following Marx, and sharing Keller's new goal, Harding reconfig-
ures objectivity along scheme/content lines. Strong objectivity is described
as the critical examination of the linguistic or social filters, "the powerful
background beliefs," that continually block our knowledge-seeking of the
nonlinguistic, natural realm.

Before I assess this new feminist reconfiguration of objectivity, I want briefly to offer one more example of the trend in Longino's now classic writings in feminist science studies "Can There Be a Feminist Science?" (1987) and *Science as Social Knowledge* (1990).[3] Longino argues against some feminist accounts that equate objectivity with value-free scientific method (Longino 1987, 60). Longino suggests, instead, that objective, good science is always biased with contextual values that come from our "interpretive frameworks," such as the interpretive frameworks of particle physics that guide observations of elementary particles in cloud chambers (54). Much of science, she claims, is guided by these interpretive contextual values, so diagnoses of bad science as that which is biased by contextual values won't fully capture the problem (56). What we need to do is redefine objectivity as that feature of scientific method that allows us to better examine the influence of these interpretive frameworks. She explains,

> We cannot restrict ourselves simply to the elimination of bias, but must expand our scope to include the detection of limiting and interpretive frameworks and the finding or construction of more appropriate frameworks. We need not, indeed should not, wait for such a framework to emerge from the data. (1987, 60)

On her model, the prescribed focus for feminist work in science then becomes a search for better conceptual filters (or schemes), as distinct from, and more coherent than, the search for better evidence (or content). The scheme/content split appears also in her explanation that the data of the external world are "dumb" and that it is only through subjective conceptual schemes that they are given voice as evidence for a particular hypothesis or theory (Longino 1990, 111).

The problem here is that when one conceives of a split between an inner conceptual world of values and interpretive frameworks and an outer world of unanalyzed data, one invites an unanswered, and unanswerable, skepticism about the relationship between evidence and theory. While Longino is surely correct that evidence of elementary particles, for example, is not simply given by nature, I do not think that we then have to redirect our project away from questions of evidence and toward some nonevidential investigations of interpretive frameworks. Feminists would be better served by a Davidsonian model that conceives of interpretive frameworks, norms, and values as holistically of a piece with other evidential considerations.

To be sure, Longino argues that suitable conceptual schemes are those likely to arise within a scientific community that respects objective approaches to evidence gathering. Such a community would be one that creates recognized avenues for the criticism of evidence, employs shared standards that critics can invoke, is responsive to criticism, and shares intellectual authority equally among qualified practitioners (Longino 1990, 76). To the extent that we are able to create such communities and work from within suitable conceptual schemes, then our resulting theories will have the normative property of being maximally objective. Note, however, that this is just one more variation on an epistemic theme—a theme that invites the same skeptical queries as have any number of previous normative accounts. In this case the skeptic is invited to ask how we know that even the most suitable conceptual frameworks produced within the most ideal communities aren't, for all that, still partial and subjective. I take up Longino's response to this skeptical concern in the next section.

FROM OBJECTIVISM TO RELATIVISM

Though Longino, Harding, and Keller rightly reject the claims that objective method involves impartial (value-, social-, and culture-free) detection of one-to-one correspondence, they do not spend as much time criticizing the metaphysical gap of representationalism that correspondence sets out to bridge. As we have seen with Keller's earlier work, if we criticize objectivist attempts to detect correspondence, but are insufficiently critical of the metaphysical confines of representationalism, then we end up with a begrudging acceptance of skepticism, especially its relativist variants.[4] This phenomenon is manifest in the arguments provided by each of these three theorists.

While each has taken great care to distance her work from relativism, as well as from objectivism, each is left with a watered-down prescription for feminist scientific method that is restricted to detecting how the filter of culture intervenes between the world and scientific knowledge. All our knowledge becomes relativized to our conceptual filters. Once our new maximally objective method has helped us identify the values, culture, and politics that comprise the conceptual scheme guiding our theories, the best we can do is pick the theory screened through the most appealing (to feminists) and/or least partial conceptual scheme.

For each theorist this new method results in a resigned skepticism. Longino admits that her criticism of the possibility of direct correspondence between theory (or hypothesis) and evidence relativizes what counts as evidence, and that "by relativizing what counts as evidence to background beliefs or assumptions, hypothesis acceptance on the basis of evidence is also thus relativized" (Longino 1990, 61). While Longino does not abandon objectivity, her contextualized account results in a restricted notion of "objectivity by degrees" that is relative to the social dynamics of various science communities (1990, chapter 4). Keller, too, concedes that in the absence of any one-to-one correspondence between representations and reality, our feminist decisions between representations should be made relative to the differing political "interventions" each representation affords (Keller 1992c, 76). Nature is ultimately unrepresentable (Keller 1987). Similarly, because Harding argues that *all* beliefs are filtered through the social standpoint of the believer, she disavows the claim that the standpoints of women or feminists will produce true beliefs about reality—just less partial, less distorted ones than those produced by "anti-liberatory interests" (Harding 1991, 185, 149).

These begrudging concessions to relativism evoke a dangerous level of self-directed skepticism. Again, this is not the fallibilistic worry that our theories might not be as well supported by the evidence as they should, or that new evidence might be found that contradicts our theories. These local empirical doubts are important and appropriate. The skepticism with which I am concerned is pitched at a much higher level of abstraction. Here, the worry is that if the empirical content of our theories is relative to the filtering effects of our political schemes and values, then we lose our ability to empirically adjudicate between competing theories. I argue that such concessions to relativism are only necessary if one is insufficiently attentive to the role of representationalism in epistemology.

Although Longino is the only one to use the term "underdetermination," the problems with relativism encountered in the writings of Harding, Keller, and Longino all seem to stem from a representationalist use of the underdetermination thesis. This is the thesis, often associated with Willard Van Orman Quine, that every scientific theory is underdetermined by the evidence brought forward in its support; that is, theoretically, any particular piece of evidence can be used to support an infinite number of theories. Conversely, for any theory that fits the available evidence, there may be another theory that fits the same evidence equally well (Quine 1981, 28–29). The representationalist elements of the underdetermination thesis arise from an apparent corollary; namely, given that some scientific theories *are* chosen over others, these choices must be *relative* to a political "worldview," "explanatory scheme," or "paradigm," rather than just the evidence; there can be no objective adjudication on the basis of how any one theory simply corresponds to the empirical evidence.[5] Again, this sort of relativism involves the conceptual splitting of the empirical evidence, that is, the content, from the conceptual filter of politics or culture, that is, the scheme. Aspects of the arguments of Longino, Keller, and Harding support this relativist interpretation of the underdetermination thesis, which they introduce as an improvement over the objectivist claims of one-to-one correspondence between theory and evidence.

One example in Longino's work comes from her analysis of competing anthropological theories for interpreting the use of ancient chipped stones (Longino 1990, 103–11). One theory, highlighting the role of the male hunter, interprets the stones as hunting tools. The other, competing, theory includes the role of the female gatherer and interprets the stones as implements for gathering and preparing edible vegetation. According to Longino, the available data support both theories equally well, so the choice of the male-focused model or the more inclusive model must be relative to an underlying political commitment—namely, to androcentrism or feminism, respectively (e.g., Longino 1990, 109). Here we have an example of the representationalist claim that political values screen or filter the empirical data about which we form beliefs, but that the values are not themselves beliefs with empirical content.

Longino and others who use this relativist version of underdetermination theory make a compelling case for the reasonableness of the position, especially as a negative point against objectivist correspondence theories of truth. However, in my view, it is still too much of a conceptual danger for feminists to suggest that political values (including feminist political values) are distinct from, because filters for, empirical data.

The relativist account of underdetermination theory is premised on the representationalist view that "data" and "political considerations" emanate from two metaphysically separate spheres—the first from the objective, external world; the second from the subjective, internal mind (or minds, as when political views are said to be socially constructed). On Davidson's account, discussed in the next chapter, underdetermination does not have to have the relativist implications of the representationalist model, because his account does not rely on a metaphysical split between outer and inner worlds.

I now return to Longino's representationalist use of underdetermination theory to chart more explicitly the development of an unnecessary level of relativism in what is, otherwise, a highly compelling discussion of feminist science.

LONGINO AND FEMINIST SCIENCE

In Longino's 1987 essay "Can There Be a Feminist Science?" she previews the major themes of her book *Science as Social Knowledge: Values and Objectivity in Scientific Inquiry* (1990). One of these themes is the debate over the criteria for what makes feminist science "feminist." As I discuss further on, Longino convincingly argues against some feminist claims that feminist science is marked either by a "feminine" style of reasoning or by theoretical content that matches the "feminine" propensity for "interactionist" rather than "linear" causal explanations. In *Science as Social Knowledge* she articulates alternatives to both these feminist accounts and to the traditional accounts of objectivity in science (Longino 1990).

As an alternative to traditional objectivist accounts, she argues that scientific knowledge is a social product, which sometimes, of course, can weaken objectivity, but often can actually *increase* objectivity. She writes,

> I will argue that there are standards of rational acceptability that are independent of particular interests and values but that satisfaction of these standards by a theory or hypothesis does not guarantee that the theory or hypothesis in ques-

tion is value- or interest-free. . . . [T]he development of knowledge is a necessarily social rather than individual activity, and it is the social character of scientific knowledge that *both protects it from and renders it vulnerable to* social
and political interests and values. (1990, 12; emphasis mine)

In other words, objectivity in science can be increased by the local community exchange of ideas and criticism that balances out the biases of any one
individual.[6] This makes good sense to me.

Another attractive feature of Longino's account is that she argues against
the conflation of a "feminist" science with scientific theories that are characterized as "feminine" or "female"—a conflation I noted in the earlier writings
of Keller and that Longino finds in the work of Bleier:

Some theorists have written as though a feminist science is one whose theories
encode a particular worldview, characterized by complexity, interaction, and
holism. Such a science is said to be feminist because it is the expression and val-
orization of a female sensibility or cognitive temperament. Alternatively it is
claimed that women have certain traits (for example, dispositions to attend to
particulars and interactive and cooperative social attitudes and behaviors rather
than individualist and controlling ones) that enable them to understand the true
character of natural processes (which are complex and interactive). (1987, 52)

Longino is appropriately concerned that this approach to feminist science
uncritically embraces and reifies gender stereotypes (1987, 53).

Longino goes on to criticize the associations of "feminist" with "feminine"
or "female" not only in characterizations of certain theories, but in characterizations of scientific method as well, especially as the associations appear
in feminist standpoint theories (Longino 1987, 53; 1993). I think these criticisms can be applied to Keller's earlier descriptions of the association between dynamic objectivity and female, or nonmale, cognitive traits.

While critical of the proposed "feminine" derivation of these standpoints,
Longino also criticizes the very idea that women share a standpoint, irrespective of its etiology. She writes that "women are too diverse in our experience to generate a single cognitive framework" (Longino 1987, 53). While
Harding, too, is clearly aware of this diversity, her own work on standpoint
theory is less consistent than Longino's in this respect.

Finally, Longino is also appropriately critical of the idea that feminist science aims to "reveal the truth that is hidden by masculine 'bad' science"
(1987, 53). Paralleling Keller's change of heart on this subject, Longino argues that even good, objective science is value-laden.

The details of Longino's negative project mark important advances in feminist science studies. My criticisms concern her positive articulation of science, including feminist science. What makes Longino's approach to science
"feminist," she claims, is not an alignment with research or methodology

that is gendered "feminine," but an alignment with research or methodology that explicitly supports feminist political values and goals. It is the scheme/content duality in her characterization of feminist political values that has me concerned.

Longino outlines two sorts of values that, she claims, are part of even the best science: those values that are constitutive of scientific practice and those that affect the context in which science is practiced (1987, 54). The constitutive values govern "what constitutes acceptable scientific practice" (54). The contextual values are the background values, explanatory schemes, or political commitments that each scientist might bring to her laboratory.

Against more traditional philosophers of science, and paralleling, to some extent, the work of Thomas Kuhn (1972 [1960]), Longino argues that the second set of values—the contextual values—plays an active role not only in what some call the context of discovery, but also in "the inner workings of scientific inquiry" or the context of justification (1987, 54). These contextual values have a function similar to that of "paradigms" in Kuhn's writings.[7] She discusses the example of the highly theoretical values that guide the otherwise indirect observations in particle physics (Longino 1987, 54). Contextual values must play a role in scientific justification and theory choice, she argues, because we can't choose theories on the basis of the data alone. Given that theories are underdetermined, theory choice, even "objective" theory choice, is always based on something more than data (54).

Thus, Longino explains, there is "no formal basis for arguing that an inference [from data to theory that is] mediated by contextual values is thereby bad science" (1987, 55). It *could* be bad science, but the presence of contextual values is not the deciding factor. Indeed, she argues, the influence of contextual values in "the inner workings of science" can be part and parcel of good science as usual (56). From here she proceeds to describe feminist science and feminist science criticism—two sites of contextual values at work—as good science. She claims that feminist scientific practice will be good, objective science *insofar as* it "admits political considerations as relevant constraints on reasoning, which, through their influence on reasoning and interpretation, *shape content*" (61; emphasis mine).

As I have suggested earlier, I believe this formulation to be unnecessarily weak. As with Harding and Keller, Longino provides a sophisticated critique of correspondence theory and the objectivism end of the objectivism/relativism debate. However, without a more thoroughgoing critique of the representationalist model on which the debate is premised, her arguments against objectivism end up conceding too much to the skeptic's relativism. As becomes clearer in chapters 6 and 7, I suggest that we view political considerations as further elements of evidential reasoning, rather than as "constraints on reasoning." By making this shift, we can more adequately treat the vestiges of relativism that remain in Longino's account.

SYMPTOM: RELATIVISM; DIAGNOSIS: REPRESENTATIONALISM

There are a number of other representationalist elements in Longino's move toward the relativist corollary of the underdetermination thesis. For example, illustrating how the contextual values of our worldview play a role in science, Longino discusses the role of feminist and nonfeminist background assumptions in the "woman-the-gatherer" versus "man-the-hunter" interpretations in anthropology and in the selection of interactionist versus linear models used to "mediate data" within sex-hormone research (e.g., Longino 1990, chapters 6–7; 1987, 58).

In the latter case, the interactionist model of the influence of sex hormones highlights the two-way interaction between the presence of prenatal hormones and resulting physiological changes at the pre- and postnatal cellular and macrolevels. Linear models focus on a more deterministic, one-way relationship where the prenatal presence of hormones are assigned all, or most, of the causal power, with little or no causal attention given to the feedback from the rest of the system either pre- or postnatally. This linear model is very similar to the "master molecule" model that Keller described as masculine (Keller 1982).

Longino is also critical of the linear model, but not because she identifies it with any particular gender symbolism. Examining the competing hormonal theories, Longino and her research partner Ruth Doell found sexism and androcentric bias in many aspects of the linear theory research, though they did not find that sexism or androcentric bias affected the inferences from data to theory in any straightforward way (Doell and Longino 1988). Instead, they claim that the inferences were affected at a deeper level by prior commitments to patriarchal political ideals, which, in turn, affected commitments to the linear explanatory model. Inferences from data to theory within the level of the linear explanatory model were found to be sound. The linear explanatory model itself, they claim, is not biased by gender symbolism one way or the other.

Longino describes the patriarchal contextual values, and the linear explanatory model associated with them, as screens or filters in the process of scientific justification. She writes,

> In the conduct of research [explanatory models] serve as background assumptions against which data are ordered, in light of which data are given status as evidence for particular hypotheses and as a context within which studies gain significance. (1990, 135)

Objectionable, patriarchal politics favored commitments to the linear hormonal explanatory models, which in turn resulted in a one-way, deterministic view of prenatal hormones in control of adult human behavior.

Longino characterizes the linear model as a patriarchal, hierarchical view of human behavior that limits understanding of "human capacities for self-knowledge, self-reflection, [and] self-determination" (Longino 1987, 58). Longino prescribes the nonlinear, interactionist model instead, because self-knowledge, self-reflection, and self-determination are part of a feminist political vision or worldview (59).

I agree with Longino when she argues that being a woman or a feminist does not remove the political bias involved in the choice of an interactionist model over a linear one, nor does it, *pace* Harding, make the choice "less partial" or "maximally objective." I also agree when she argues that our reasons for choosing interactionist models should not be based on a perceived relation between interactionist approaches and "women's nature" (1987, 61). However, when she writes that an interactionist model should be chosen by feminists, "because of explicitly political considerations" (61), her representationalism weakens her case. Here, again, "political considerations" seem to be distinct from evidential considerations, just as the representationalist model distinguishes scheme from content.

Recall that Longino makes this argument because of her commitment to a relativist understanding of the underdetermination thesis. Leaving aside, for the moment, the problematic split between feminist politics and evidence, it has proved difficult to document the existence of two theories that are underdetermined, because supported *equally well* by all the available data (Bergström 1993, Brown 1995). This is not to argue against the relativist problem of underdetermination theory in principle, but to suggest that examples of competing hypotheses are hard to come by in the real world. Typically, one theory is supported by some aspects of the data, while a competing theory is supported by other aspects. At this point, the choice between the theories can proceed on an empirical discussion of which aspect of the data is the most relevant. As I argued in chapter 1, feminists are particularly good at criticizing previously held beliefs about relevance.

But in the case of the interactionist versus linear models of sex hormones, there does indeed seem to be empirical data (however conceived) that the interactionist model *is* better than the linear model.[8] The models are not equally well supported by the same body of data. Even Longino writes that the interactionist model "allows not only for the interaction of physiological and environmental factors but also for the interaction of these with a continuously self-modifying, self-representational (and self-organizing) central processing system"—something that the linear model *cannot* do (1987, 58). But, says Longino, this is not enough. "Obviously model-choice is also constrained by (what we know of) reality, that is, by the data. But reality (what we know of it) is, I have already argued, inadequate to uniquely determine model choice" (61).

My sense is that Longino's use of the hedge "what we know of reality" is the same sort of skepticism we find in the arguments of Harding and the later

Keller. It is the skepticism that results from conceiving of a metaphysical gap between the raw data of the world, out there waiting, and our organizing schemes primed to filter the waiting data. The organizing filters of feminism or androcentrism block unmediated knowledge of reality, serving as pre-conceived explanatory frameworks that organize the raw data of sex hormones, for example. In Longino's words, again, explanatory models "serve as background assumptions against which data are ordered, in light of which data are given status as evidence" (1990, 135).

Longino's description of feminist scientific practice as one that "admits political considerations as relevant constraints on reasoning, which, through their influence on reasoning and interpretation, shape content" (1987, 61) parallels the writings of Keller and Harding, who split the "political" (what Keller calls "culture," and Harding calls "social standpoint") from the "data." The political serves as a conceptual scheme that filters the data as evidence, so we can never be guaranteed against massive error in our scientific theories. If this is the case, then, Longino is right: When choosing between representations that are underdetermined by the data, the best we can do is choose between those that have been screened according to our feminist political inclinations.

But wait. We shouldn't give up on the potentially decisive role of empirical data so soon. Just because correspondence doesn't bridge the metaphysical gap doesn't mean we have to be resigned to this level of relativism. We need instead to more fully deconstruct the traditional epistemological project by dismantling the representational metaphor of the gap. So say Richard Rorty and Donald Davidson, or so, at least, I have been hinting. It is time, now, to make good on the promise to illustrate a nonrepresentationalist model that would free feminist science studies from the epistemological ties that bind.

NOTES

1. More recent work from Harding includes *Is Science Multicultural? Postcolonialisms, Feminisms, and Epistemologies* (1998). For a comparison of Harding's more recent arguments with her earlier epistemological prescriptions, see my review "Thinking Globally, Progressing Locally: Harding and Goonatilake on Scientific Progress across Cultures" (Clough 2001).

2. Paralleling my concerns with Ruth Bleier's work, I wonder whether Harding's more detailed description of science as bourgeois, homophobic, sexist, white, and Western is an improvement, given that science is and historically has been practiced in a number of non-Western countries, by nonwhite peoples. Perhaps the science practiced in these countries is not the sort of science Harding is criticizing, but then we have little evidence that these countries are free from bourgeois, homophobic, and sexist science. We need to be more cautious in our explanations of wherein the

difference between "Western" and "non-Western" science lies; careful in particular about romanticizing Eastern cultures. Harding herself has begun to address this particular concern (*Is Science Multicultural?* Harding, 1998). See also Edward Said's classic discussion of the Western romanticization of the (Middle) East, *Orientalism* (1978).

3. Longino's more recent book-length writings include *The Fate of Knowledge* (2002). Here, she departs from her earlier concerns with feminism and science, to address more generally the splitting of the rational and social that continue to inform science studies.

4. For a parallel analysis, see Ilkka Niiniluoto's essay "The Relativism Question in Feminist Epistemology" (1997).

5. Quine's own views on this corollary are hard to pin down; see Lars Bergström (1993) for a review of this point.

6. Similar points about objectivity and values have been made by Ernest Nagel (e.g., *The Structure of Science,* 1961, 489). Regarding the role of the scientific community, similar points can be found in Karl Popper's theory of "inter-subjective agreement" (Popper 1959).

7. Longino's differences with Kuhn are discussed in chapter 2 of her book *Science as Social Knowledge* (1990).

8. Lynn Hankinson Nelson makes the same observation about Longino on this point (Nelson, *Who Knows? From Quine to a Feminist Empiricism,* 1990, 238–39; see also Nelson 1993). See chapter 2 for a discussion of my differences with Nelson's analysis.

6

A Pragmatist, Davidsonian Perspective

As I argue in chapter 2, "representationalism" names the most comprehensive diagnosis of the skepticism plaguing epistemology. In the representationalist model, beliefs are conceived as representations of their objects. In the most elementary cases these beliefs are said to be the subjective end-product of a sensory process whereby the objective content from our world is sensed and then screened through our interpretive schemes (the filters of our worldview or language). This argument was most apparent in the selections from Willard Van Orman Quine and also from Ruth Bleier. Theories are viewed as the combination or systematization of beliefs. Sometimes the resulting theory is said to feed back into the filtering system, so that our allegiance to the theory affects our ability to perceive new data. Selections from Ruth Hubbard and Bleier supported this view, as did the underdetermination thesis as used by Evelyn Fox Keller, Sandra Harding, and Helen Longino.

The representational conception of beliefs as filtered representations of the world explains the skepticism that fuels epistemology. If there is a metaphysical distinction between inner, subjective beliefs and the outer objective world, then some sort of epistemic bridge is needed to link the two. However, if beliefs do not arise from direct access to the world, if a bridge is needed to link them, then we have injected the possibility of global error. All our representations could be inaccurate because our bridge might be blocked by the filters of our perceptual apparatus, language, cultural worldview, and/or theory allegiance.

Objectivists on the epistemological continuum argue that (ideally) we can provide objective reasons for thinking our representations are accurate, by checking for the presence of normative relational properties—for example, by checking whether the bridge between our representations and the world represented allows a clear relation of correspondence or whether it is blocked by conceptual filters. There is some disagreement between more straightforward objectivists and empiricists about how we check for relational properties in theories containing nonobservational language, but most agree that it can be done for theories containing observational language, at least. Some of Bas van Fraassen's work supports this view, as does the work of the early Quine and of some feminists who make use of Quine's theory. With respect to theories containing observational language, they all agree that the method for detecting the relation can be objective—it is an empirical checking method available to all (qualified) participants—and that the method detects the presence of objectivity, or some normative functional equivalent, in our theories.

However, as Richard Rorty argues, when we articulate general methodological norms for "objectivity-indicativeness," the philosophical skeptic is invited to ask, "But how do you *know* that your epistemic criteria *really* signal objectivity (or truth, or evidential justification)?" (Rorty 1995). Both the objectivist and the empiricist must continually chase after recalcitrant methodological features; always one step behind the skeptic.

Tellingly, there has been little progress within the various objectivist or empiricist programs with respect to addressing skepticism. Certainly, all the feminists whose work I surveyed came to argue against objectivism as a live epistemological option. And while some feminists have been supportive of empiricism, the problems with skepticism remain.

One way to describe the futility of the epistemological debate is to note that skepticism is invited from any position on the continuum, from objectivism to relativism. If one takes an optimistically objectivist position, one invites the skeptic to second-guess one's normative criteria. However, as I argued in the case of Keller, Harding, and Longino, if one is critical of objectivism, but insufficiently critical of the representationalism under which it is subsumed, then skepticism reappears, this time in its relativist guise.

Relativism becomes an epistemological option as soon as doubts about objectivism are expressed in terms of doubts about the clarity of relational bridges and doubts about the objectivity involved in detecting the presence of such bridges. Here we encounter the view that our subjective conceptual schemes filter the detection process just as they filter the belief-acquisition process. However, because this relativist view entails that something like a correspondence relation is *needed* to bridge the representationalist gap, the relativists' doubts about the ability to detect such bridgework apply equally to the relativists' own epistemological claims. This is, indeed, the reflexive skeptical worry introduced in the works of Keller, Harding, Longino, and earlier in Bleier.

I have suggested, however, that there are more persuasive arguments against objectivism (*and* relativism)—arguments that show that the representationalism on which the entire epistemological continuum is based is optional.[1] In particular, Donald Davidson argues for an alternative to representationalism that is not premised on the coherence of skepticism. If we are convinced that, on Davidson's model, global skepticism is a nonstarter, then we no longer have any motivation for continuing the epistemological debate about how best to address skepticism. I hope that the previous four chapters have provided some support for my claim that removing our motivation for the epistemological debate would be a liberating project, especially for feminist science studies. An explanation of Davidson's role in this liberatory project, follows.

"A REASON FOR A BELIEF THAT ISN'T EVIDENCE FOR THAT BELIEF"

As discussed in chapter 2, Davidson makes a number of points against the representationalist model that informs epistemology. Paralleling the work of Longino, in particular, he argues against the claim that the objective detection of sensory data can be used to justify or stand as evidence for beliefs that represent those data. Davidson notes that for the justification process to work, we have to be aware of the detection of sense data, and this awareness is simply another belief. His argument undercuts the objectivist attempt to construe awareness of sensory data as an evidential entity that stands independent from our beliefs.

It might seem, however, that in revealing the incoherence of harnessing sensations as independent evidence, Davidson has removed any justificatory scheme for our empirical beliefs. This seems to leave us with the skepticism Davidson's nonrepresentationalist model is supposed to avoid. If explanations appealing to the sensory origins of our beliefs don't justify those beliefs, how do we know that we are not globally mistaken about the world? In this section I make use of Davidson's "radical interpreter"—a heuristic device that provides a "*reason* for supposing most of our beliefs are true that is not a form of *evidence*" (Davidson 1991a [1983], 127).

It is important to make clear that the term "most" in the previous quotation is not meant as a quantificational claim guaranteeing, for example, that a certain number of our beliefs must be true. Rather, Davidson uses the concept of the radical intepreter to support a philosophical claim—the detection of false beliefs *requires* that we have a background of true beliefs against which the error of the false beliefs can be measured. This latter claim undercuts the global skeptic who wants to make error a general concern, that is, who wants to deny or question the existence of norms against which errors can be measured.

The radical interpreter—an adult interpreter faced with a completely foreign language—is an idealized concept Davidson borrows from his mentor, Quine. Quine introduced the character in his explanation of how we would have to proceed to learn a completely foreign language when no "translation manual" is available (e.g., Quine, "*Ontological Relativity,*" 1969). I argue that if we analyze meaning from the perspective of the radical interpreter, a whole host of traditional epistemological problems can be set aside.[2]

Davidson equips the radical interpreter with the abilities of a competent adult speaker of a language. Parachuted into the midst of a foreign land, she has general expectations about how to proceed. She has a sense of basic logical structure (i.e., she understands the implications of those elements of a language ["and," "if . . . , then," etc.] that gives the sentences that contain them their particular logical form). She also has the ability to discern when the speakers of the foreign language are making assertions, that is, expressing, in the form of sentences, beliefs held true, even though, in the beginning, she has no idea what those sentences mean.

Davidson notes that in order to make any progress in her new world, the radical interpreter must watch for correlations between types of sounds uttered by the native speakers and the kinds of events in their shared world that caused the utterances. In the beginning this is all she has to go on. She does not have any preconceived notion of the particular semantic role that is played by any particular noises uttered by the native speakers. Rather, at this early stage, it is the radical interpreter's successful (accurate) identification of the environmental reference that prompted the native speakers' noises, that provides those noises with semantic content in the first place.

Imagine the rural radical interpreter encountering her object language in an urban setting, focused on the vagaries of public transportation. The interpreter's understanding of the meaning of the native speaker's utterance "There's the bus!" is provided by the shared causal relationship between the arrival of a bus in the visual (or aural) fields of the interpreter and the native speaker, and the native speaker's utterance.[3] The foreign noises that express basic or simple beliefs, in sentences such as "There's the bus!" are the starting points for the radical interpreter.

These basic beliefs are expressed in what Quine called "occasion sentences" (Quine 1960). Occasion sentences are those sentences the truth values of which change depending on precise, salient variables such as the time and place the sentences are uttered and who utters them. The truth of the sentence "There's the bus!" for example, will depend on the presence of a bus at the time the sentence is uttered. For these "basic" beliefs expressed in occasion sentences, it is possible for the radical intepreter to make an educated guess about the truth conditions of the native utterance, because she has such immediate access to the truth values of her guesses.

Quine contrasts these occasion sentences with "standing sentences," such as "The bus to the university usually stops here." These latter sentences will be true depending on much more general variables, such as the presence of the appropriate bus at any number of times prior to the sentence being uttered. What makes occasion sentences, as opposed to standing sentences, the basic entry points for the radical interpreter is not the epistemic simplicity of the terms involved in the sentences, but the relative ease with which a non-native speaker can guess the truth conditions of the native occasion sentences.

Quine goes on to distinguish a subclass of occasion sentences, the observation sentences, in order to make a number of empiricist claims (as discussed in chapter 2). Like some of the more traditional foundationalists such as Carl Hempel (1965), Quine tries, at times, to use the empirical simplicity of occasion sentences as an epistemological grounding for claims about more complex sentences. As I argue further in the next section, Davidson's discussion of occasion sentences has no such epistemological implications.

The causal triangular relationship between the interpreter, the native speakers' utterances of occasion sentences, and the objects and events in their world requires that the interpreter assume the natives are speaking about their beliefs truthfully. While the adult language user has the ability to recognize when a native speaker is making an assertion, this recognition does not guarantee that the native speaker's assertion is true. But, says Davidson, at the beginning, the radical intepreter must *assume* that the native speaker's assertions are true. For interpretation to occur, she must assume that the same relation between belief and truth holds for those she interprets, as for herself—what Davidson and Quine have called "the principle of charity." In other words, starting with the most simple utterances such as "There's the bus!" the radical interpreter must assume that she and the native speakers agree about what would make those utterances true (e.g., the presence of a bus).

Why is this agreement necessary at the beginning when the interpreter is collecting sentences in the native language and correlating them with the sorts of environmental conditions that prompted the sentences? It is necessary, says Davidson, because in order to identify her teachers as having *any* beliefs, she must assume the beliefs they hold are true. Once she has established an empirical base of correlations between their sentences and hers, *then* she can start to make judgments of inconsistency and falsehood. Before that point, identifying her teachers' beliefs as false would deplete the empirical base from which she needs to begin her interpretative project in the first place. As one Davidson commentator explains, assigning "too much falsity among beliefs undermines the possibility of identifying beliefs at all" (Malpas 1992, 159). Identifying falsehoods and misconceptions is "parasitic" on an established coordinate of shared meaning.[4] We are getting closer, then, to explaining Davidson's "anti-" skeptical claim about the necessity of having true beliefs for the identification of false beliefs.

It might still be unclear, however, why the existence of a "shared coordinate of meaning" between the native speaker and the radical intepreter guarantees, in Davidson's words, that "it cannot happen that most of our plainest beliefs about what exists in the world are false" (1991b, 195). Just because there must be *agreement* between the radical interpreter and the native speakers about the truth of basic beliefs does not guarantee that those beliefs are, *in fact,* true. Davidson responds by examining the concept of truth it-self. Where, he asks, do we come up with the concept of objective truth? The answer is in shared language. "Unless a language is shared there is no way to distinguish between using the language correctly and using it incorrectly; only communication with another can supply an objective check" (Davidson 1991c, 157). And communication with another can only start by assuming agreement on what makes utterances true—the principle of charity.

Davidson's apologists note that the principle of charity is unfortunately named, because it does not operate as advice that we could choose to follow or not (e.g., Ramberg 1989; Malpas 1992). Ramberg emphasizes this point:

> The principle of charity . . . offers no advice to us as interpreters, it yields no in-terpretational strategy. It is not a heuristic device, nor is it, accordingly, some-thing we could get by without; it is a *condition of the possibility* of interpreta-tion. (Ramberg 1989, 74)

Ramberg notes, too, that "just as we have no choice, if we want to make sense of what others say, but to regard them as on the whole speaking the truth, so we have no choice but to regard *ourselves* as largely speakers of truth" (Ramberg 1988, 643). But, again, applying the principle of charity to our own utterances is not to be seen as a cognitive compliment (however de-served). Ramberg continues, "It has, rather, a somewhat deflationary effect on our self-esteem insofar as it implies that we cannot lie even if we try. Can-not lie very much, that is, just as we cannot be dramatically and romantically mistaken about how things are" (643).

Again, this last comment should not be taken as a claim about the truth of any *number* of beliefs. If, within a system of beliefs or theories, we interpret "dramatically mistaken about our beliefs" as "mistaken about a pretty large number of beliefs," it is quite clear that Aristotelian physics, for example, did get the world *dramatically* wrong. But note that the skeptic's claim that we could be globally mistaken is not proved by showing that Aristotle's particu-lar theories turned out to be false. Stated positively, all we need to diffuse the coherence of the skeptic's claims is to express the force of "cannot be dra-matically mistaken" in pragmatic, behavioral terms. That Aristotle was in pos-session of true beliefs is illustrated by the fact that he had some objective un-derstanding of the norms against which he measured error; for example, he was able to move about in his world with roughly the same success that we move about in ours. There is a background of true beliefs that we continue to *share* with Aristotle. This shared background of beliefs includes all those be-liefs that enable us to say that Aristotle's views are *about,* or explanatory *of,* features of our shared world—features such as the motion of falling bodies—and that with regard to those features, his views are false.[5]

If the principle of charity is a precursor for successful interpretation, this means that truth must be held primitive for words and sentences to be meaningful. This takes us back to the example of the radical interpreter correlating environmental circumstances with basic native utterances—for example, "There's the bus!" The radical interpreter has no initial preconceptions about how to link a native utterance with specific semantic content. Rather, her attention to the correct (true) reference of the native sentence is what provides her with clues to the meaning of the utterance in the first place. The meaning of an utterance is given by its truth conditions and not the reverse.[6]

TELLING THE SKEPTIC TO GO AWAY

Davidson uses these points about the radical intepreter to support his extensionalist claim that in the simplest cases of beliefs—that is, those expressed in occasion sentences—the events and objects that cause those beliefs (the *extension* of the beliefs) also determine their contents, or meaning (the *intension* of the beliefs) (Davidson 1989a, 164; 1989b; 1991a [1983]; 1991b, 195). This means that in the simplest cases, there cannot be wholesale slippage between our understanding of the meaning of a sentence and our understanding of the conditions that would make that sentence true. Davidson describes this approach to meaning further in the following passage:

> As long as we adhere to the basic intuition that in the simplest cases words and thoughts refer to what causes them, it is clear that it cannot happen that most of our plainest beliefs about what exists in the world are false. The reason is that we do not first form concepts and then discover what they apply to; rather, in the basic cases, the application determines the content of the concept. (1991b, 195)

Davidson's extensionalist approach to meaning excludes the possibility that the speech of the radical intepreter could be, in principle, indistinguishable from her teachers *and* idiosyncratic with respect to meaning. In the simplest cases of beliefs expressed in occasion sentences, the meaning of her utterances is determined by their being used correctly in the presence of another speaker and the event in the world that caused the utterance. Taking a holistic approach to build from the simpler cases of beliefs to beliefs expressed in more complex theories, any idiosyncrasies in the radical interpreter's meaning are, in principle, available for her correction through a purely extensional examination of how she has applied her references. Somewhere along the line, any discrepancies can, in principle, be revealed. There is no "subjective" "inside" to her beliefs that is metaphysically separate and inaccessible from the viewpoint of the native speakers in the "objective" "outer" world.

Imagine, for example, that the radical interpreter observes the urban women speakers of her object language negotiating their place in line for a bus and comes to interpret "She's assertive" in the native language as "She's aggressive" in her own language. On Davidson's account the difference in meaning between the two sentences could, in principle, be revealed to her. The two words "aggressive" and "assertive" are linked in a weblike fashion to different, simpler concepts, which, in turn, have different causes. The two utterances are correctly applied on different occasions—this is what gives them different meanings.

Using the model of the radical intepreter, Davidson's causal analysis of belief provides us less-than-radical interpreters with a presumption in favor of the truth of any particular belief. However, a presumption is not a guarantee. He cheerfully admits that the truth of each belief is up for grabs, though not all or even most of these beliefs can be up for grabs at once. It is the veridicality of beliefs generally, as understood through his causal account, that makes "meaningful disagreement" over particular beliefs possible (Davidson 1984 [1974], 196–97). Our beliefs have no content unless we have established a common convergence between ourselves, another speaker, and a shared environmental stimulus. Occasion sentences provide the entry points for this convergence. Once we have established a pattern of successful convergence, a pattern of semantic "firmness," then we can say of any particular belief that it is false. You have to be right about a large background of beliefs before you can critically examine the validity of particular ones. Similarly, successful communication with others indicates that you know many things about your world (Davidson 1989a; 1990a, section III).

We now have a way to explain how, on Davidson's view, skepticism does not arise as a coherent option that needs addressing. Davidson does not show that global skepticism is wrong; he simply argues that on the model of the radical intepreter, a metaphysical gap between language users and the world is unthinkable. On the representationalist view, beliefs are conceived as an "inner" non-natural, subjective representation of the outer, natural realm. In contrast, Davidson asks us to try viewing belief as the production of a triangular causal relationship between three naturalized entities, namely, ourselves, other speakers, and our shared environment. From the perspective of the radical intepreter, our ability to use language comes from *direct, unmediated, causal contact* with the world, which, in turn, guarantees that we have an established background of true beliefs against which our false beliefs can be measured. As Davidson writes, "Communication begins where causes converge" (1991a [1983], 132). If we want to doubt in a wholesale, global fashion the causal etiology of our beliefs, we must also "give up language" (Ramberg 1989, 97).

While Davidson's views have enjoyed a certain amount of sympathy within mainstream philosophy of language, they have also been met with criticism. I cannot do justice to the details of the critical reception of his work, referring readers instead to Ernest LePore's edited collection devoted to the subject (LePore 1986). However, in the next section I set out to defend Davidson's project from certain criticisms that arise when he is construed as presenting an alternative epistemology—a defense that is potentially damaging to my claim that Davidson provides a good *non*epistemological option for feminist science studies.

EVALUATING DAVIDSON'S ESCAPE FROM EPISTEMOLOGY

On balance, Davidson's causal account of meaning supports neither objectivist nor relativist understandings of truth. Davidson's theory is not of truth but of meaning. This latter claim is a pragmatist interpretive point supported by Rorty (1991a [1986]; 1991b [1988]) and Ramberg (1989, 1993b). Though again, Rorty and Ramberg both point out that Davidson's holistic focus on interpretive practice or pragmatics should not be construed as a pragmatic *theory* of truth. Davidson supports this nonepistemic reading of his work in his "Afterthoughts" to "A Coherence Theory of Truth and Knowledge" (Davidson 1991a), but, aside from the importance of author's intention, there are a number of arguments that favor this particular reading. I begin by arguing against the view that Davidson's work supports objectivism, often referred to in the Davidsonian literature as "realism."[7]

First, while Davidson's causal theory of meaning provides us with an explanation how it is that we have a background of true beliefs against which false beliefs are assessed, it does not attempt to function as an epistemological method independent from the local empirical process of justifying *particular* beliefs. Rather, he claims, the background of true beliefs is necessary before "meaningful disagreement" over particular beliefs is *possible* (Davidson 1984 [1974], 196–97). Jeffrey Malpas reinforces this point:

> Davidson claims that, as beliefs are in their nature veridical, all beliefs are justified in this sense. This leaves open, as an empirical question, the issue of whether any particular belief, or set of beliefs [is] justified in some particular context. But what is closed off is the question as to whether all our beliefs might be unjustified and unjustifiable. . . . Local error is admissible, so long as global truth is preserved. (Malpas 1992, 218)

Unlike the objectivist, Davidson argues that the causal connections between our beliefs and the world cannot be used as independent justifications of our beliefs. Empirical evidence in favor of a particular claim cannot be used as a belief-independent justification for that claim. We have to perceive any causal sensations that make up the empirical evidence in support of our claim, and this perception is itself another belief. Justifying any particular belief can be made only by appeal to other beliefs. It is between beliefs, conceived in holistic, weblike fashion, that the important justification process proceeds, not between beliefs and some nonbeliefs we call "the evidence."

To be sure, we can, and do, use some of our beliefs to provide evidential support for other beliefs, but we can't construe this evidence as an epistemological "nonbelief" entity. Davidson refers to the evidential support provided for one belief by other beliefs as a "reason" for that one belief (as when he promotes his causal account as a "*reason* for supposing most of our beliefs are true that is not a form of *evidence*"). Davidson's position on the causal relationship between our words and the world is epistemologically benign, then. It does not support any positive claims about objectivism or realism. Rather, it functions largely as a negative claim against the relativist's skepticism (Davidson 1990a, section II). As Ramberg explains,

> If we think we understand what people say, we must also regard most of our observations about the world we live in as correct. Davidson does not provide metaphysical [or epistemological] assurance of our connection with reality, he simply makes the point that if we try to give up the world, we must also give up language. (Ramberg 1989, 47)

Davidson also argues against the empiricist elements in the theories of van Fraassen and the early Quine. Recall that empiricists highlight the causal role of empirical sensations with respect to "observables" only (or sentences containing only observable terms). Nonobservable terms (or sentences containing them), they claim, do not have this same causal relationship with empirical sensations. For Davidson, however, there is no sense in which empirical data play a causal role in the acquisition of *some* beliefs (say, those beliefs expressed in observation sentences) but not other beliefs (those expressed in nonobservation sentences). He makes the holistic point that empirical data plays a causal role in establishing the content of *all* beliefs. Again, however, his view of the role of empirical, causal relations is to be distinguished from the representationalist understanding that causal connections to the empirical world are normative properties contained by those beliefs we call true or maximally objective. On Davidson's nonrepresentationalist view of belief, causal connections play no epistemological or justificatory role.

Davidson emphasizes that there is an important distinction to be maintained between (a) acknowledging that empirical data provide the *only* basis for knowing (a point that he shares with Quine) and (b) giving an empirical theory of which particular data are going to be the *right* basis for knowing (Davidson 1991b). Davidson's brand of externalism involves sticking with the acknowledgment that external, empirical data provide the only basis for knowing. At the same time he denies the coherence of the claim that one can use empiricism as an epistemological theory for deciding which particular data are normatively foundational. That is, he denies the coherence of the theory that certain beliefs will be true or maximally objective, insofar as they are justified by their relation to empirical evidence. As I note in chapter 2, this distinction is sometimes blurred in Quine's empiricism, even in his more naturalist moments, and it is purposefully blurred in more straightforwardly objectivist accounts.

According to Davidson, "empiricism is the view that the subjective [i.e., individual sense experience] is the foundation of objective empirical knowledge. I am suggesting that empirical knowledge has no epistemological foundation and needs none" (1989a, 166). Davidson shares John Dewey's pragmatic annoyance with philosophical theories that view truth as "correspondence between thought and reality inaccessible to experimental research and ordinary practice" (Davidson 1990a, 279).

Another more general difference to note between Davidson's account of meaning and epistemological accounts of truth, such as correspondence, is that, according to Davidson, our successful language use indicates that we must have some working knowledge of how to apply the predicate "true" *before* we can interpret new utterances. His causal theory of meaning cannot be used to explain how we should *apply* the truth predicate, as correspondence theories claim to do. Malpas explains this point here:

> Most of our beliefs must always be true prior to any attempt to compare beliefs or reality with "the facts." The attempt to make such comparison presupposes the identification of the beliefs to be compared, and that already presupposes a background of mostly true belief—a broader horizontal setting—against which the identification can be made. So it is not correspondence with the world or the facts that, in general, makes our beliefs true. It is rather the truth of those beliefs in general that makes correspondence itself possible. (Malpas 1992, 242)

In other words, we cannot, at the beginning steps of our translation project, understand an utterance and then test whether it truthfully refers to its object. Truth must have been imported much earlier in the process. This is a point against those who, like Jerry Fodor (1987), support causal theories of how our words come to refer to their objects and suggest that we isolate meaning and *then* test for truth. In the following passage Ramberg describes further the question-begging nature of these causal theories:

> While we might be able to formulate a causal theory of reference without using the concept of truth (or some similar predicate), *testing* such a theory presupposes knowledge of the truth-value of sentences, knowledge which we have come by independently of the theory to be tested. . . . If this is true, a causal theory of reference cannot give rise to the sorts of empirical predictions that we want a semantic theory to generate; they are always ad hoc explanations of meaning already known. (Ramberg 1989, 27–28; emphasis mine)

Rorty explains further that although the radical interpreter will eventually end up with a number of correspondence or "satisfaction" relations between the native speakers' words and events in the world, "these links will not be

the basis for the translation. Rather they will be fallout from the translation"
(Rorty 1991a [1986], 137).

The opposite sort of misunderstanding of Davidson's theory is the argument that his theory supports relativism, rather than objectivism. According to this view, Davidson's criterion of truth for our beliefs is
whether they cohere with our other beliefs, which, the critics point out,
leaves the external world disturbingly unaccounted for.[8] While the title of
Davidson's essay, "A Coherence Theory of Truth and Knowledge" (1991a
[1983]), lends prima facie support to this interpretation, the essay contains
passages such as the following: "It should be clear that I do not hope to
define truth *in terms of* coherence and belief" (Davidson 1991a, 122; emphasis mine). Critics who label Davidson a coherence theorist typically fail
to appreciate his claims about the direct causal connections between our
simplest empirical beliefs and the world those beliefs are about. Those of
Rorty's critics who claim he is a relativist similarly fail to see his allegiance
to Davidson on this point.[9]

For Rorty, relativism involves the three-part representationalist claim that
(a) those representations we call true or objective are not fully constrained
by the empirical world; that the empirical world leaves our representations
underdetermined, perhaps; (b) the criteria then available for judging truth
or objectivity must come from within us (our cultural filters, historical biases, values, etc.); and finally (c) relative to the equivocal nature of the empirical world, any one representation is as good as any other. Again, while
Rorty and Davidson are critical of representationalism and epistemic notions of normative properties making our beliefs true or objective, they explicitly argue that our true beliefs are *indeed* constrained by the world (and
so, a fortiori, any one belief is *not* as good as any other). In an earlier version of "The Structure and Content of Truth" Davidson responds to these
relativist concerns:

> What we hold true, what we believe, determines what we mean, and thus, in-
> directly, when our sentences are true. Believing doesn't make it so, but it cre-
> ates a presumption that it is so. This is not because belief creates a world, as co-
> herence theories and various forms of idealism maintain . . . it is because the
> contents of beliefs are in centrally important ways determined by the causes of
> those beliefs. (Davidson 1988, 7)

Believing that we do not "create" our world does not, for Davidson, entail
a metaphysical independence between our thoughts about the world,
screened through conceptual schemes, and the world "as it is" in its "natural" "unrepresented" form. This representationalist view involves a conceptual separation between belief, meaning, and truth that is anathema to
Davidson's extensionalist approach to meaning and leads to skepticism.[10]

On Davidson's nonrepresentationalist view, our explanatory models, values, political commitments, or worldviews are best conceived, not as conceptual schemes through which the evidence from the external world is filtered; not as underdetermined representations of the evidence; but as further strands in our web of belief. The veridical nature of belief tells against the skeptical view that the world could remain "ultimately unrepresentable" by us (assuming that by "unrepresentable" we mean "unknowable") or that "for all we know" the world could turn out to be completely different from how we, in fact, conceive it to be.

In one pragmatic swoop, Davidson shows how epistemological theories such as objectivism are unnecessary (and, so far, failed) responses to skepticism, while allowing room for meaningful disagreement on the truth or falsity of particular beliefs. His model of language use has no need for objectivist epistemology; and, similarly, he avoids taking the "for all we know . . . so anything goes" position of relativism.

NOTES

1. Karen Barad makes similar suggestions based on the philosophy of Neils Bohr (Barad 1997). From my own preliminary assessment of Bohr's work on this point, I believe Davidson's diagnosis to be more thorough.

2. Joseph Rouse presents an account of Davidson's antirepresentationalism that parallels my own. Chapter 8 of his book *Engaging Science* (Rouse 1984) is particularly helpful in this respect.

3. Charlene Haddock Seigfried reminds me that an even more thoroughgoing pragmatist interpretation would involve pairing the sentence "There's the bus!" with a whole host of public transit practices—riding the bus, smelling the bus fumes, and so forth. I think Davidson would appreciate the addition of these other practical, experiential details.

4. My thanks to Bjørn Ramberg for this characterization.

5. My thanks to Norman Swartz for pressing me about the importance of error. The fact that we can detect error is the primary weapon in the arsenal of those who argue against the coherence of skepticism.

6. Some logical positivists used this verificationist claim to support a reductive epistemological agenda. See C. J. Misak (1995, 144–51) and Ramberg (unpublished manuscript) to distinguish Davidson's (and Quine's) interpretive points about extension and truth from the verificationism associated with the logical positivists.

7. For a realist interpretation of Davidson, see Simon Evnine's book *Donald Davidson* (Evnine 1991, especially chapter 9). Ramberg's critical response to Evnine on this point provides a helpful explication of the pragmatist reading of Davidson (Ramberg 1993b).

8. See, for example, the criticisms by Michael Williams (1991), 230–32, and much of chapter 7; and by Vrinda Dalmiya (1990). Linda Alcoff, too, interprets Davidson as a coherence theorist (Alcoff 1996).

9. See, for example, the criticisms of Bruce Aune (1972), Milton Fisk (1976), Tibor Machan (1993), Harry Veatch (1985, especially page 318), Thomas McCarthy (1990a), and the exchange that follows (Rorty 1990; McCarthy 1990b), Susan Haack (1993, chapter 9, especially page 187), and Rorty's response (1995).

10. See Davidson (1984 [1974]) for further criticisms of conceptual schemes. For a very clear discussion of Davidson's arguments on this point, see Michael Hymers's *Philosophy and Its Epistemic Neuroses* (Hymers 2000, especially chapter 5).

7

Feminist Science Studies from a Pragmatist Perspective

It is my hope that by removing the skeptic's motivation for epistemology, the energy of feminists engaged in science studies will be freed up to return to the other important empirical projects that remain in our critiques of science. The empirical task of analyzing the connections between our scientific beliefs, and the causal connections between beliefs and the world, is a political and sociocultural project to which feminist contribution is crucial. As Sandra Harding counsels, we need to identify all the causes for our various beliefs, in all their, often ignoble, specificity (Harding 1991, 147). We will run into the difficulties I have documented only if we attempt an epistemological meta-analysis of which of our causal accounts are true, or least partial, or maximally objective.

As Donald Davidson has shown, we must also be careful that our causal analysis does not metaphysically bifurcate political reasons for scientific beliefs from empirical causes of these beliefs. This advice is particularly relevant for addressing the relativist aspects of underdetermination encountered by Helen Longino, Harding, and Evelyn Fox Keller. Recall that each argued that when (or because) empirical support is equivocal, we have to choose between theories on the basis of our political values. However, this construal presumes the representationalist view that the empirical data and our feminist political values emanate from two metaphysically separate spheres—the first from the objective, external world; the second from the subjective, internal mind (or minds). The empirical data is construed as (ideally) providing independent, objective support for a theory, while political values are viewed as dependent and subjective filters through which the data pass.

DAVIDSON ON UNDERDETERMINATION THEORY

In response to this representationalist claim about the independence of empirical data, Davidson reminds us that when we marshal empirical data in support of a belief or theory, we need first to be *aware* of the data, and that awareness is itself another belief. In the project of marshaling epistemic justification for our individual beliefs, there is no independent, "nonbelief" entity to which we can appeal. Any evidential datum supporting a belief must itself be a belief. It is also important to see that both our political values and our more straightforwardly empirical commitments can function as beliefs of this evidential sort. On Davidson's model even our feminist political beliefs must have some weblike relation to beliefs about empirical data, if they are to have any content.

There are a number of ways in which feminist political values can interact with and support the more straightforwardly empirical commitments that, together, make up our growing web of beliefs about the oppressive aspects of science. Recall Longino's discussion of the role of political values in choosing between competing archaeological interpretations of chipped stones (see chapter 5). One theory, highlighting the role of the male hunter, interprets the stones as hunting tools. The other, competing, theory highlights or includes the role of the female gatherer and interprets the stones as implements for gathering and preparing edible vegetation. According to Longino, the available empirical data support both theories equally well, so the choice between the male-focused model or the more inclusive, female-focused model must be relative to an underlying political commitment—namely, to androcentrism or feminism, respectively (e.g., Longino 1990, 109). I argue, instead, that feminist political values are *themselves* beliefs with empirical content that can in turn provide *good evidential support* for preferring the "woman-the-gatherer" interpretation over the "man-the-hunter" interpretation.

Feminist analysis of past scientific practices has revealed what is by now a well-documented pattern—namely, that theories of human bodies and/or behavior that ignore *women's* bodies and/or behavior have proved to be inaccurate. The all-male studies of the effects of stress on "humans," referred to in chapter 1, are illustrative here (Muller 1992). The feminist archaeologist who holds to her "woman-the-gatherer" theory, in spite of the equivocal evidence provided by the chipped stones, still has good inductive evidence, based on her feminist political views, to support her decision. The "man-the-hunter" theory leaves out the role of women in the human development of technology and culture. The feminist archaeologist who chooses to interpret the chipped stones on the basis of a theory that includes or even highlights the role of female agrarian behavior is making her choice based on past empirical evidence that to ignore the role of women is to get the "human" story drastically wrong. Her decision does not have to be construed as relative to the nonempirical world of feminist politics, brought in when all the objective, empirical data are equivocal. Rather, it is a decision well supported by inductively observed instances of past scientific errors.[1]

On my view, then, the "man-the-hunter" and the "woman-the-gatherer" interpretations are not equally well supported by the empirical data. The latter is *better* supported than the former by feminist analyses of past scientific practice. It is not the case that, faced with interpretations equally well supported by beliefs about evidence, we are forced to the inner nonevidential world of politics to make our choice—both realms form part of our web of belief.

Following the web metaphor, our empirical beliefs have no better metaphysical links than do our political beliefs to the outer, independent objective world, just as our political beliefs are no more closely related than our more straightforwardly empirical beliefs to our inner subjective world. But this is because there is no inner or outer world; there is no metaphysical bifurcation. There is only one world, an objective view of which can be made meaningful only by the language users who are part of it.

While it is certainly possible that some of the political beliefs that make up our belief webs might be more *geographically* remote from the empirical beliefs at the edge of our webs, the holism of Davidson's model indicates that the political beliefs are still connected, by some threads, to those empirical beliefs. When we examine meaning on the model of the radical intepreter, we see that changes in empirical beliefs can, and must, in principle, affect more theoretical beliefs, even if the effect is only slight. For the radical interpreter, no two theoretical beliefs can both conflict with each other in drastic ways *and* have the same truth conditions.

Of course, even though Longino might not have found one, there still might be cases where we want to say that from the point of view of us nonradical interpreters, two conflicting theories are equally well supported by the empirical data. Here, if we are careful to construe both the empirical and political data in support of any theory, as themselves beliefs, we might say that both types of belief can be epistemically underdetermined by their causal relationship with the external world. But, in principle, the radical intepreter must be able to identify the precise causal history of any individual belief, even if we less-than-radical interpreters cannot.

In the skeptic's world, the fear is that the metaphysical separation between us and the world makes coherent the worry that we are, *in principle,* unable to speak with confidence about the causal links between our representations and the world represented. Davidson's point is not to offer comfort to the skeptic that her representations are indeed accurate, but to rethink the "beliefs as representations" model itself. He uses the radical intepreter to give life to an alternate view of the relationship between language users and the world. On this alternate view, all we have, and all we need, is an interconnected web of empirical and theoretical/political beliefs, where for any one attribution of error, that potentially false belief must be connected sufficiently firmly to a sufficiently rich background of true beliefs, before we can even identify it as being false *about* some feature of the world.

Applying the idealized concept of the radical interpreter to the everyday practices of scientists, however, still might invite a number of concerns. For example, Steve Fuller argues that the pragmatist science prescriptions found in Richard Rorty's work, and by extension, Davidson's, support a "quietism" that undermines our ability to be critical of science (Fuller 1992, 390). Fuller traces this quietism to Rorty's use of a Davidsonian-type principle of charity. In Fuller's interpretation, and in many others', the principle of charity demands that we interpret scientists, for example, as more or less rational creatures, thereby removing our ability to make critical, normative claims about their work.

Recall that for Davidson, the possibility of a skeptical gulf between inner, subjective selves and the outer, objective world is belied by the ease with which we use language to communicate with each other about shared features of our world. But once again, "ease" should be read here as an idealized description. Communication in practice is often difficult, especially for those working for social change. We are constantly battling misinterpretation, using a language we know to be amenable to ideological concealment. How, then, can we square our experience of misinterpretation with Davidson's idealized descriptions of the transparency of communication?

Davidson's arguments about linguistic communication center on the concept of interpretational charity; however, as I have argued in the previous chapter, his use of the concept is often misunderstood. If, with Fuller, we understand the principle of charity as the prescription that we view our interlocuters as speaking truthfully at all times, then not only do we encounter an inconsistency between our experiences of misinterpretation and Davidson's idealized account, we also lose the normative stance required for critical science studies. In this next section, I examine further Davidson's principle of charity, showing how it is consistent with, and even encouraging of, a critical approach to science studies.

REVIEWING CHARITY

To say that the principle of charity mandates that we view others as rational at all times is to misinterpret the role of the principle for the radical interpreter. Davidson's claim amounts to the point that for interpretation to begin, the radical interpreter must initially assume that the same relationship between truth and belief holds between those she is interpreting as it does for herself. The radical interpreter needs to assume this agreement at the start, not because she's a quietistic, charitable sort who doesn't want to cause any trouble, but because at this point, assigning too much falsity robs her of the empirical base necessary to identify the foreign speakers as having beliefs about anything at

all. Once she has acquired a sufficient number of utterances, *then* she can begin to identify false ones by sifting for inconsistencies, and so forth.

However, while Fuller does not point to it, there might still be a lingering
sense of conflict between Davidson's principle of charity and the possibility
of diagnosing the linguistic concealment of truths, especially the concealment practiced by those in positions of dominance who want to keep their
power. If we say that meaning is given simply by externally available truth
conditions, then it is, in principle, impossible to address the ways that socially oppressive forces work to control and *conceal* truth conditions.

Bjørn Ramberg responds to precisely this concern in his essay "Charity
and Ideology" (1988). He approaches the problem by analyzing the differences in theories of meaning given by Michael Dummett and Davidson.
Ramberg argues that Dummett is right that language involves conventions.
We don't always—in fact, we seldom—look to truth conditions when interpreting each other. However, Ramberg is faithful to Davidson's claim that
language isn't essentially convention-driven (indeed, this is one of the points
we learn from the practices of the radical interpreter). Part of what keeps us
from being idealized radical interpreters is that we do so often rely on conventions in meaning, rather than on always testing for truth conditions. Ramberg argues that it is this semantic laziness on our part that explains how ideological concealment becomes possible (1988, 647).

To better illustrate Ramberg's point, I return to the argument made by some
scientists in the early 1900s that unlike white men, white women should not
be encouraged to pursue secondary education (e.g., Hall 1904). The justification given was typically characterized as being in the best interest of all
concerned—that, for example, men and women of the higher races have each
evolved with inherent differences and these differences need to be identified
if we are to treat the members of each sex fairly and encourage them to rise to
levels of excellence appropriate to their natural capacities (revised from Ramberg). Ramberg acknowledges that merely identifying this claim as false does
not help us. The claim has meaning precisely because it trades on various linguistic conventions, such as our agreement about the meaning of the words
"treat fairly" and "encourage levels of excellence." Ramberg argues that here
the ideology at work produces a "a three-way tension between the subject's
perception of the world, her perception of the conventions of her language,
and her perception of the meaning of the description" (648), in this case the
description of human evolution. Ideology, he continues, "both uses and undermines the present conventions of a language, and thereby gradually alters
the conventional meanings of the words, or rather, the truth-conditions of sentences" (649).

Confronting the alteration of truth conditions requires vigilance on the
part of those wishing to criticize oppressive ideology. Such normative critique is difficult but not impossible, and certainly not constrained by the

principle of charity. Ideological critique, writes Ramberg, "is a never-ending labour, a continuous struggle to clarify meaning, to recapture the efficacy of language" (649). From a Davidsonian perspective, normative critique of science as elsewhere, is not only possible but desirable.

FEMINIST SCIENCE WITHOUT EPISTEMOLOGY

I have argued that feminist science criticism is the most successful when it is kept internal to specific science projects, and because these projects are always in flux, the prescriptions are best kept ad hoc and dynamic. The criteria for what constitutes the proper prescription will always be undergoing adjustment as new information comes in, for us, as for the radical interpreter. This is what separates a pragmatist interpretive project from epistemological theories that attempt to provide, a priori, general criteria for identifying normative properties.

Returning to the distinction with which I began this chapter, between the innocuous empirical question "Is this scientific theory true?" and the troublesome epistemological questions "By which criteria might we adjudicate between competing knowledge claims?" and "Do these criteria indicate the presence of normative properties such as truth, or something other than truth, such as maximal objectivity or least partiality?" Ramberg explains that we will encounter problems only when we think that answers to this latter set of questions will provide answers to the former question (Ramberg 1989, 9). For, as Rorty reminds us, no matter what normative relational property we identify in a particular theory, we still must fallibilistically acknowledge that future evidence might show the theory to be false (Rorty 1995, 149).

However, epistemologists have in mind the higher standard of satisfying any and all future skeptics. Objectivists and empiricists hope to approach this standard by articulating, a priori, or from a naturalized perspective, those properties of our methods and theories that would indicate truth or a normatively functional variant such as objectivity. The trouble is that when feminist epistemologists link the mundane question of the truth or objectivity of a particular claim ("the Darwinian variability hypothesis about women is false") to any given set of normative properties, the fact that the claim might *have* those normative properties and *still* turn out to be false introduces a devastating and unnecessary skepticism to the equation. Keller's early work encountered precisely these problems.

Critics of objectivism often end up biting the skeptic's bullet. They admit the standard can never be reached; that, for all we know, nature is ultimately unrepresentable. I examined theories of Longino, Harding, and the later Keller that fall in this category. Longino's epistemology suggests that scientific theories are underdetermined by the data, and that the normative key becomes the examination of how the data are filtered as evidence. In the face of the relativism of underdetermination theory, she prescribes the use of feminist, rather than some other, political, filters. I argued that this was an unnecessarily weak formulation that conceded too much to the skeptic.

If we abandon these meta-searches for truth and/or objectivity, and the skepticism such searches engender, we are left, instead, with our everyday empirical practices of testing our claims against our past experiences and our ongoing bodies of theories. The claim that the Darwinian variability hypothesis is false is well supported by these practices. Of course, this empirical study remains a fallibilistic project—we might come up with new evidence that falsifies our own claims. But scientists and others in the business of producing knowledge claims have never had any more assurance than that provided by the best evidential support available at the time.

Arthur Fine provides a similar reminder of the limitations of epistemology for science, arguing that epistemologists "see science as a set of practices in need of an interpretation, and they see themselves as providing just the right interpretation" (Fine 1989, 100; see also Fine 1984, 1991). However, Fine continues, "science is not needy in this way. Its history and current practice constitute a rich and meaningful setting. In that setting questions of goals or aims or purposes occur spontaneously and *locally*" (1989, 100).[2] Fine's epistemic description is very similar to Davidson's own take on science and truth. Fine continues,

> Truth cannot be "explained" or "given an account of" without circularity. Nor does it require anything of the sort. The concept of truth is open-ended, growing with the growth of science. Particular questions (Is this true? What reason do we have to believe in the truth of that? . . .) are addressed in well-known ways. The significance of the answers to those questions is rooted in the practices and logic of truth-judging . . . but that significance branches out beyond current practice along with the growing concept of truth. . . . There is no saying, in advance, how this will go. (Fine 1989, 101)

Fine's point is related to my concern that the feminist move from scientist to epistemologist is typically accompanied by a shift in focus toward overgeneral accounts of "science" and/or "method" and away from the specific agents responsible for harming people. Some feminist discussions of science often proceed as if science was a monolithic, homogenous institution. Prescribing a local, ad hoc approach to the study of specific scientific projects, as is suggested by Davidson and Fine, helps address this group of concerns.[3]

I should also note that while I believe that feminist science critics should reprioritize the focus on epistemology and return to specific science projects, I do not base this prescription on the view that scientists, feminist or otherwise, are epistemologically special, that they have a privileged access to truth detection. I recommend, instead, Rorty's view of scientific inquiry, expressed in essays such as "Is Natural Science a Natural Kind?" (Rorty 1991d [1988]) and

"Science as Solidarity" (Rorty 1991c [1987]). Here, Rorty identifies the uniqueness of scientific practices not in any new method for establishing the truth of particular scientific claims, but rather in the democratic, moral tenor of ideal scientific investigations (Rorty 1991c, 39). His pragmatic view of scientific investigation as a set of democratic values still allows him to speak of the truth of various scientific claims, but, he writes, to say that "truth will win" in the open, democratic scientific encounter "is not to make a metaphysical claim about the connection between human reason and the nature of things. It is merely to say that the best way to find out what to believe is to listen to as many suggestions and arguments as you can" (1991c, 39). Again, this is set against his belief that as language users we have and are constrained by direct causal contact with our world—we can't and don't just "make it all up."

Rorty's critique of the traditional representationalist view of scientific method complements much feminist science criticism, insofar as both Rorty and feminist theorists deconstruct the "scientist-as-priest" myth. Rorty describes this as the myth that the world speaks "God's language" and that scientists have a special method for tuning in to "God's voice." Against this myth, Rorty is critical of demarcating science versus the arts and humanities along the traditional fault lines of "rational versus irrational," "hard versus soft," or "objective versus subjective" (Rorty 1991c, 36). Returning to his view of scientific investigation as ideally exemplifying democratic virtues, he explains how these virtues can and should be evident in *all* disciplines. "On this construction, to be rational is simply to discuss any topic—religious, literary, or scientific—in a way which eschews dogmatism, defensiveness, and righteous indignation" (Rorty 1991c, 37).

A PRAGMATIST VIEW OF SEX/GENDER CATEGORIES

Returning to my criticisms of epistemology and the use of epistemological theorizing in feminist science studies, not only was I concerned that feminists often target a monolithic version of science, I was also concerned with the overgeneralized sex/gender categories that often accompany feminist epistemological projects. I argued that the preference for these overgeneralizations over more complex alternatives was evidence of the ontological rigidity often required by objectivist or empiricist accounts. What if, instead, we applied a pragmatic, nonrepresentationalist approach to the ontological status of our categories of analysis?

Nelson Goodman's analysis of the confirmation of scientific hypotheses provides just the sort of alternative we need. Although there have been no satisfactory epistemological responses to Goodman's "grue" riddle, Goodman himself came up with a reasonable pragmatic solution. According to Goodman, we decide that a theory or hypothesis is confirmed by its positive instances if the theory contains categories or predicates that our linguistic *practices* have allowed us to habitually "project" (Goodman 1955). Projectible predicates, or hypotheses containing those predicates, are those that have been "entrenched," through practice or habit, in language use. To use his famous example, the hypothesis "All emeralds are green" is confirmed by instances of green emeralds, whereas "All emeralds are grue" is not similarly confirmed. "Grue" is not a projectible predicate, by Goodman's linguistic criteria, while "green" is. "Grue" has not had a history of use in inductive generalizations about emeralds. "Green" has.[4]

Paralleling Davidson's holism, Goodman claims that the legitimacy of any new predicates "has to be decided on the basis of their relationship to older predicates" (1955, 98).[5] Keeping in mind Davidson's causal account of meaning, the fact that projectible predicates are those that have been entrenched in our linguistic practices does not need to be equated with the view that "we create our world." Our language use tells us that our predicates or categories arise from firm causal links with our world, though these causal links cannot be used to objectively verify the criteria by which we identify any *particular* category.[6] As one Goodman commentator explains further:

> Entrenchment is a linguistic fact, but it's not just a linguistic fact. Entrenchment is neither accidental nor the result of an arbitrary decision. Whether a term is entrenched, or rather can become entrenched, depends essentially on the way the world is. (Rheinwald 1993, 69)

Otto Neurath's boat metaphor is helpful for expanding on this point. Imagine that we are floating in a boat at sea, but we occasionally discover that the hull of our boat is not water-tight. The boat represents our theories about the world, with each plank in the hull representing the different categories or predicates we have projected in our theories. The difference between a "contrite fallibilism" about the sea-worthiness of our boat and a complete or global skepticism is that on Neurath's model *our boat is floating,* so most of the planks must be water-tight; most of the categories that we habitually project must successfully refer. And even if we can't immediately specify which planks are leaky or which will *become* leaky, we can still repair the leaks as we discover them (see, for example, Goodman 1955, 98–99).

So, then, how do the categories "women" and "men" fare in our hypotheses and theories? I think that for the most part they fare just as well as do "green" and "blue," but let's examine the case of "green" and "blue" more closely.

Serendipitously, while looking for Helen Thompson Woolley's review article on the psychology of sex differences (Woolley 1910), I came across a neighboring article in the same volume entitled "The Puzzle of Color Vocabularies" (R. S. Woodworth 1910). Here I was delighted to find an anthropological discussion of the color names "green" and "blue"—more particularly, a discussion of the *absence* of these color names among the majority of human languages, especially ancient languages. Anthropologist Geiger describes his discovery of this phenomenon in the Bible and also in the *Vedas*. Of the latter he writes,

> These hymns, consisting of more than 10,000 lines, are nearly all filled with descriptions of the sky. Scarcely any subject is more frequently mentioned; the variety of hues which the sun and dawn display in it, day and night, clouds and lightnings, the atmosphere and the ether, all these are with inexhaustible abundance exhibited to us again and again in all their magnificence; only the fact that the sky is blue could never have been gathered from these poems by any one who did not already know it himself. (Geiger [1880], cited in Woodworth 1910, 325)

Geiger provides similar examples regarding "green." Woodworth is careful to point out that when tested, most adult humans, even those speaking languages that had no names for "green" or "blue," can still *distinguish* between these and most other colors on the spectrum, so citing these observations is not meant to support linguistic determinism. Words do not "create our world," for Woodworth (nor do they for Goodman or Davidson). Woodworth hypothesized, instead, that the people speaking these languages simply had no use for the color names "green" and "blue" (Woodworth 1910, 333–34).[7]

As I note in chapter 4, there is a growing literature by and about transsexuals who find the categories "women" and "men" similarly unhelpful, searching, perhaps, for some new middle category (e.g., Rothblatt 1995; Herdt 1994; and Bornstein 1994). Anne Fausto-Sterling supports a similarly complicated view of sex/gender in her essay "The Five Sexes: Why Male and Female Are Not Enough" (1993). However, many feminist theorists continue to be concerned that such creative deconstruction invites a relativist approach to the very categories around which feminism is focused, and, therefore, a relativist approach to the politics of feminism (e.g., Stoljar 1995; Okin 1994). As I argue in chapter 4, I believe, with Cressida Heyes (2000), that these particular worries can be assuaged by approaching our analytic categories from a pragmatist perspective; a perspective that complements Heyes's own Wittgensteinian analysis. If we take a pragmatic approach to our categories of analysis, whether they be categories of color or sex/gender, we are reminded, without fear of relativism, that the categories can be refined, we can rethink their range of application, and over time, when necessary, we can discard them. A Davidson/Goodman account of the projectibility of our predicates allows for an openness in our hypothesis testing that is beneficial for any rational investigation, whether it is science or feminist science studies.

Some might still be inclined to worry that even if this pragmatist approach is coherent, it is beside the point; that feminism *requires* some essential difference between the categories "women" and "men," by definition, and that this difference is endangered by those who claim that simple sex categories fail to capture their own sense of themselves or their own experience of oppression. Denise Riley addresses precisely this sort of feminist concern in her book *"Am*

I That Name?" Feminism and the Category of "Women" in History (1988). She writes compellingly of the history of Western feminism as a group of movements constantly struggling to both deconstruct and reconstruct the category "woman," depending on the political needs of the time (Riley 1988). She argues that "woman" (and even moreso, "women") is an "unstable" category; "that this instability has a historical foundation, and that feminism is the site of the systematic fighting-out of that instability" (Riley 1988, 5). I agree with Riley when she writes that the "systematic fighting out" doesn't have to be seen as a problem for feminism; rather, it is what feminism is all about (5).

Similarly, Chandra Talpade Mohanty is critical of the view that the categories "men" and "women" are naturally given and that all that is left for feminists to do is to analyze the role of men and women in the science lab, the "Third World," the workforce, or any of a variety of social settings (Mohanty 1991). She argues that the categories "men" and "women" are constructed *within* each of these settings.

> The problem . . . is [one of assuming] that men and women are already constituted as sexual-political subjects *prior* to their entry into the arena of social relations. Only if we subscribe to this assumption is it possible to undertake analysis which looks at the "effects" of kinship structures, colonialism, organisation of labor, etc., on women, who are identified, *in advance*, as a group. The crucial point that is forgotten is that women are produced through these very relations as well as being implicated in forming these relations. (Mohanty 1991, 59; emphasis mine)

Within feminist science criticism, the more local and specific the targets, the more flexible and dynamic our approach, the less likely we are to require ontological rigidity in our categories of analysis. This is yet another reason why feminist critics of science should spend more time with specific, though necessarily messy, studies of particular scientific theories and practices. As Mohanty counsels, her arguments are not "*against* generalizations as much as they are *for* careful, historically specific generalizations responsive to complex realities" (Mohanty 1991, 69; emphasis mine).

SUMMARY

"Right conduct in belief," to borrow an old pragmatist phrase, has been achieved in the sciences and in feminist science studies, not through adherence to a priori epistemological searches for normative criteria, but, however fallibly, through adherence to ad hoc, site-specific rules, such as these time-honored suggestions for laboratory experiments:

> Always repeat an experiment a few times.
> Have a few other folks try to repeat your experiment.

To this list can be added the rules suggested by Longino:

> Create recognised avenues for the criticism of evidence.
> Employ shared standards that critics can invoke.
> Always be responsive to criticism.
> Share intellectual authority equally among qualified practitioners. (Adapted from
>   Longino 1990, 76)

Recall from chapter 5 that in the context of Longino's own epistemological project, these rules are substantially weakened by skepticism. I diagnosed the skeptical symptoms as arising from her representationalist understanding of evidence and objectivity. That is, Longino prescribes these rules because, in her view, they allow for the most objective, critical exploration of the contextual values at work filtering the scientific evidence. Once we see that even our most objective theories and models are underdetermined by the data, then, she argues, all we can make of the concept of objectivity is the critical exploration of contextual values and their influence on explanatory models. She comes to choose certain scientific theories, not necessarily because of their relationship to the empirical data, but because they have been constructed with contextual values that best suit feminist politics. As I noted, however, this more relativist analysis weakens the role of empirical data and evidence and so invites skepticism.

A nonrepresentationalist understanding of contextual values or worldviews would conceive of them, not as filters through which the empirical data pass, but as further important strands in our web of belief. When we justify particularly crucial elements of our feminist worldviews, such as our beliefs about oppression and justice, our appeals to (beliefs about) the empirical data have been well documented and are powerfully persuasive as a result. There is no need for us to doubt the empirical evidence for our feminist political values, as long as we conceive of the evidence as that which is provided by other beliefs in our web.

Again, it is important to remember that, when I refer to the relationship between beliefs about our political views and beliefs about empirical evidence, I am using the term "about" in a metaphysically neutral sense. This neutral usage contrasts with the metaphysically laden notion within representationalism whereby uninterpreted interpreters view their inner, subjective beliefs as being "about" the external, objective world. Rorty gives examples of other nonrepresentationalist uses of "aboutness" as when we speak of the rings on tree trunks representing the age of the tree. But, he explains, in these cases "we use the term 'about' as a way of directing attention to the beliefs which are relevant to the justification of other beliefs, not as a way of directing attention to [the relationship between inner beliefs and external data]" (Rorty 1991e, 97).

While coherence or relativist theories of epistemology make similar claims about the justificatory relationship between beliefs, these epistemic theories are best understood in terms of their representationalist commitments. According to coherence or relativist theories of truth, if we had direct access to sensory data, then interbelief comparison would become unnecessary. All our beliefs would mirror the sensory world they represent and could be justified with respect to their fidelity. However, because our subjective conceptual schemes impede the objective flow of sensory content, interbelief comparison is all we have. By limiting the role of sensory content, coherence or relativist theories of truth invite skepticism about the relationship between our beliefs and the world.

In contrast, recall Davidson's argument that assigns a firm causal role to the sensory data our beliefs are about. Problems arise only when, with the epistemologist, we try to harness the world of sensation as independent justification for our beliefs. As both Davidson and Rorty remind us, interbelief comparison is where all justification happens. And it is this interbelief comparison, understood against a firm causal network of sensory evidence, that allows us to make stronger claims than those allowed by the epistemological theories of Longino (or Harding or Keller). Our scientific theories and our beliefs about oppression and justice are not merely relative to our feminist conceptual schemes; they are justified by the evidence and they are true.

NOTES

1. Richmond Campbell's work on feminist empiricism makes the very same point here (Campbell 1994, 1998). He argues that feminist motivation can *contribute* to objective evidence gathering. Objectivity, in the sense of rationally assessing the evidence, should not be equated with political neutrality (1994, 100). However, as I've argued in chapter 2, insofar as Campbell uses this holistic point to defend a realist epistemic version of feminist norms, his project invites skepticism about the very feminist projects he defends.

2. Fine relies on the view that scientists are not "naturally" inclined to take epistemological positions such as objectivism or relativism, realism or antirealism (see also Fine 1991). This has brought him a lot of criticism from philosophers such as Ernan McMullin (1991) and Richard Schlagel (1991), though I haven't seen any criticisms from scientists themselves (scientists are probably just not reading the philosophy journals in which Fine speaks on their behalf). While I agree with Fine's anti-epistemological points, I do not commit myself to the view that all scientists are free from epistemological leanings.

3. See John Dupré (1990, 1993) for similar points on the pluralism of the sciences.

4. See Rosemarie Rheinwald (1993, 73) for further discussion of the relationship between beliefs about the causal structure of the world and the entrenchment of certain predicates.

5. Davidson has argued against "projectibility" as a satisfactory criterion for distinguishing between grue and green (see the appendix to "Mental Events," Davidson 1980 [1970]). But I believe that for the purposes of my argument, his differences with

Goodman do not make a difference. Davidson's own views about "salience," for example, are very similar to "projectibility." Davidson argues that successful triangulation between the radical interpreter and native speaker suggests that both must be
able to co-calibrate their sense of salience with respect to relevant features of the environment.

   6. Ludwig Wittgenstein makes similar points about identifying color categories in
his *Philosophical Investigations* (e.g., 1958, IIxi, 226–27). This is the "family resem-
blance" approach to categories that Cressida Heyes models for her extremely helpful
discussions of sex/gender categories (Heyes 2000).

   7. Woodworth explains his views about the low functional utility of the color names
"green" and "blue" by first addressing the question of the functional utility of color
names generally. He hypothesizes that color categories are introduced to help identify
objects and to distinguish them from their backgrounds. But, he argues, other sorts of
words often serve the same function—"We speak of a berry as ripe, rather than red, of
meat as well done or underdone rather than brown or red. In such cases the color is
the mark by which the condition of the thing is known, but what is named is the condition rather than the mark" (1910, 333). There is a lack of function, then, for many
color names, which, he believes "accounts for the widespread poverty of languages in
such names" (333). With respect to "green" and "blue," in, particular, he notes that they
are themselves primarily background colors. "Red" and "yellow" are the colors of objects that need to be distinguished from this background, and so are bound to be more
functional than "blue" and "green" (333).

8

A Pragmatist Case Study:
Back to the Theory of Evolution

In this book I have documented a number of examples of the problems encountered by feminist critics of science when they employ epistemological strategies based on a representationalist model of minds and language. This model forces a questionable metaphysical split between our subjective, political beliefs and the objective world of empirical data, which, in turn, makes global skepticism about our political beliefs a coherent concern. I then offered a pragmatized reading of Donald Davidson's philosophy of language as an alternative model that avoids the questionable metaphysics. On Davidson's non-representationalist model, skepticism is not a coherent option, so epistemology understood as a response to skepticism, becomes radically unmotivated.

If we are persuaded by this pragmatized Davidsonian model, we can abandon the seemingly endless epistemological battle with skepticism and return to our feminist science studies as chemists, biologists, sociologists, and so forth. In these specific science forums we can continue the project at which feminist theorists have always excelled—that is, the construction of empirical, sociological accounts designed to weed out the oppressive genealogy of the terms, theories, and models used by scientists. And, importantly, we can continue to question how the documenting of an oppressive genealogy bears on the issue of the *truth* of the scientific claim under consideration.

Within the traditional literature on the epistemology of science, the beliefs about the genealogy of a scientific hypothesis (e.g., the pragmatic and political beliefs that led to its introduction) are said to belong to the context of scientific discovery. In turn, beliefs about the truth of the hypothesis (e.g., its relationship to beliefs about sensory evidence) belong to the context of scientific justification. Traditionally, the two contexts are kept separate. However, by employing a Davidsonian understanding of meaning, belief, and truth, we can collapse the distinction by viewing both discovery and justification as naturalized elements of the equation, which are, *both,* in principle, constrained by beliefs about empirical evidence.

In chapter 5, I argue that in their classic writings in feminist science studies, Helen Longino and Sandra Harding retain a problematic metaphysical split between the political values that lead to the discovery of a hypothesis and the empirical beliefs that lead to its justification. Both argue that subjective political values, from the context of discovery, screen or filter evidential testing in the context of justification (see, e.g., Longino 1987, 54; Harding 1991, 143–44). When Longino argues that the nonempirically constrained realm of politics is always bound to influence the underdetermined, empirical realm of justification, her account paradoxically serves to underscore the view that each realm is conceptually distinct. Her argument reinforces, at a more general level, the very split between the subjective/political realm of discovery and the objective/evidence realm of justification that she seeks to deconstruct.[1] I argue that the reinforcement of this traditional split damages our own, well-justified, *and* politically motivated criticisms in and of science. Davidson's nonrepresentationalist perspective successfully removes this danger by showing how both the discovery and the justification of a theory are constrained by evidence.

However, while Davidson's nonrepresentationalist view supports the claim that both contexts are constrained by evidence, it does not support the objectivist claims of a "logic" or epistemological method in either one or both levels. If we are no longer motivated to search for general accounts of normative properties such as truth or maximal objectivity, we should likewise abandon our search for an epistemic method that would indicate the *presence* of such properties. Searching for evidential relations to guide our scientific examinations, genealogical or otherwise, is largely an ad hoc task that proceeds in well-known ways ("Have someone else check your results," "Use double-blind research designs where possible"). If we attempt to "precipitate out" the features of these well-known methods that make them objective methods for identifying truth, we will be continually chasing after recalcitrant features. Recall the convoluted changes Evelyn Fox Keller was forced to make to her account of "dynamic objectivity" in the face of the recalcitrance of Barbara McClintock's gender (see chapter 4).

To further illustrate my nonrepresentationalist prescription for the construction of pragmatic, feminist genealogies in science, I now return to the evolutionary topics with which I began the book. In the next section I introduce a pragmatist evolutionary account of biological function. I apply this account, first, to the function of the allegedly superior (European) male physique and intellect; and second, to the function of menstruation. In both cases I highlight a number of entry points for feminist genealogical criticism.

EVOLUTIONARY ACCOUNTS OF BIOLOGICAL FUNCTION

Earlier, in chapter 3, I favorably discuss Helen Montague and Leta Stetter Hollingworth's empirical criticisms of Darwin and his functionalist claims about sex differences in intelligence (e.g., Montague and Hollingworth 1914; Hollingworth 1914). Recall that Charles Darwin argued that human males, especially European males, had superior mental and physical secondary sexual characteristics. Darwin claimed that this superiority was functional, insofar as it helped males to attract and defend female mates (Darwin 1981 [1871], vol. 2, 327–28). Darwin hypothesized that the selection of superior characteristics in European males was aided by the fact that these males vary more from the "generic human form" than do males of the "lower races," and adult females of any race, on any number of physical and mental measures (Darwin, vol. 1, 275). In turn, he hypothesized that the greater physical and mental variability in European males resulted from the fact that the females in our prehistoric past were more choosy about mates than were the males. The highly variable male, especially the "civilised" European male, was viewed as the "engine of evolution." Recall that, for Darwin, female mate choice was frustrated prehistorically in certain "lower races," thereby decreasing the effects of male variability and, subsequently, male superiority, in contemporary members of those races (see Darwin 1981, vol. 2, 358–67).

Montague and Hollingworth provided empirical criticisms of the Darwinian functionalist claims, arguing that prior studies of sex differences had failed to capture inherent, biological variability; that the results had been unduly influenced by sexist distinctions in social practices such as child rearing. They argued that "the lives of men and women are lived under conditions so different as to constitute different environments" and that these environments needed to be controlled before they could be confident about the reliability of empirical research (Montague and Hollingworth 1914, 343). Accordingly, they chose to research infants, assuming that measurements at infancy would best reflect inherent, biological causes, rather than social or cultural pressures.

Hollingworth and Montague examined records of the weight, length, and cranial size of a large, ethnically diverse population of infants. They noted that the ethnic diversity should not be a problem, insofar as the diversity extended to infants of both sexes. I think this marks a misunderstanding of Darwin's claims about variability. He would have objected to racial populations being mixed, because the lesser variability between the sexes of the "lower races" would have lowered the correlation coefficients measured between sexes of the "higher races." However, the two ethnicities mentioned by Montague and Hollingworth, "Italian" and "Greek," would probably have fallen relatively high on Darwin's scale of European supremacy, not as high as "British" but certainly qualifying as superior to the "lower races" of Africa, Asia, and the Indian subcontinent.

Despite the European demographics of their sample, Montague and Hollingworth found no significant sex differences in physical variability; the Darwinian claim was not supported by the empirical evidence (Montague and Hollingworth 1914). Hollingworth also criticized the claim that greater male variability in *mental* traits is inherent (if indeed such variability can be found), arguing instead for the value of sociological explanations that detailed the discriminatory treatment of girls and women (Hollingworth 1914).

I would like to expand the target of this empirical critique to extend not only to the details of the functional thesis of European male superiority, but also to the larger, philosophical debates about biological functions more generally. Feminists have not yet made significant critical inroads in the mainstream philosophical debates about biological function, and I think we should start.

THE ETIOLOGICAL ACCOUNT AND SOME PRAGMATIC CONSIDERATIONS

Within the philosophy of biology the main explanation of a mechanism's function is given by appeal to the evolutionary or etiological history of the mechanism in question. To cite a favorite example in the etiologist literature, the function of the heart is to pump blood, because an evolutionary account reveals that the heart was naturally selected to pump blood. The heart was not selected to produce heartbeats, so noise production is a nonfunction, or a side effect. Various versions of this etiological position are taken by philosophers such as Larry Wright (1972, 1973), Ruth Millikan (1989), Karen Neander (1991), and Peter Godfrey-Smith (1994).[2] According to this approach, a mechanism is functional insofar as it was selected to perform that function in the past. The term "etiological" refers to the historical course of the functional mechanism's evolution by natural selection.

The functional analysis provided by philosophers such as Robert Cummins (1989 [1975]), Christopher Boorse (1976), and Elizabeth Prior (1985) presents a set of pragmatic issues that can be seen as conceptually prior to the evolutionary analyses offered by the etiologists. These more pragmatic philosophers often support the view that the evolutionary course of a functional mechanism is an important aspect to study.[3] However, they argue that we cannot arrive at this course by simply reading off the evolutionary facts of nature, independent of a contextual analysis of the goals of the larger system within which the mechanism in question is said to function. While they may agree with the etiologists that the heart functions to pump blood, and that a sophisticated adaptationist analysis can provide a good explanation of how the heart came to be functional in this way; they add that using evolutionary theory to ascribe functional status to a mechanism is always relative to a number of pragmatic, or second-order, considerations about the systems within which that mechanism is situated. We must have individuated some features of an organism into "functional" systems and mechanisms working within that system, before we can begin to analyze the evolutionary history of the functional features. According to these more pragmatically inclined philosophers, functions are "those effects of the components of [a] system, reference to which provides us with our best account of some high-level capacity of that system" (Prior 1985, 311).

A second-order analysis reveals a number of variables that influence the focus of our interest in some systems rather than others. For example, Derek Turner has recently argued that biologists have trouble making functional ascriptions unless they have available a familiar functional analogue for the mechanism in question (Turner 2001). If this is true, then it is likely that human interests and cultural context will (and have) influenced what sort of analogues are available and salient.[4]

I should note that when the more pragmatically minded philosophers of biology speak of the importance of "human interests," it is easy to read them as making the relativistic claim that we can make up whatever functional accounts interest us, the objective facts of natural selection come what may. Recall, however, the origins of objectivity as explained through the radical interpreter. According to Davidson, an objective delineation of a category is the product of two or more speakers noticing, that is, taking some interest in, the same features of the environment and grouping those features into the same linguistic category ("functions" and "effects"). On Davidson's model, human interests are naturalized and made part of the scientific equation. Far from forming some metaphysically separate, subjective viewpoint relativized to separate knowers, human interests are part and parcel of the objective categorization of the world, including the categorization of functions.

Nelson Goodman has written extensively on this process, using the term "entrenchment" where I have used "human interest" and Davidson uses "salience." Goodman's work focuses on the study of confirmation, specifically on difficulties in distinguishing between hypotheses that are confirmed by their instances and those that are not. The hypothesis that copper conducts electricity seems properly supported by instances of copper conducting electricity. That copper conducts electricity is a lawlike generalization, says Goodman. Compare this generalization to the hypothesis that every woman in my logic class is a third daughter. Here, the discovery that one of the female students was indeed a third daughter would not increase the credibility of the hypothesis as it stands. This latter hypothesis, says Goodman, is accidental rather than lawlike.

How then to tell the difference? Traditional accounts of confirmation demand a decision algorithm based on objective features of the hypothesis in question, that is, an algorithm based on syntactical features. Goodman argued, convincingly, that nonsyntactical features play more of a role in confirmation than was first supposed (Goodman 1955, 73). Specifically, he showed that the predicates used in any given hypothesis must be well behaved—that is, "projectible"—before those hypotheses could be confirmed by their instances; projectibility, it turns out, is largely an issue of entrenchment in linguistic usage.

Like Davidson, Goodman has a number of arguments to support his confidence in the positive correlation between linguistic descriptions and the world described (Goodman 1955, 1978) and I return to these arguments shortly. For now, it is important to note that his confidence still leaves room for interesting questions about how the world is individuated through linguistic usage. Which systems of an organism strike us as functional? Which functional hypotheses are subsequently confirmed by evolutionary data about the natural selection of mechanisms within that system?

I argue that when attributing functional status to elements of a biological system, both the system and the capacities of that system can be viewed as predicates that need to be well entrenched in the appropriate linguistic sphere before functional hypotheses containing those predicates are themselves projectible and capable of empirical confirmation.[5]

Returning to the biological study of the well-entrenched circulatory system, for example, we have a number of components such as the heart, the veins, and the arteries, all of which produce a number of different effects. Once a capacity of that system has been similarly entrenched, such as the capacity "circulates nutrients/disposes of wastes," those effects of the components that contribute to our *explanations* of that capacity can be identified as functions, the rest (such as production of heartbeats) as mere effects. In other words, the historical entrenchment of the capacity "circulates nutrients/disposes of wastes" helped to decide which of any competing functional hypotheses about hearts were later analyzed using natural selection accounts of the circulatory system. The various components of the vertebrate circulatory system and their contribution to its circulatory capacities were well entrenched and well understood, even before natural selection accounts of the system were in place. The high frequency of the use of the capacity predicate "circulates nutrients" (or a nearly coextensive term like "pumps blood") positively influenced the projectibility of the functional hypothesis "the heart functions to pump blood" in later selection accounts.[6] Given that no other capacities of the system have been entrenched, no evolutionary story can be told that would ascribe to the heart a function other than pumping blood. The production of heartbeats, for example, is properly described as a side effect of the functioning of the heart (see figure 8.1).

Entrenched System	**Components of Entrenched System**
Vertebrate circulatory system	*Heart, veins, arteries*

Entrenched *Capacity* of System:
Circulates nutrients/disposes of wastes

Function of Heart	**Side Effect of Heart**
(relative to entrenched capacity)	(relative to entrenched capacity)
Pumps blood	*Produces heartbeats*

Figure 8.1.   Function of Heart Relative to Capacity for Circulation

At the moment, then, biologists are inclined to say that the hypothesis about pumping blood is true, while the hypothesis about producing heartbeats is false. Articulating the relationship between projectibility and truth is tricky, but it seems clear that projectibility is needed before a hypothesis can become *confirmed* by its positive instances. The obvious representationalist worry that arises from this formulation is that if we define a true hypothesis as that which is well confirmed, and we believe that confirmation depends on entrenchment in our previous linguistic usage, rather than in "the world," then we could be globally mistaken about what is true.

There are a number of ways to respond to this representationalist worry. First, the nonrepresentationalist view of the radical interpreter illustrates that false beliefs—about functional hypotheses, for example—have content only in relation to a background of true beliefs against which the false beliefs are compared. Global error is incoherent on this model. Beliefs are not potentially erroneous representations about nonbelief entities.[7] But, of course, individual beliefs—about functions, for example—can indeed be false. Second, Goodman notes that it is only when one *defines* truth, in some epistemological sense, as "those hypotheses well-confirmed by observations of positive instances" that skepticism about the relationship between "projectibility" and "truth" becomes a problem (Goodman 1955, 99). Goodman, Richard Rorty, and Davidson support instead the "cautionary" use of true—found, for example, in the phrase "This hypothesis is 'well-confirmed' but it might not turn out to be 'true'" (see, for example, Rorty 1995, 149). Problems arise if, in an attempt to defeat some future skeptic, we define projectible hypotheses as those that will *continue* to be true (Goodman 1955, 99). If, instead, we are fallibilistic about our hypotheses, we can acknowledge that "produces heartbeats" may indeed become entrenched within biology, and "the heart functions to produce heartbeats" might turn out to be true. Even though the pragmatic model of the radical

intepreter makes a general skepticism incoherent, we still need to be falli-
bilists about our particular truth claims.

Imagine, for example, that heart sounds and stethoscope technology evolve
together over the next few millennia, with the effect that cardiac diagnostic accuracy is markedly increased. It might then be possible to give an etiological
account detailing the selective pressures on the production of heart sounds.
However, if Goodman is right about projectibility, then some system *other* than
that of vertebrate circulation would have to become entrenched before heartbeat production could be given an adaptationist account—that is, before
heartbeat production could become a projectible function of the heart.

THE FUNCTION OF "EUROPEAN MALE SUPERIORITY"

Returning to Hollingworth's empirical critique of variability, we can make
use of this pragmatic, Goodmanesque approach to produce a genealogical
account of the function of "European male superiority." Darwin hypothesized that intellectual and physical superiority helped the "civilised" European male to attract mates, a claim supported recently by Doreen Kimura
(1992). More pragmatic-minded philosophers such as Elizabeth Prior might
suggest that an examination of the capacities or features of the system to
which the component "European male superiority" contributes might reveal
to us the reasons for the tenacity of such a sexist claim.

"European male superiority" is a component of the well-entrenched system of sexual selection. One of the well-entrenched capacities of this system
is that it features the phenomenon of "female mate-choice" (see figure 8.2).

Entrenched System   **Components of Entrenched System**
Sexual selection   *European male superiority, female and*
non-European male inferiority

Entrenched *Capacity* of System:
Encourages female mate-choice
(in "higher races," at least)

Function of European male superiority
(relative to entrenched capacity)
Helps these males attract mates

**Figure 8.2.   Function of European Male Superiority Relative to Capacity for Encourag-
ing Female Mate-Choice**

Here it becomes clear that "helps males attract mates" contributes to our explanations about "female mate-choice." But why, we might ask, is female mate-choice a projectible, that is, entrenched, feature of sexual selection? Here is one site where feminists can contribute a crucial genealogical examination.

In our androcentric society, it might seem odd that "female mate-choice" is well entrenched at all, because the predicate suggests that at some earlier point in the evolutionary record, human females exerted some power (of choice) over their male partners (at least, Darwin argued, in the "higher races"). One explanation might be found in an examination of the concept of the "oversexed," "eager" male. This characterization of the male is crucial for female mate-choice to be successful and provides a useful genealogical entry point for feminists. Generalizations about the (European) female lack of desire, and concomitant male eagerness, continue from Victorian times to the present, and they can obviously be interpreted in numerous ways. Surprisingly, Havelock Ellis provided a prescient feminist account of this phenomenon when he explained that a woman's lack of desire may, in part, be due to the fact that her partner has not understood her sexual needs (Ellis 1936 [1897–1928], vol. 3).[8]

Donna Haraway has made some more recent inroads on this question when she argues that "female mate-choice" paradoxically requires "female passivity" (Haraway 1989, 364). Female passivity is, of course, as well entrenched a predicate as one can find in Western, androcentric evolutionary biology, irrespective of the species under study. Haraway explains that Darwin viewed our prehistoric male ancestors as competitors in access "to the means of reproduction," that is, females. This means that in the "higher races" at least, the female becomes the "limiting resource" (Haraway, 364). Haraway notes that, unfortunately, the limiting resource "always runs the risk of being nothing but the prize, not a player (agent) in its (her) own right" (364). The choosy female is reduced to a passive object of desire.

The relationship between male hypersexuality, female passivity, and female mate-choice (all within the context of European colonialist understandings of racial differences within sexual selection) might help explain why female mate-choice is as entrenched as it is in androcentric biology. It might also help explain why "helps males attract mates" is the accepted function of one component of sexual selection, namely, European male "superiority." "Attracts mates" contributes to our explanations of the component "encourages female mate-choice" (at least in the "higher races"). In the next section I examine these pragmatic, genealogical analyses of function in more depth, utilizing a recent evolutionary theory of the function of menstruation (see also Clough 2002).

THE FUNCTION OF MENSTRUATION

In 1993, biologist Margie Profet captured the attention of the popular press with the publication of her controversial thesis: Menstruation functions as a defense against pathogens transported by sperm (Profet 1993).[9] There has been less response in scientific journals, and what little there is has failed, I argue, to address adequately her main point (see J. Clarke 1994, C. A. Finn 1994, Beverly Strassmann 1996). Profet hypothesizes that all internally fertilizing mammals menstruate because menstruation is necessary for clearing the female reproductive tract of sperm-borne pathogens. Menstruation, she argues, has been naturally selected as a pathogen defense. She also argues that traditional accounts fail to describe menstruation as functional because, prior to her work, no one had thought to perform an evolutionary analysis of menstruation (Profet 1993, 336). The traditional view of menstruation as a preparation for the implantation of a newly fertilized egg is not a functional thesis, she claims; rather, it views menstruation as a "nonfunctional byproduct of reproductive cycling" (336).

In support of her functional thesis, Profet reviews the microscopy evidence that pathogens are transported by sperm to the uterus (Profet 1993, 341). These pathogens may originate in the vagina, in the cervix, or in the male reproductive system. She then describes an array of female defenses against sperm-transported pathogens in the vagina, cervix, and uterus (342–43). Of course, she notes, the aggressiveness of this defense system must be balanced with the need to make sperm welcome for reproductive purposes. The balance generally involves increased defenses somewhat during, but especially after, the female's period of sexual receptivity—that is, during and after exposure to sperm and the accompanying pathogens (342).

During and after sexual receptivity, the walls of the vagina become cornified or scale-like, "hindering sexually transmitted pathogens from colonizing vaginal tissue" (342). In the cervix, thick, acidic mucous accumulates to keep sperm and the accompanying pathogens from proceeding to the uterus. During sexual receptivity, this particular defense must be weak to allow sperm through to fertilize eggs, but before and especially after sexual receptivity this defense is particularly strong. The uterus and oviducts have similarly well-timed defenses (343–44), such as "nonmenstrual forms of normal uterine bleeding" (348). Concluding this section of her argument, she writes, "The female reproductive organs have a cascade of defenses designed to protect them against sexually-transmitted pathogens. I propose that menstruation is one such defense" (344).

Profet argues that menstruation protects against pathogens both mechanically and immunologically (345). In the mechanistic process, pathogens attached to the endometrium (uterine lining) are expelled as the endometrium is sloughed off. "Pockets of menstrual blood form hematomas at the base of the endometrium, which lift, stretch, and help to shed it" (345). In the immunological process, pathogens are fought with leukocytes. "Menstrual blood delivers large concentrations of leukocytes to bacteria-infested endometrial tissue. Leukocytes directly combat pathogens and also phagocytise [envelope] potentially infected necrotic tissue" (345).

Profet then anticipates and counters a possible problem with her thesis. Pathogens such as bacteria actually *require* iron to survive. It might seem unlikely then, that an iron-rich substance such as menstrual blood has the function of *combating* bacteria (346). Profet responds with two arguments. The first is that the substance lactoferrin, which is found in both menstrual and circulatory blood, chemically sequesters the iron, making it unavailable to bacteria. Levels of lactoferrin in circulatory blood have been shown to increase prior to menstruation, and it is inferred that the levels are high in menstrual blood as well (346). The second is that, during menstruation, iron levels are low in circulatory blood anyway. Again, it is inferred that these lower levels are mirrored in those of menstrual blood. She also notes that iron levels in menstrual blood might be *less* than those in circulatory blood, which would mean that the iron loss during menstruation, calculated by measuring circulatory levels, is overestimated (347).[10]

Profet is, arguably, the first researcher to examine these individual mechanisms as part of a female defense *system,* certainly the first to provide a detailed evolutionary examination of the individual responses and the system in which they play a part. Although the medical and biology journals have not focused much attention on her work, it would seem that Profet has described the function of menstruation in a way that newly synthesizes a variety of immunological and physiological research previously thought to be unrelated. Such a project seems long overdue. Furthermore, Profet's functional arguments about menstruation have potentially significant clinical implications. Menstrual blood is often seen as a contributing factor in uterine infections, so current clinical practice favors treating some uterine infections by artificially inhibiting menstruation. According to Profet, menstruation actually *combats* such infection. If she is right, inhibiting menstruation at these times is contraindicated. Current clinical practice, she says "blames the firemen for the fire."

However, it is one thing to argue that a particular mechanism can be thought of as currently "functioning" in a particular way. Physiologists and clinicians make these sorts of functional claims all the time, with little or no interest in the evolutionary history of the mechanism in question. But it is much more difficult, both empirically and conceptually, to argue that a particular mechanism has been naturally selected *for* any given function. These difficulties are often used by physiologists and clinicians to support the claim that natural selection accounts are not necessary tools for studying disease mechanisms (Gammelgaard 2000).[11]

Leaving aside debates about the place of evolutionary theory in current clinical practice, it is certainly the case that the weakest parts of Profet's project involve her natural selection account.[12] She often conflates accounts of recent selection pressures, within, say protohuman ancestry, with the selection pressures faced by mammals generally, as when she defends her functional thesis from a competing view that menstruation functions to decrease levels of iron that would otherwise lead to heart disease (337). In her criticism of this competing thesis, she abruptly switches the level of analysis from the ancestral selection pressures faced by early mammals to the more recent pressures faced by "hunter-gatherer women, and by extension our Pleistocene ancestors." She argues that these women would have had no need to have their iron levels reduced, as they "seldom lived long enough to suffer degenerative diseases of old age" (337). However, one could just as easily use the selection pressures faced by these women to argue against Profet's thesis. Menstruation would be an unlikely aid to women who were usually pregnant during their reproductive years. These and other concerns with her evolutionary account are discussed further on.

Most of my discussion, however, focuses on a set of pragmatic concerns that, in the case of functional explanation, prove to be conceptually prior to questions of evolutionary detail. In the case of functional hypotheses, empirical attention often needs to be paid not just to the selection history of the mechanism in question, but also to the pragmatic details that underwrite our interest in and characterization of both the mechanism and the contribution of the mechanism to the working order of the larger system of which it is a part. The need for examining these pragmatic considerations becomes particularly obvious when the hypothesis is new or controversial, as is the case with Profet's account.

Recall Profet's claim that the reason a functional account of menstruation has proved elusive is because biologists have failed to subject menstruation to an evolutionary analysis. Once the selection pressures on female mammals are made clear, she implies, the pathogen-defense function of menstruation would be equally transparent. However, the cool reception of her hypothesis by her peers suggests otherwise. I argue that pragmatic considerations such as those introduced by feminist studies of biology might better explain why Profet's arguments for menstruation sound so revolutionary and why her work has largely been ignored in the science literature.

"THE PHYSIOLOGY OF MENSTRUATION SHOWS ADAPTIVE DESIGN"

Unencumbered by the pragmatic details of projectibility, Profet's argument focuses on explaining the presence of menstruation by showing that menstruation was naturally selected to perform its function of removing sperm-transported pathogens. Profet cites George Williams's (1966) two-part investigation for identifying whether a process is a functional mechanism (i.e., whether it has been naturally selected) or not (Williams, in Profet 1993, 336). The first part of the investigation involves "identifying the problem that the candidate mechanism was designed to solve." The second part involves "elucidat[ing] design—that is, show[ing] that there is an adaptive fit between the mechanism and the problem that is too close to be merely the product of chance or the by-product of other mechanisms" (Profet 1993, 336).[13]

To satisfy the first part, Profet itemizes a number of candidate problems, besides her own preferred one, that menstruation may have been designed to solve. One such problem is the build-up of plant toxins in the uterus. Menstruation might remove these toxins. Another is the strain on the cardiovascular system that results from high iron levels. Again, iron loss through menstruation might be thought to keep these levels healthful (337).

She then continues with part two of her investigation by illustrating how menstruation as a defense against pathogens shows an adaptive fit that is not found with menstruation as a removal of plant toxins or as a reduction of iron. She argues that natural selection cannot explain these other competing options. In the case of plant toxins, she points out that they can be removed without endometrial breakdown. It is in her arguments against the selection of menstruation for iron reduction that she switches the burden of proof from the selection pressures faced by ancestral mammals to pressures faced more recently by protohumans. Accordingly, she argues that our protohuman ancestors "rarely live[d] long enough to suffer degenerative diseases of old age" such as heart disease (337), which would make iron reduction an unlikely functional candidate.

In arguing that menstruation as a pathogen defense shows the adaptive fit "too close to be merely the product of chance," Profet points out that menstruation *must* be an adaptation (i.e., it must be a functional mechanism) because it is too costly to have lasted unless it also offered some selective advantage (337). "If menstruation were both costly and functionless, natural selection surely would have eliminated it long ago" (336). According to Profet, menstruation is costly both nutritionally (through iron and tissue loss) and reproductively (through the reduction of the number of reproductive opportunities in any one breeding season). Furthermore, the uterus wall is lined with specialized spiral-shaped arteries "that constrict and dilate in a sequence timed to induce menstruation" (339). Finally, menstrual blood differs from venous blood such that in menstrual blood, clotting is reduced (339). Profet believes that this efficient, precise, and complex system points to adaptation. She writes, "If menstruation were merely a functionless by-product of cyclic hormonal flux [i.e., if menstruation were not naturally selected], there would be no mechanisms [the spiral arteries] specifically designed to cause it, nor would the constituents of menstrual and circulatory blood differ significantly [such that circulatory blood clots but menstrual blood does not]" (338).

THE ETIOLOGY OF MENSTRUATION
AS A PATHOGEN DEFENSE: SOME CONCERNS

On Profet's account, if menstruation were both costly and functionless, natural selection would have eliminated it long ago. Menstruation *is* costly. Menstruation has not been eliminated. Therefore, menstruation has a function (i.e., has been naturally selected). In specifying the *exact* function, Profet argues that pathogen defense is the only functional hypothesis that can explain the presence of menstruation. That menstruation has the function of removing sperm-transported pathogens explains the presence of menstruation (and the requisite physiology such as spiral arteries and low levels of coagulant).

There are numerous problems with the inferences she makes here. As Carl Hempel has argued, identifying a problem to be solved—in this case, combating sperm-borne pathogens—does not countenance an inference to any *particular* functional solution (Hempel 1965). Indeed, Profet's description of the defense system of the female reproductive tract includes a number of other components such as vaginal cornification, mucous plugs in the cervix, and nonmenstrual bleeding in the uterus, any or all of which could be solutions to the problem of sperm-borne pathogens. Knowing there's a problem to be solved does not guarantee that a particular solution will be selected in any given case.[14] At most Profet can infer some general sort of defense mechanism, with the built-in redundancy of the functional equivalents, but she cannot, at this point, infer menstruation in particular.

As mentioned earlier, Profet also neglects the evolutionary details necessary to move from the ancestral selection pressures faced by all mammals to the more recent pressures faced by protohumans. Unless she wants to claim that every mammal species evolved menstruation independently, she needs the ancestral account to support her claims about the universality of menstruation in mammals. But she also needs the more recent selection account to support her clinical prescriptions for treating uterine infection in contemporary human females. Details of both accounts and the historical links between them are lacking.

It could be possible, for example, that pathogen defense is a "piggyback" trait that has no selection history except through its close connection to another trait that has itself been selected.[15] Pathogen defense might also be a result of what Paul Griffiths calls "exadaptation," where a mechanism originally selected for one function comes to have another (Griffiths 1992). All of these issues are relevant to the etiological question of menstruation's function, and they require far more examination than Profet provides. However, in addition to the incredibly difficult evolutionary questions that confront her project, Profet needs also to address the lack of entrenchment of the containing system within which her functional account of menstruation is situated—namely, the distinctively female system of sperm-borne pathogen defense.

A PRAGMATIC PRESCRIPTION

The more pragmatic, contextual approach of Cummins and others helps to address these second-order, contextual questions. Cummins argues that, typically, we don't appeal to functions to explain the presence of the mechanism in question; rather, we appeal to functions in order to explain the capacities of some "containing system," whether that system be an organism, a system of organisms, or a system within an organism (Cummins 1989 [1975], 501). In Goodman's terms, the containing system predicate needs to be entrenched, as do predicates or categories of the system's capacities, before an evolutionary account can be given (see figure 8.3).

The containing system of Profet's functional account is the female reproductive tract, which is, itself, well entrenched. But what about Profet's hypothesized capacity of that system—the capacity of defense against sperm-borne pathogens? How well is this capacity entrenched in contemporary evolutionary biology? How often has this capacity been used in making inductive generalizations? An examination of the literature indicates not well, and not often.

According to the pragmatic, contextual considerations outlined previously, there are three levels of "interest" or entrenchment required to get a

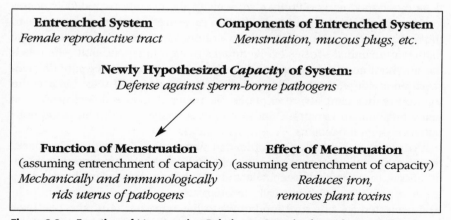

Figure 8.3.   Function of Menstruation Relative to Capacity for Pathogen Defense

functional account projected and subsequently tested, and Profet's account is missing two. The first element is some established research interest in a particular containing system. In Profet's example, this is the system of the female reproductive tract, and this system is well entrenched. The second is the entrenchment of a capacity of the containing system; that is, the capacity, or some extensional equivalent, has to have appeared in a sufficiently large number of hypotheses in evolutionary biology. In Profet's case, this would mean established research interest in the capacity of the female reproductive tract to defend itself against sperm-borne pathogens. The third element is some understanding of how individual components of that system contribute to our explanations of the capacities of that system. For Profet, this would involve projectible hypotheses about the role of menstruation in the healthy operation of the sperm-borne pathogen-defense system. These last two elements are currently absent in Profet's case—hypotheses containing the predicates "defends the female against sperm-borne pathogens" are not currently projectible. As Profet laments, there has been little established research interest in the sperm-borne pathogen-defense system of the female reproductive tract, and as a consequence there is little understanding of how the components of that system work together.

However, Profet also argues that the reason we don't think of menstruation as functional is simply because we have never viewed menstruation from an evolutionary perspective. There are two potential issues of contention here. The first has been mentioned earlier and concerns the debate between those who argue that we should expand the etiological approach to better understand functional claims in physiology and medicine and those who argue that we should continue to keep evolutionary explanations separate from functional claims in physiology and medicine; indeed, that in these latter spheres, evolutionary etiology is often beside the point. Williams and Randolph Nesse have championed the former position, as documented in their book *Evolution and Healing: The New Science of Darwinian Medicine* (Nesse and Williams 1995), and Profet is clearly supportive of their cause. She argues that understanding the selected function of menstruation "is essential for making good [clinical] decisions about whether and when to interfere with menstruation (1993, 368). Against Nesse and Williams, Anne Gammelgaard and a number of physiologists have argued that etiological/natural selection accounts are not necessary tools for physiologists and others who study disease mechanisms (Gammelgaard 2000). Unlike Profet, some etiologists have accepted this sort of boundary setting, admitting that an etiological account of functions might be better suited to evolutionary biology than it is to medicine and physiology.[16]

Whether Profet will find herself on the winning side of this particular issue is an empirical question, though there are no signs that it will be decided any time soon. As I have noted, however, a second point of contention remains. When Profet argues that the function of menstruation will be clear once we take an evolutionary perspective, she fails to consider that, in this case in particular, there are a number of second-order concerns about the larger system within which her menstruation hypothesis is contained. A quick examination of Beverly Strassman's response to Profet is illustrative of the problem here (Strassman 1996). Strassman's is the only substantial response to Profet's thesis published to date. She follows up Profet's study with an explicitly evolutionary analysis of menstruation, as Profet prescribes. She concludes, however, that menstruation is not itself functional; that it is a by-product of the highly functional endometrial shutdown that occurs during periods of nonsexual receptivity. Interestingly, Strassman spends only half of a page of her thirty-two pages of text considering the role of menstruation in any larger system of female pathogen defense. And here she looks only at Profet's claims about the sperm barrier provided by cervical mucous; no other aspects of the system are discussed. The female pathogen-defense system that forms the larger context of Profet's thesis is not given any significant treatment; in other words, it does not seem particularly projectible or salient, as far as Strassman is concerned.[17]

Here, then, is a site for a pragmatic examination of how second-order contextual issues inform what can come under the purview of etiological functional analysis. In this case we might not be surprised to discover that a particular kind of masculine bias has informed the choice about which physiological systems and capacities of those systems are salient and entrenched. A number of compelling feminist studies of biology provide significant grist for the mill here (see, for example, Anne Fausto-Sterling's *Myths of Gender: Biological Theories about Women and Men*, 1992 [1985]). While there has been no feminist analysis of this particular issue, it does not seem overly provocative to suggest that certain strains of androcentrism may have negatively influenced the amount of research directed at the female system of sperm-borne pathogen defense.

In this respect it is interesting to compare the lack of entrenchment of Profet's functional thesis, and the female defense capacity to which it is hypothesized to contribute, with another more thoroughly entrenched account—namely, the view that menstruation prepares the womb for the implantation of a fertilized egg. *Pace* Strassman and Profet, this latter account can still be, and often is, thought of as a functional account. And unlike Profet's account, it fits within the well-established, well-researched system of the female reproductive tract. In Goodman's terms, the predicate "prepares the uterus for the implantation of a new egg" is an "old-timer," well entrenched in the linguistic conventions of physiologists, mostly through its relation to the well-entrenched capacity predicate "pregnancy"—a capacity that we are likely to associate with female reproduction (see figure 8.4).

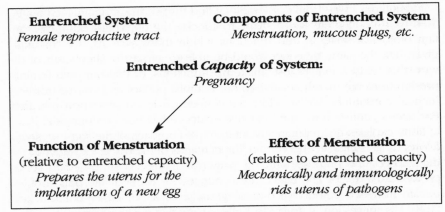

Figure 8.4. Function of Menstruation Relative to Capacity for Pregnancy

Again, a pragmatic, contextual analysis points us in directions of inquiry that are not quite so obvious on a more simplistic version of the etiological account. Examinations of the historical context of particular sorts of masculine bias in biology and physiology (as elsewhere) might help answer how the pregnancy predicate came to be of interest—that is, how it came to be entrenched in physiology and evolutionary biology—while the sperm-borne pathogen-defense predicate did not. Indeed, whenever a functional claim involves controversial ideas that capture public attention, a second-order analysis of the entrenchment of the system within which that function is situated is bound to be revealing.

In Profet's particular case, it seems clear that feminist studies of sexism in science provide good prima facie support for further examination of her functional hypothesis. It is only through an increase in the frequency with which we use the predicate "protects females from sperm-transported pathogens" that her functional hypothesis can become projectible and tested against evolutionary data about menstruation. Recall that Profet's account has been met with very little response in the medical and biology journals. We need to get started. Entrenchment is neither an apolitical nor an overnight process.

CONCLUSION

I have argued that as feminist scientists and science critics, we should keep in mind Goodman's view of the relationship between projectibility, entrenchment, and linguistic practice and Davidson's view of the relationship between linguistic practice, belief, and truth. If we can reorient our science commentaries away from epistemology and toward these pragmatic themes, then we'd be in pretty good shape to criticize the objectivist claim that certain biological systems, and functions within those systems, are "naturally given." At the same time we would be able to avoid the skepticism of the view that sexist scientists just "make up" functions, or that our own feminist prescriptions are merely relative to our feminist politics and/or free from evidential constraints. We should have confidence in our empirical research. For over a century now, the inductive evidence has been on our side.

Rorty explains that a pragmatist interpretive approach of the sort I prescribe allows us to "switch attention from 'the demands of the object [of study]' to the demands of the purpose which a particular inquiry is supposed to serve" (Rorty 1991e, 108). "The effect," he continues, "is to modulate philosophical debate from a methodologico-ontological key into an ethico-political key" (108). His suggestion is similar to Keller's view that we should turn our focus to the cultural and political interventions allowed and/or prescribed by various scientific inquiries. Freed from the representationalist framework within which her view was initially articulated, this pragmatist suggestion serves perfectly the demands of feminist science and science criticism.

NOTES

1. As I note in chapter 5, Longino's more recent writings argue against this split (Longino 2002), though she does not address how this new articulation might influence feminist science studies.

2. Many of these essays have recently been anthologized in *Nature's Purposes: Analyses of Function and Design in Biology* (C. Allen, M. Bekoff, and G. Lauder, eds., 1998).

3. Cummins is idiosyncratic in this regard, discussing functions in nonevolutionary contexts. For an excellent discussion of the appropriateness of Cummins's work for evolutionary biology, see Ron Amundsen and George Lauder (1998).

4. See also Peter Machamer, Lindley Darden, and Carl Craver (2001), who argue that historical context is important for the intelligibility of various mechanisms employed within scientific explanations (21).

5. Goodman's discussion of predicates similarly extends from simple color categories like "blue" to more complex capacity categories like "conducts electricity" and "is radioactive" (Goodman 1955, 97).

6. Goodman explains that the coextensions of a predicate are equally projectible, even if they are not as familiar to us. Projectibility cannot be reduced to mere familiarity—unfamiliar predicates might become projectible (1955, 95–96).

7. Israel Scheffler proposes a different response to concerns about the relationship between human interests, categories, and hypotheses about those categories (Scheffler 1967, 37–39). He acknowledges that human (subjective) interests might influence what categories we choose to study, but, he claims, we can still be objective about the testing of our hypotheses *about* those categories. This makes sense to me, as long

as we do not construe the objective test of those categories as a comparison between a nonbelief entity (the external evidence) and a belief entity (our subjective hypothesis about the category).

8. When more feminist attention is paid to Darwin's racist sexism, we will need to be more fluent in the ways that the concept of the "oversexed" male has been differentially applied across races. Similarly for the "passivity" of females.

9. See, for example, the articles in the *New York Times* (Natalie Angier 1993), *Time* (Anastasia Toufexis 1993), *Newsweek* (Jean Seligmann 1993), *People* (William Plummer 1993), *Shape* (Joseph Amodio 1994), *Glamour* (Glamour editorial staff 1994), *New Scientist* (Rosie Mestel 1993), and *Omni* (Shari Rudavsky 1994), all of which feature Profet as the "maverick" scientist with the "radical" thesis.

10. Profet notes that the research on levels of both lactoferrin and iron typically assumes that the levels in circulatory blood will be the same as that found in menstrual blood, though these claims are not tested (Profet, 347).

11. Indeed, if Profet is right about the current clinical importance of menstruation as a pathogen defense, many clinicians might be inclined to say that debates about the selection history of menstruation, while interesting, are entirely beside the point.

12. Though, certainly, insofar as she argues that the selection history of menstruation is causally related to her clinical prescriptions for the treatment of uterine infection, any weaknesses in her evolutionary account similarly weaken her important clinical claims.

13. Williams's own account is more sophisticated than this, offering an iterative process for recognizing adaptations prior to this two-step process. Contemporary accounts would require an even more stringent set of criteria (see Massimo Pigliucci and Jonathan Kaplan 2000).

14. This point is argued further in Matthew Ratcliffe's essay "Cognitive Adaptation and Truth" (2001).

15. For more on "piggyback" traits, see Karen Neander (1991, 179–80).

16. This more pluralist account of functions is discussed by Philip Kitcher (1993) and David Buller (1998).

17. A helpful discussion of the Profet/Strassman debate can be found in Natalie Angier (2000), though, tellingly, Angier downplays the larger context of the female pathogen-defense system once the discussion moves to Strassman (Angier, 109–16).

Works Cited

Abir-Am, P. G., and D. Outram, eds. 1987. *Uneasy Careers and Intimate Lives: Women in Science, 1789–1979.* New Brunswick, N.J.: Rutgers University Press.

Ainley, Marianne Gosztonyi. 1990. *Despite the Odds: Essays on Canadian Women and Science.* Montreal: Vehicule.

Alcoff, Linda. 1996. *Real Knowing: New Versions of the Coherence Theory.* Ithaca, N.Y.: Cornell University Press.

Alcoff, Linda, and Elizabeth Potter, eds. 1993. *Feminist Epistemologies.* New York: Routledge.

Allen, C., M. Bekoff, and G. Lauder, eds. 1998. *Nature's Purposes: Analyses of Function and Design in Biology.* Cambridge, Mass.: MIT Press.

Amodio, Joseph. 1994. "Profet-ing from a Dream." *Shape* 13 (6): 29.

Amundsen, Ron, and George Lauder, eds. 1998. "Function without Purpose: The Uses of Causal Role Function in Evolutionary Biology." In *The Philosophy of Biology,* ed. David Hull and Michael Ruse. Oxford: Oxford University Press.

Angier, Natalie. 1993. "Radical New View of Role of Menstruation." *New York Times,* September 21, B5-6.

———. 2000. *Woman: An Intimate Geography.* New York: Anchor.

Antony, Louise. 1993. "Quine as Feminist." In *A Mind of One's Own: Feminist Essays on Reason and Objectivity,* ed. Louise M. Anthony and Charlotte Witt. Boulder, Colo.: Westview.

Antony, Louise, and Charlotte Witt, eds. 1993. *A Mind of One's Own: Feminist Essays on Reason and Objectivity.* Boulder, Colo.: Westview.

Aune, Bruce. 1972. "Rorty on Language and the World." *Journal of Philosophy* 69: 665–67.

Barad, Karen. 1997. "Meeting the Universe Halfway: Realism and Social Constructivism without Contradiction." In *Feminism, Science, and the Philosophy of Science,* ed. Lynn Hankinson Nelson and Jack Nelson. Dordrecht, Holland: Kluwer.

Bar On, Bat-Ami. 1993. "Marginality and Epistemic Privilege." In *Feminist Episte-mologies,* ed. Linda Alcoff and Elizabeth Potter. New York: Routledge.

Benhabib, Seyla. 1991. "Feminism and Postmodernism: An Uneasy Alliance." *Praxis International* 11 (2): 137–47.

Bergström, Lars. 1993. "Quine, Underdetermination, and Skepticism." *Journal of Philosophy* 90 (7): 331–58.

Bernstein, Richard. 1983. *Beyond Objectivism and Relativism: Science, Hermeneutics, and Praxis.* Philadelphia: University of Pennsylvania Press.

Blackwell, Antoinette Brown. 1875. *The Sexes throughout Nature.* New York: G. B. Putnam's Sons.

Bleier, Ruth. 1984. *Science and Gender: A Critique of Biology and Its Theories on Women.* New York: Pergamon.

———. 1986a. "Lab Coat: Robe of Innocence or Klansman's Sheet?" In *Feminist Studies/ Critical Studies,* ed. Teresa de Lauretis. Bloomington: Indiana University Press.

———, ed. 1986b. *Feminist Approaches to Science.* New York: Pergamon.

Bordo, Susan. 1987. *The Flight to Objectivity: Essays on Cartesianism and Culture.* Albany, N.Y.: SUNY Press.

Boorse, Christopher. 1976. "Wright on Functions." *Philosophical Review* 85: 70–86.

Bornstein, Kate. 1994. *Gender Outlaw: On Men, Women, and the Rest of Us.* New York: Routledge.

Brown, James Robert. 1995. "Underdetermination and the Social Side of Science." *Dialogue* 34 (1): 147–62.

Buller, David. 1998. "Etiological Theories of Function: A Geographical Survey." *Biology and Philosophy* 13: 505–27.

Butler, Judith. 1991. "Contingent Foundations: Feminism and the Question of 'Postmodernism.'" *Praxis International* 11 (2): 150–65.

———. 1992. *Gender Trouble: Feminism and the Subversion of Identity.* New York: Routledge.

Calkins, Mary. 1896. "Community of Ideas of Men and Women." *Psychological Review* 3 (4): 426–30.

Campbell, Richmond. 1994. "The Virtues of Feminist Empiricism." *Hypatia* 9 (1): 90–115.

———. 1998. *Illusions of Paradox: A Feminist Epistemology Naturalized.* Lanham, Md.: Rowman & Littlefield.

Carnap, Rudolph. 1939. "Theories as Partially Interpreted Formal Systems." In *Foundations of Logic and Mathematics.* Chicago: University of Chicago Press.

Cattell, James McKeen. 1903. "A Statistical Study of Eminent Men." *Popular Science Monthly* 62: 359–77.

Chodorow, Nancy. 1978. *The Reproduction of Mothering: Psychoanalysis and the Sociology of Gender.* Berkeley: University of California Press.

———. 1981. Reply to "On *The Reproduction of Mothering:* A Methodological Debate." *Signs* 6 (3).

Clark, Ann. 1993. "The Quest for Certainty in Feminist Thought." *Hypatia* 8 (3): 84–93.

Clarke, J. 1994. "The Meaning of Menstruation in the Elimination of Abnormal Embryos." *Human Reproduction* 9: 1204–7.

Clough, Sharyn. 1998. "A Hasty Retreat from Evidence: The Recalcitrance of Relativism in Feminist Epistemology." *Hypatia* 13 (4): 88–111.

———. 2001. "Thinking Globally, Progressing Locally: Harding and Goonatilake on Scientific Progress across Cultures." *Social Epistemology* 15 (4): 379–416.

———. 2002. "What Is Menstruation For? On the Projectibility of Functional Predicates in Menstruation Research." *Studies in the History and Philosophy of the Biological and Biomedical Sciences* 33 (4): 719–32.

Code, Lorraine. 1981. "Is the Sex of the Knower Epistemically Significant?" *Metaphilosophy* 12: 267–76.

———. 1991. *What Can She Know? Feminist Theory and the Construction of Knowledge.* Ithaca, N.Y.: Cornell University Press.

Cope, Edward Drinker. 1974 [1887]. *The Origin of the Fittest* and *The Primary Factors of Organic Evolution.* Reprint, with advisory editor Keir B. Sterling. New York: Arno.

Cummins, Robert. 1989 [1975]. "Functional Analysis." Reprinted in *Readings in the Philosophy of Science,* 2nd edition, ed. Baruch A. Brody and Richard E. Grandy (495–511). Englewood Cliffs, N.J.: Prentice Hall.

Dalmiya, Vrinda. 1990. "Coherence, Truth, and the Omniscient Interpreter." *Philosophical Quarterly* 40: 86–94.

Darwin, Charles. 1962 [1859]. *The Origin of Species by Means of Natural Selection, or the Preservation of Favoured Races in the Struggle for Life.* Reprint. New York: Collier.

———. 1981 [1871]. *The Descent of Man and Selection in Relation to Sex.* 2 vols. Princeton, N.J.: Princeton University Press.

Davidson, Donald. 1980 [1970]. "Mental Events." Reprinted in *Essays on Actions and Events.* Oxford, U.K.: Clarendon.

———. 1984 [1974]. "On the Very Idea of a Conceptual Scheme." Reprinted in *Inquiries into Truth and Interpretation.* Oxford, U.K.: Clarendon.

———. 1986. "A Nice Derangement of Epitaphs." In *Truth and Interpretation: Perspectives on the Philosophy of Donald Davidson,* ed. Ernest LePore. Oxford, U.K.: Basil Blackwell.

———. 1988. "Epistemology and Truth." Proceedings of the 4th PanAmerican Philosophy Conference.

———. 1989a. "The Myth of the Subjective." In *Relativism: Interpretations and Confrontations,* ed. Michael Krausz. Bloomington: Indiana University Press.

———. 1989b. "The Conditions of Thought." In *The Mind of Donald Davidson,* ed. Johannes Brands and Wolfgang Gombocz. *Grazer Philosophische Studien* 36. Amsterdam: Editions Rodopoi.

———. 1990a. "The Structure and Content of Truth." *Journal of Philosophy* 87 (6): 279–328.

———. 1990b. "Meaning, Truth, and Evidence." In *Perspectives on Quine,* ed. R. Barrett and R. F. Gibson Jr. Oxford, U.K.: Basil Blackwell.

———. 1991a [1983]. "A Coherence Theory of Truth and Knowledge." Reprinted in *Reading Rorty: Critical Responses to Philosophy and the Mirror of Nature (and Beyond),* ed. Alan Malachowski. Oxford, U.K.: Basil Blackwell.

———. 1991b. "Epistemology Externalized." *Dialectica* 45 (2–3): 191–202.

———. 1991c. "Three Varieties of Knowledge." In *A. J. Ayer Memorial Essays,* ed. A. Phillips Griffiths. Cambridge: Cambridge University Press.

Dennett, Daniel. 1982. "Contemporary Philosophy of Mind: Comments on Rorty." *Synthese* 53: 349–55.

Dinnerstein, Dorothy. 1976. *The Mermaid and the Minotaur: Sexual Arrangements and Human Malaise*. New York: Harper & Row.

Doell, Ruth, and Helen Longino. 1988. "Sex Hormones and Human Behavior: A Critique of the Linear Model." *Journal of Homosexuality* 15 (3/4): 55–79.

Dupré, John. 1990. "Scientific Pluralism and the Plurality of the Sciences: Comments on David Hull's *Science as a Process*." *Philosophical Studies* 60: 61–76.

———. 1993. *The Disorder of Things: Metaphysical Foundations of the Disunity of Science*. Cambridge, Mass.: Harvard University Press.

Duran, Jane. 1998. *Philosophies of Science/Feminist Theories*. Boulder, Colo.: Westview.

Ellis, Havelock. 1894. *Man and Woman: A Study of Human Secondary Sexual Characteristics*. London: Walter Scott.

———. 1903. "Variation in Man and Woman." *Popular Science Monthly* 62: 237–53.

———. 1936 [1897–1928]. *Studies in the Psychology of Sex*. Rearranged, with a new foreword. 4 vols. New York: Random House.

Evnine, Simon. 1991. *Donald Davidson*. Stanford, Calif.: Stanford University Press.

Fausto-Sterling, Anne. 1992 [1985]. *Myths of Gender: Biological Theories about Women and Men,* 2nd ed. New York: Basic.

———. 1993. "The Five Sexes: Why Male and Female Are Not Enough." *The Sciences* (March/April): 20–24.

Fee, Elizabeth. 1982. "A Feminist Critique of Scientific Objectivity." *Science for the People* 14 (5–8): 30–33.

Feldberg, Georgina. 1992. "From Anti-Feminine to Anti-Feminist? Students' Reflections on Women and Science." *Women and Therapy* 12 (4): 113–25.

Fine, Arthur. 1984. "The Natural Ontological Attitude." In *Scientificrealism*, ed. J. Leplin. Berkeley: University of California Press.

———. 1989. "And Not Antirealism Either." In *Readings in the Philosophy of Science,* 2nd ed., ed. Baruch Brody and Richard Grandy. Englewood Cliffs, N.J.: Prentice Hall.

———. 1991. "Piecemeal Realism." *Philosophical Studies* 61 (1–2): 79–96.

Finn, C. A. 1994. "The Meaning of Menstruation." *Human Reproduction* 9: 1202–3.

Fisk, Milton. 1976. "Idealism, Truth, and Practice." *Monist* 59: 373–91.

Fodor, Jerry. 1987. *Psychosemantics*. Cambridge, Mass.: MIT Press.

Foss, Jeffrey. 1996. "Is There a Natural Sexual Inequality of Intellect? A Reply to Kimura." *Hypatia* 11 (3): 24–46.

Fraser, Nancy. 1989. *Unruly Practices: Power, Discourse, and Gender in Contemporary Social Theory*. Minneapolis: University of Minnesota Press.

———. 1991. "False Antitheses: A Response to Seyla Benhabib and Judith Butler." *Praxis International* 11 (2): 166–77.

Fritzman, J. M. 1993. "Thinking with Fraser about Rorty, Feminism, and Pragmatism." *Praxis International* 13 (2): 113–25.

Frye, Marilyn. 1983. *The Politics of Reality: Essays in Feminist Theory*. Freedom, Calif.: Crossing Press.

Fuller, Steve. 1992. "Social Epistemology and the Research Agenda of Social Studies." In *Science as Practice and Culture,* ed. Andrew Pickering. Chicago: University of Chicago Press.

Galison, Peter, and David Stump, eds. 1996. *The Disunity of Science: Boundaries, Contexts, and Power*. Stanford, Calif.: Stanford University Press.

Gammelgaard, Anne. 2000. "Evolutionary Biology and the Concept of Disease." *Medicine, Health Care, and Philosophy* 3: 109–16.

Garry, Ann, and Marilyn Pearsall. 1996 [1989]. *Women, Knowledge, and Reality: Explorations in Feminist Philosophy,* 2nd ed. New York: Routledge.

Geddes, Patrick, and J. Thomson. 1890. *The Evolution of Sex.* New York: Scribner and Welford.

Geiger. 1880. *Contributions to the History of the Development of the Human Race,* trans. D. Asher. London.

Glamour editorial staff. 1994. "The Important Questions One Woman Asked." *Glamour* 92 (1): 47.

Godfrey-Smith, Peter. 1994. "A Modern History Theory of Functions." *Nous* 28 (3): 344–62.

Goodman, Nelson. 1955. "The New Riddle of Induction." In *Fact, Fiction, and Forecast,* 2nd ed. Indianapolis, Ind.: Bobbs-Merrill.

———. 1978. *Ways of Worldmaking.* Indianapolis, Ind.: Hackett.

Grant, Judith. 1993. *Fundamental Feminism: Contesting the Core Concepts of Feminist Theory.* New York: Routledge.

Griffiths, P. 1992. "Adaptive Explanation and the Concept of a Vestige." Pp. 111–32 in *Trees of Life,* ed. P. Griffiths. Dordrecht, Holland: Kluwer.

Gross, Paul, and Norman Levitt. 1994. *Higher Superstition: The Academic Left and Its Quarrels with Science.* Baltimore: Johns Hopkins University Press.

Grünbaum, Adolf. 1984. *The Foundations of Psychoanalysis: A Philosophical Critique.* Berkeley: University of California Press.

Haack, Susan. 1993. *Evidence and Inquiry: Towards Reconstruction in Epistemology.* Cambridge, U.K.: Blackwell.

———. 1997. "'We Pragmatists . . .' Peirce and Rorty in Conversation." *Partisan Review* 64 (1): 91–107.

Hacking, Ian. 1983. *Representing and Intervening.* Cambridge: Cambridge University Press.

Hall, Granville S. 1904. *Adolescence: Its Psychology and Its Relations to Physiology, Anthropology, Sociology, Sex, Crime, Religion, and Education.* 2 vols. New York: Appleton.

Hanen, Marsha, and Kai Nielsen, eds. 1987. *Science, Morality, and Feminist Theory, Canadian Journal of Philosophy,* supplementary volume 13. Calgary, Alberta: University of Calgary Press.

Haraway, Donna. 1989. *Primate Visions: Gender, Race, and Nature in the World of Modern Science.* New York: Routledge.

Harding, Sandra. 1986a. *The Science Question in Feminism.* Ithaca, N.Y.: Cornell University Press.

———. 1986b. "The Instability of the Analytic Categories of Feminist Theory." *Signs: Journal of Women in Culture and Society* 11 (4): 645–64.

———, ed. 1987. *Feminism and Methodology.* Bloomington: Indiana University Press.

———, 1991. *Whose Science? Whose Knowledge? Thinking from Women's Lives.* Ithaca, N.Y.: Cornell University Press.

———, ed. 1993a. *The "Racial" Economy of Science: Toward a Democratic Future.* Bloomington: Indiana University Press.

———. 1993b. "Rethinking Standpoint Epistemology: What Is 'Strong Objectivity'?" In *Feminist Epistemologies*, ed. Linda Alcoff and Elizabeth Potter. New York: Routledge.

———. 1998. *Is Science Multicultural? Postcolonialisms, Feminisms, and Epistemologies*. Bloomington: Indiana University Press.

Harding, Sandra, and Merrill B. Hintikka, eds. 1983. *(Dis)covering Reality: Feminist Perspectives on Epistemology, Metaphysics, and Philosophy of Science*. Dordrecht, Holland: D. Reidel.

Harding, Sandra, and Jean F. O'Barr, eds. 1987. *Sex and Scientific Inquiry*. Chicago: University of Chicago Press.

Hartsock, Nancy. 1985. *Money, Sex, and Power: Toward a Feminist Historical Materialism*. Boston: Northeastern University Press.

———. 1987 [1983]. "The Feminist Standpoint: Developing the Ground for a Specifically Feminist Historical Materialism." Reprinted in *Feminism and Methodology*, ed. Sandra Harding. Bloomington: Indiana University Press.

Hein, H. 1981. "Women and Science: Fitting Men to Think about Nature." *International Journal of Women's Studies* 4: 369–77.

Hempel, Carl G. 1965. *Aspects of Scientific Explanation and Other Essays in the Philosophy of Science*. New York: Free Press.

Herdt, Gilbert, ed. 1994. *Third Sex, Third Gender: Beyond Sexual Dimorphism in Culture and History*. New York: Zone.

Heyes, Cressida. 2000. *Line Drawings: Defining Women through Feminist Practice*. Ithaca, N.Y.: Cornell.

Hollingworth, Leta Stetter. 1914. "Variability as Related to Sex Differences in Achievement." *American Journal of Sociology* 19: 510–30.

hooks, bell. 1981. *Ain't I a Woman: Black Women and Feminism*. Boston: South End.

———. 1989. *Talking Back: Thinking Feminist, Thinking Black*. Boston: South End.

Hubbard, Ruth. 1983 [1979]. "Have Only Men Evolved?" Reprinted in *Discovering Reality: Feminist Perspectives on Epistemology, Metaphysics, and Philosophy of Science*, ed. Sandra Harding and Merrill B. Hintikka. Dordrecht, Holland: D. Reidel.

Hull, Gloria T., Patricia Bell Scott, and Barbara Smith, eds. 1982. *All the Women Are White, All the Blacks Are Men, but Some of Us Are Brave*. New York: Feminist Press.

Hymers, Michael. 2000. *Philosophy and Its Epistemic Neuroses*. Boulder, Colo.: Westview.

Keller, Evelyn Fox. 1982. "Feminism and Science." *Signs: Journal of Women in Culture and Society* 7 (3): 589–602.

———. 1983 [1978]. "Gender and Science." Reprinted in *(Dis)covering Reality: Feminist Perspectives on Epistemology, Metaphysics, and Philosophy of Science*, ed. Sandra Harding and Merrill B. Hintikka. Dordrecht, Holland: D. Reidel.

———. 1985. *Reflections on Gender and Science*. New Haven, Conn.: Yale University Press.

———. 1987. "The Gender/Science System or, Is Sex to Gender as Nature Is to Science?" *Hypatia* 2 (3): 37–49.

———. 1992a. Introduction to *Secrets of Life, Secrets of Death: Essays on Language, Gender, and Science*. New York: Routledge.

———. 1992b. "Gender and Science: An Update." In *Secrets of Life, Secrets of Death: Essays on Language, Gender, and Science*. New York: Routledge.

———. 1992c. "Critical Silences in Scientific Discourses." In *Secrets of Life, Secrets of Death: Essays on Language, Gender, and Science.* New York: Routledge.

———. 2000. *The Century of the Gene.* Cambridge, Mass.: Harvard University Press.

———. 2002. *Making Sense of Life: Explaining Biological Development with Models, Metaphors, and Machines.* Cambridge, Mass.: Harvard University Press.

Kimura, Doreen. 1992. "Sex Differences in the Brain." *Scientific American* 267 (September): 118–25.

Kitcher, Philip. 1993. "Function and Design." *Midwest Studies in Philosophy* 28: 379–97.

Kuhn, Thomas. 1972 [1960]. *The Structure of Scientific Revolutions,* 2nd ed. Chicago: University of Chicago Press.

Kohlstedt, Sally Gregory, and Helen Longino, eds. 1997. "Women, Gender, and Science: New Directions." *Osiris* 12 (Special Issue).

LePore, Ernest, ed. 1986. *Truth and Interpretation: Perspectives on the Philosophy of Donald Davidson.* Oxford, U.K.: Basil Blackwell.

Lewis, C. I. 1956 [1929]. *Mind and the World Order.* Republication of the first edition with corrections. New York: Dover.

Lloyd, Genevieve. 1984. *The Man of Reason: "Male" and "Female" in Western Philosophy.* Minneapolis: University of Minnesota Press.

Lloyd, Elisabeth. 1997. "Science and Anti-Science: Objectivity and Its Real Enemies." In *Feminism, Science, and the Philosophy of Science,* ed. Lynn Hankinson Nelson and Jack Nelson. Dordrecht, Holland: Kluwer.

Longino, Helen. 1987. "Can There Be a Feminist Science?" *Hypatia* 2 (3): 51–64.

———. 1990. *Science as Social Knowledge: Values and Objectivity in Scientific Inquiry.* Princeton, N.J.: Princeton University Press.

———. 1993. "Review Essay: Feminist Standpoint Theory and the Problems of Knowledge." *Signs: Journal of Women in Culture and Society* 19 (1): 201–12.

———. 2002. *The Fate of Knowledge.* Princeton, N.J.: Princeton University Press.

Lovibond, Sabina. 1989. "Feminism and Postmodernism." *New Left Review* 178: 5–28.

———. 1992. "Feminism and Pragmatism: A Reply to Richard Rorty." *New Left Review* 193: 56–74.

Machamer, Peter, Lindley Darden, and Carl Craver. 2001. "Thinking about Mechanisms." *Philosophy of Science* 67 (1): 1–25.

Machan, Tibor. 1993. "Some Reflections on Richard Rorty's Philosophy." *Metaphilosophy* 24: 123–34.

Malpas, Jeffrey, E. 1992. *Donald Davidson and the Mirror of Meaning.* Cambridge: Cambridge University Press.

Martin, Biddy, and Chandra Mohanty. 1986. "Feminist Politics: What's Home Got to Do with It?" In *Feminist Studies/Critical Studies,* ed. Teresa de Lauretis. Bloomington: Indiana University Press.

Marx, Karl, and Frederick Engels. 1964. *The German Ideology.* Ed. and trans. C. J. Arthur. New York: International.

McCarthy, Thomas. 1990a. "Private Irony and Public Decency: Richard Rorty's New Pragmatism." *Critical Inquiry* 16 (Winter): 355–70.

———. 1990b. "Ironist Theory as Vocation: A Response to Rorty's Reply." *Critical Inquiry* 16 (Spring): 644–55.

McMullin, Ernan. 1991. "Comment: Selective Anti-Realism." *Philosophical Studies* 61: 97–108.

Mestel, Rosie. 1993. "Are Periods a Protection against Men?" *New Scientist* 140: 1893.

Millikan, Ruth. 1989. "In Defense of Proper Functions." *Philosophy of Science* 56: 288–302.

Misak, C. J. 1995. *Verificationism: Its History and Prospects*. Routledge: New York.

Mohanty, Chandra Talpade. 1991. "Under Western Eyes: Feminist Scholarship and Colonial Discourses." In *Third World Women and the Politics of Feminism*, ed. Chandra Talpade Mohanty, Ann Russo, and Lourdes Torres. Bloomington: Indiana University Press.

Montague, Helen, and Leta Stetter Hollingworth. 1914. "The Comparative Variability of the Sexes at Birth." *American Journal of Sociology* 20: 335–70.

Muller, Charlotte. 1992. *Healthcare and Gender*. New York: Russell Sage.

Nagel, Ernest. 1961. *The Structure of Science: Problems in the Logic of Scientific Explanation*. New York: Harcourt, Brace and World.

Neander, Karen. 1991. "Functions as Selected Effects: The Conceptual Analyst's Defense." *Philosophy of Science* 58: 168–84.

Nelson, Lynn Hankinson. 1990. *Who Knows? From Quine to a Feminist Empiricism*. Philadelphia: Temple University Press.

———. 1993. "A Question of Evidence." *Hypatia* 2 (8): 172–89.

Nelson, Lynn Hankinson, and Jack Nelson, eds. 1997. *Feminism, Science, and the Philosophy of Science*. Dordrecht, Holland: Kluwer.

Nesse, Randolph, and George C. Williams. 1995. *Evolution and Healing: The New Science of Darwinian Medicine*. London: Phoenix.

Newman, Louise, ed. 1985. *Men's Ideas/Women's Realities: Popular Science, 1870–1915*. New York: Pergamon.

Nicholson, Linda, ed. 1990. *Feminism/Postmodernism*. New York: Routledge.

———. 1999. *The Play of Reason: From the Modern to the Postmodern*. Ithaca, N.Y.: Cornell University Press.

Niiniluoto, Ilkka. 1997. "The Relativism Question in Feminist Epistemology." In *Feminism, Science, and the Philosophy of Science,* ed. Lynn Hankinson Nelson and Jack Nelson. Dordrecht, Holland: Kluwer.

Okin, Susan Moller. 1994. "Gender Inequality and Cultural Difference." *Political Theory* 22 (5).

O'Brien, Mary. 1981. *The Politics of Reproduction*. Boston: Routledge and Kegan Paul.

Pearson, Karl. 1897. "Variation in Man and Woman." In *The Chances of Death*, vol. 1. London: Edward Arnold.

Pigliucci, Massimo, and Jonathan Kaplan. 2000. "The Fall and Rise of Dr. Pangloss: Adaptationism and the Spandrels Paper 20 Years Later." *Trends in Ecology and Evolution* 15 (2): 66–70.

Plummer, William. 1993. "A Curse No More." *People Weekly* 40 (15) (October 11): 75.

Popper, Karl. 1959. *The Logic of Scientific Discovery*. New York: Harper and Row.

———. 1962. *Conjectures and Refutations*. New York: Basic.

———. 1974. "Replies to My Critics." In *The Philosophy of Karl Popper,* ed. P. A. Schilpp, book 2. LaSalle, Ill.: Open Court.

Prior, Elizabeth. 1985. "What Is Wrong with Etiological Accounts of Biological Function?" *Pacific Philosophical Quarterly* 66: 310–28.

Profet, Margie. 1993. "Menstruation as a Defense against Pathogens Transported by Sperm." *Quarterly Review of Biology* 68 (3): 335–86.

Quine, Willard Van Orman. 1960. *Word and Object*. Cambridge, Mass.: MIT Press.

——. 1969. *"Ontological Relativity" and Other Essays*. New York: Columbia University Press.

——. 1981. "Empirical Content." In *Theories and Things*. Cambridge: Belknap.

——. 1990a. "Comment on Davidson." In *Perspectives on Quine*, ed. R. Barrett and R. F. Gibson Jr. Oxford, U.K.: Basil Blackwell.

——. 1990b. "Comment on Haack." In *Perspectives on Quine*, ed. R. Barrett and R. F. Gibson Jr. Oxford: Basil Blackwell.

——. 1990c. "Let Me Accentuate the Positive." In *Reading Rorty: Critical Responses to Philosophy and the Mirror of Nature (and Beyond)*, ed. Alan Malachowski. Oxford, U.K.: Basil Blackwell.

Ramberg, Bjørn. 1988. "Charity and Ideology: The Field Linguist as Social Critic." *Dialogue* 27: 637–51.

——. 1989. *Donald Davidson's Philosophy of Language: An Introduction*. Oxford, U.K.: Basil Blackwell.

——. 1993a. "Strategies for Radical Rorty (but Is It *Progress?*)." In *Meta-Philosophie/Reconstructing Philosophy? Canadian Journal of Philosophy*, supplementary volume 19, ed. Jocelyne Couture and Kai Nielsen. Calgary, Alberta: University of Calgary Press.

——. 1993b. "Interpreting Davidson." *Dialogue* 32: 565–71.

——. (unpublished manuscript). "Metaphysics and Metaphor: Verificationism and Pragmatism," in Carnap, on the one hand, and in Rorty and Dennett, on the other.

Ratcliffe, Matthew. 2001. "Cognitive Adaptation and Truth: A Sceptical View." Paper presented at the *International Society for History, Philosophy, and Social Studies of Biology*, Quinnipiac University, Connecticut, July 19.

Rheinwald, Rosemarie. 1993. "An Epistemic Solution to Goodman's New Riddle of Induction." *Synthese* 95: 55–76.

Riley, Denise. 1988. *"Am I That Name?" Feminism and the Category of "Women" in History*. Minneapolis: University of Minneapolis Press.

Rorty, Richard. 1979. *Philosophy and the Mirror of Nature*. Princeton, N.J.: Princeton University Press.

——. 1990. "Truth and Freedom: A Response to Thomas McCarthy." *Critical Inquiry* 16 (Spring): 633–43.

——. 1991a [1986]. "Pragmatism, Davidson, and Truth." Reprinted in *Philosophical Papers, Vol. 1. Objectivity, Relativism, and Truth*. Cambridge: Cambridge University Press.

——. 1991b [1988]. "Representation, Social Practise, and Truth." Reprinted in *Philosophical Papers, Vol. 1. Objectivity, Relativism, and Truth*. Cambridge: Cambridge University Press.

——. 1991c [1987]. "Science as Solidarity." Reprinted in *Philosophical Papers, Vol. 1. Objectivity, Relativism, and Truth*. Cambridge: Cambridge University Press.

——. 1991d [1988]. "Is Natural Science a Natural Kind?" Reprinted in *Philosophical Papers, Vol. 1. Objectivity, Relativism, and Truth*. Cambridge: Cambridge University Press.

——. 1991e. "Inquiry as Recontextualization: An Anti-Dualist Account of Interpretation." In *Philosophical Papers, Vol. 1. Objectivity, Relativism, and Truth*. Cambridge: Cambridge University Press.

———. 1991f [Spring 1991]. "Feminism and Pragmatism." Reprinted in *Radical Philosophy* 59 (Autumn): 3–14.

———. 1995. "Response to Haack." In *Rorty and Pragmatism: The Philosopher Responds to His Critics,* ed. H. J. Saatkamp. Nashville, Tenn.: Vanderbilt University Press.

———. 1998. "Antiskeptical Weapons: Michael Williams versus Donald Davidson." In *Truth and Progress: Philosophical Papers, Vol. 3.* Cambridge: Cambridge University Press.

———. 1999 [1994]. "Truth without Correspondence to Reality." Reprinted in *Philosophy and Social Hope.* London: Penguin.

Rose, Hilary, and Steven Rose, eds. 2000. *Alas Poor Darwin: Arguments against Evolutionary Psychology.* New York: Harmony Books.

Rossiter, Margaret. 1982. *Women Scientists in America: Struggles and Strategies to 1940.* Baltimore: Johns Hopkins University Press.

Rothblatt, Martine. 1995. *The Apartheid of Sex: A Manifesto on the Freedom of Gender.* New York: Crown.

Rouse, Joseph. 1984. *Engaging Science: How to Understand Its Practices Philosophically.* Ithaca, N.Y.: Cornell University Press.

Rudavsky, Shari. 1994. "Interview with Margie Profet." *Omni* 16 (8) (May): 69.

Russett, Cynthia Eagle. 1989. *Sexual Science: The Victorian Construction of Womanhood.* London: Harvard University Press.

Said, Edward. 1978. *Orientalism.* New York: Pantheon.

Scheffler, Israel. 1967. *Science and Subjectivity.* Indianapolis, Ind.: Bobbs-Merrill.

Schiebinger, Londa. 1989. *The Mind Has No Sex? Women in the Origins of Modern Science.* Cambridge, Mass.: Harvard University Press.

———. 1999. *Has Feminism Changed Science?* Cambridge, Mass.: Harvard University Press.

Schlagel, Richard H. 1991. "Fine's Shaky Game (and Why NOA Is No Ark for Science)." *Philosophy of Science* 58 (2): 307–23.

Seigfried, Charlene Haddock. 1996. *Pragmatism and Feminism.* Chicago: University of Chicago Press.

———. 2001. "Beyond Epistemology: From a Pragmatist Feminist Experiential Standpoint," in *Engendering Rationalities,* ed. Nancy Tuana and Sandra Morgen. Albany, N.Y.: SUNY Press.

Seligmann, Jean. 1993. "Rethinking Women's Bodies." *Newsweek* 122 (14) (October 4): 86.

Sellars, Wilfred. 1963. *Science, Perception, and Reality.* London: Routledge and Kegan Paul.

Shields, Stephanie A. 1975. "Functionalism, Darwinism, and the Psychology of Women." *American Psychologist* 30: 739–54.

———. 1982. "The Variability Hypothesis: The History of a Biological Model of Sex Differences in Intelligence." *Signs: Journal of Women in Culture and Society* 7 (4): 769–97.

Smith, Dorothy. 1987a. *The Everyday World As Problematic: A Feminist Sociology.* Boston: Northeastern University Press.

———. 1987b [1974]. "Women's Perspective as a Radical Critique of Sociology." Reprinted in *Feminism and Methodology,* ed. Sandra Harding. Bloomington: Indiana University Press.

Sobstyl, Edrie. (unpublished manuscript). "Gender and Knowledge: Some Disquiet about the Masculine Mind of Science."

Spanier, Bonnie. 1995. *Im/partial Science: Gender Ideology in Molecular Biology*. Bloomington: Indiana University Press.

Spelman, Elizabeth. 1988. *Inessential Woman: Problems of Exclusion in Feminist Thought*. Boston: Beacon.

Spencer, Herbert. 1969 [1873]. *The Study of Sociology*. Ann Arbor: University of Michigan Press.

Sperling, Susan. 1991. "Baboons with Briefcases: Feminism, Functionalism, and Sociobiology in the Evolution of Primate Gender." *Signs* 17 (1): 1–27.

Stoljar, Natalie. 1995. "Essence, Identity, and the Concept of Woman." *Philosophical Topics* 23 (Fall): 261–93.

Strassmann, Beverly. 1996. "The Evolution of Endometrial Cycles and Menstruation." *Quarterly Review of Biology* 71 (2): 181–220.

Stroud, Barry. 1984. *The Significance of Philosophical Scepticism*. Oxford, U.K.: Clarendon.

Tanesini, Alessandra. 1999. *An Introduction to Feminist Epistemologies*. Oxford: Blackwell.

Tavris, Carol. 1992. *The Mismeasure of Woman*. New York: Simon and Schuster.

Toufexis, Anastasia. 1993. "A Woman's Best Defense?" *Time* 142 (14) (October 4): 72.

Tuana, Nancy, ed. 1989. *Feminism and Science*. Bloomington: Indiana University Press.

———. 1992a. *Woman and the History of Philosophy*. St. Paul, Minn.: Paragon.

———. 1992b. "The Radical Future of Feminist Empiricism." *Hypatia* 7 (1): 100–113.

Tuana, Nancy, and Sandra Morgen. 2001. *Engendering Rationalities*. Albany, N.Y.: SUNY Press.

Turner, Derek. 2001. "The Role of Analogy in Reverse Engineering." Paper presented at the *International Society for History, Philosophy, and Social Studies of Biology*, Quinnipiac University, Connecticut, July 21.

van Fraassen, Bas. 1980. *The Scientific Image*. New York: Oxford University Press.

Veatch, Henry. 1985. "Deconstruction in Philosophy: Has Rorty Made It the Denouement of Contemporary Analytic Philosophy?" *Review of Metaphysics* 39: 303–20.

Vogt, Carl. 1864. *Lectures on Man*, English translation. London: Longman, Green, Longman, and Roberts.

Williams, George C. 1966. *Adaptation and Natural Selection: A Critique of Some Current Evolutionary Thought*. Princeton, N.J.: Princeton University Press.

Williams, Michael. 1991. *Unnatural Doubts: Epistemological Realism and the Basis for Scepticism*. Oxford: Blackwell.

Winnicott, D. 1971. *Playing and Reality*. New York: Basic.

Wittgenstein, Ludwig. 1958. *Philosophical Investigations*. Trans. G. E. M. Anscombe. Oxford, U.K.: Basil Blackwell.

Woodworth, R. S. 1910. "The Puzzle of Color Vocabularies." *Psychological Bulletin* 7 (10): 325–34.

Woolley, Helen Thompson. 1910. "Psychological Literature: A Review of the Recent Literature on the Psychology of Sex." *Psychological Bulletin* 7 (10): 335–43.

———. 1914. "The Psychology of Sex." *Psychological Bulletin* 11 (10): 353–79.

Wright, Larry. 1972. "Explanation and Teleology." *Philosophy of Science* 39 (2): 204–18.

————. 1973. "Functions." *Philosophical Review* 82: 139–68.

Wylie, Alison. 1994. "Reasoning about Ourselves: Feminist Methodology in the Social Sciences." In *Readings in the Philosophy of the Social Sciences,* ed. Michael Martin and Lee C. McIntyre. Cambridge, Mass.: MIT Press.

————. 2002. *Thinking from Things: Essays in the Philosophy of Archaeology.* Berkeley: University of California Press.

Index

About the Author

Sharyn Clough currently holds a research fellowship in the philosophy department at the University of Tennessee, Knoxville. She has published essays in *Hypatia, Social Epistemology,* and *Studies in the History and Philosophy of Biology and the Biomedical Sciences.* She has also edited a collection of essays titled *Siblings under the Skin: Feminism, Social Justice, and Analytic Philosophy.*